JUVE!

Herbie Sykes

JUVE!

100 Years of an Italian Footballing Dynasty

YELLOW JERSEY PRESS
LONDON

Published by Yellow Jersey Press 2021

1 3 5 7 9 10 8 6 4 2

Yellow Jersey is part of the Penguin Random House group of companies
whose addresses can be found at global.penguinrandomhouse.com

First published by Yellow Jersey Press in 2020

penguin.co.uk/vintage

A CIP catalogue record for this book is available from the British Library

ISBN 9781787290518

Typeset in 11.21/14 pt Adobe Minion Pro
by Integra Software Services Pvt. Ltd, Pondicherry

All images in the picture section are © Offside Sports Photography,
with the exception of the top image on page 2 which is © Wikicommons.
Plate section design by Darren Bennett at DKB Creative Ltd
(www.dkbcreative.com).

Printed and bound in Great Britain by Clays Ltd, Eclograf S.p.A.

The authorised representative in the EEA is Penguin Random House
Ireland, Morrison Chambers, 32 Nassau Street, Dublin DO2 YH68

Penguin Random House is committed to a sustainable future for our
business, our readers and our planet. This book is made from Forest
Stewardship Council® certified paper.

For Geoffrey Sykes, bicycle repairman
25 October 1942–10 September 2018

Acknowledgements

I'm grateful to Tim Broughton for having believed in the book, and to Joe Pickering for husbanding it and getting it over the line. Thanks also to Hugh Davis for his diligence and patience, and to David Luxton, my agent, for his sterling efforts on my behalf.

Thanks, as ever, to the Sykes and Peracino families, and to everyone who was kind enough to lend me their time, wisdom and anecdotes. Thanks, overwhelmingly, to the good people of Turin; past and present, *Juventini* and otherwise. There may very well be better, more fascinating and more beautiful cities in which to live, but I can't for the life of me think of any.

Acknowledgement

Contents

In Baldissero Torinese, with My Friends Alberto (11) and Luca (8)

We're talking footy with Alberto and Luca, at their house in the hills above Turin. They're brothers and they're funny, but they're as different as night and day.

Their mother is Claudia, and the local dialect has a word for people like her. It's *bogianen*, and its literal meaning approximates to 'immovable'. It signifies stoicism, inscrutability, the age-old intransigence of a mountain people, and it's about right. Claudia's not much for travel (literal or figurative) because she understands that she's always going to end up back here. This is her place, this is where she was formed and this, whether she likes it or not, is who she is. She's quite fatalistic, but what's to be done? She's of Piedmont – literally the 'foot of the mountain' – and the mountains are much bigger than her. She's a hostage to forces – climate, geology, history – over which she has no control. The Piedmontese, they say, are predisposed to *vittimismo*, and Claudia is Piedmontese to her very marrow. She's hard-pressed against this hillside, and she knows she has to keep

1

chiselling away at it as best she can. You can't help but like her, just as you can't help but like her little Luca.

Unlike her children, Claudia is slightly detached from the quotidian psychodrama that is *calcio*. However it's implicit that she's a fan of Torino FC, just as it's implicit that her former husband isn't. His name is Gaetano, and they say that opposites attract. If she's the reason Luca is Luca then he's the reason that Albi, his big brother, categorically is not.

Gaetano's father came up from Puglia during the economic boom of the late 1950s. Like any number of Southern Italians he'd dreamed of *la dolce vita*, so he climbed aboard a hot, sweaty, heaving train headed emphatically north. He got off it wide-eyed and penniless in Turin, stared long and hard at the neo-baroque masterpiece that is Porta Nuova station, and stepped into the light. It was there that he saw – because you can't not – Turin's porticoed majesty, and resolved that one day he'd own a slab of it. Very quickly he found work (or, more accurately, work found him) and he substituted back-breaking days in arid southern fields with the greasy pole of heavy industry.

What was it they used to say about southern Italian immigrants? To know them was to love them? The northerners didn't understand Pugliese dialect, but he learned their language and sidled up to a girl. They survived a couple of Sub-Alpine winters, then what happens happened, and in 1975 little Gaetano came along. Gateano came along, and he and his family are the story of the Italian century.

How best to put it with Gaetano? We'll refrain from calling him a gobshite principally because he's not. It's just that, for all he was born here, he conforms to the unreconstructed southern stereotype. It would be difficult to argue that he's cerebral, and certainly he's not much given to reflection. He knows what he knows though, and in contrast to his ex-wife he's not at all uncomfortable talking about his accomplishments. He doesn't say anything particularly profound, but he's expansive, and still more so when the topic of conversation turns (inevitably it always seems) to him.

He's a big Juventus fan, but I guess you'd already deduced that.

Smog permitting, you can see right across town from here. In the near distance the great River Po, the bedrock upon which the Romans built Augustus Taurinorum, arcs south-west towards the Alps. The river was once the limit of the city but then, 300 years ago, the *torinesi* sent the French packing. They celebrated by building a new bridge across it and a whopping great neoclassical church the other side. In time the Gran Madre di Dio would become one of Turin's more famous landmarks, as anyone who's seen *The Italian Job* will testify.

The film, in case you hadn't noticed, is a metaphor for English isolationism. Michael Caine and his fleet of Minis are anti-FIAT, anti-Europe, anti-anything-and-anyone who's not a crafty, self-preserving, meat-and-two-veg English ignoramus. Notwithstanding the fact that Turin is a thousand kilometres from Sicily, Caine's Italian adversary is a *mafioso*. However, he's played by a former Torino midfielder named Raf Vallone, and that, given that the pretext for the heist is a football match, seems fair enough.

The Gran Madre scene sees Caine and his Luddite cronies despoil a beautifully choreographed Italian wedding scene. They launch their Minis down the church steps, onto the weir of the Po, and on through Turin's famous arcades. Later, having stolen Italy's gold, they flaunt their superiority complex in a low-speed car chase on the roof at FIAT's massive Lingotto plant.

Anyway Borgo Po, the residential area behind the Grand Madre, became very fashionable. Eager to be both in the city and out of it, Turin's middle classes began to build their homes there. The higher they built the more they paid, and the more they paid the more equanimity – imagined or otherwise – the houses bestowed. Some are very beautiful, and most are genteel like their inhabitants.

The city centre, mannered and linear, is populated by old Piedmontese families with their old Piedmontese money. It's pure Savoy, and yet its great emblem is a former synagogue. Not for nothing is Turin known as Little Paris, and the extraordinary Mole Antonelliana, transformed now into a wondrous cinema museum, looks like a precursor to the Eiffel Tower precisely because it was. It was the tallest building in Turin until they allowed a bank to defile the sight lines with a skyscraper in 2011.

Eight northern kilometres from La Mole is a place named Lucento. It's right on the north-western outskirts, and it's the Italy they never tell you about. Even the locals are hard-pushed to remember what it's called, so they just say it's Venaria because that's the closest suburb they've heard of.

Lucento doesn't look much, but it's home to a modern-day Italian icon. In 2003, Juventus bought the Stadio Delle Alpi, the 67,000-seater white elephant of Italia '90, from the city council. They demolished it just as quickly as they could, and in its stead built a much smaller, much better ground. They added Italy's best sports museum, a huge medical complex, a shopping centre and an international language school. Collectively these comprise J-Village, but it's far from finished. A five-star hotel is in the works, so too a wellness centre, and the club headquarters are shortly to be relocated from the town centre. The Allianz Stadium (the naming rights are leased to the highest bidder) is the centrepiece. Though most of the old *torinesi* I know want nothing to do with it, it's handy for the motorway, and there's a metaphor in that somewhere.

Whether they like it or not, J-Village works seamlessly. It's full immersion, the football club reinvented as a one-stop shop, and as sports marketing-branding exercises go it's exceptional. It's designed to feel holistic and ecumenical, and it's without parallel in parochial, homespun Italy.

Torino's ground, the Stadio Olimpico, is harder to make out from up here. It's near the city centre, on the corner of Via Filadelfia and Corso Giovanni Agnelli. That's the tree-lined boulevard named after FIAT's founder. It leads south-west to Mirafiori, the FIAT plant inaugurated by Mussolini in 1939. Just across the rail tracks lies Lingotto, so one way or another Toro are a bit hemmed in. Like most of Turin they're subordinate to the Agnelli power vertical, and they lease the ground from the council.

Little Luca's room is to the left and Albi's, quite a bit bigger, is to the right. They each have this season's Panini sticker album, though Albi is much further along with completing his. His mum says he's adept at wheeling and dealing, and he has an encyclopedic knowledge of who's who. He can name the full squad of any Serie A side, and those of all the big English and Spanish ones as well.

Luca tends to be a bit slower because he gets less pocket money, but also because he loses concentration. Albi thinks that's hilarious and, because he's the big brother, he wallops Luca from time to time. But that's life, and Luca puts up with it. Everyone loves him, and his mates are always coming round to play.

So Albi's impressing me with his Panini husbandry and, inevitably, we start talking about actual football. Albi's a good player because he's athletic, quick-witted and wiry, and because he understands that football is a serious business. Luca, though, doesn't seem to get it at all. He just chases after the ball like the others, and his mum says he doesn't mind whether he wins or loses.

Luca says he supports Torino because he has *fidùcia*, faith. His mum told him there's more to life than winning, and he doesn't like Juventus because they don't stand for anything. He also says there are fewer and fewer Toro fans, and a couple of his mates have switched recently. When I ask him why, he says it's because Juve have Ronaldo, Buffon and Dybala.

Albi tells his brother he appears ridiculous, but Luca counters with, 'What is Juve though? It's not even a place, so what are you supporting?'

Albi says Juve is the only club able to compete with PSG, with Manchester City and with Barcelona. He says the 'philosophy' is about winning. He asks why you'd even bother doing sport if you don't start with that attitude, and tells his brother supporting Toro 'doesn't make sense'. It's a joke club for *sfigati* (losers); the team is garbage and nothing ever happens. Toro never, ever win anything, and all their fans talk about is the *Grande Torino*. They were the greatest team in Italian history, but that was 70 years ago.

Luca doesn't really have an answer and nor, if I'm honest, does anybody else.

If you're right about something, the Italians say you 'have reason', and here Albi is incontrovertibly right.

Ha ragione, Alberto.

Chapter 1

Fratelli d'Italia

Turin is a beautiful city. Its spaciousness exceeds, I think,
everything that has ever been conceived before.

Mark Twain

At the Royal Palace, with the estimable Rudolf Obermann

The eighteenth-century writer Giuseppe Baretti had
this to say about his fellow Piedmontese: 'One of
the qualities which distinguishes them from the other
Italians is a lack of high spirits. Travellers visiting Italy
will immediately notice that its people are agreeable and
cheerful, and seem naturally disposed to noisy pleasures.
If, however, he visits Piedmont, he'll note a certain melancholy, a troubled seriousness.'

And he was right. Everyone in Italy knows the
Piedmontese are a bit starchy, but goodness knows there
were mitigating circumstances back then. Prior to the
unification of Italy, they'd been a scurvy, consumptive
lot. In itself that hadn't been an issue for the House of
Savoy, rulers of Piedmont and Sardinia, because taxing

them into penury had been company policy. The problem was that there had been wars to fight, they tended to come along thick and fast, and they needed soldiers able-bodied and stupid enough to martyr themselves for the kingdom. However, what with disease, stunted growth and grinding poverty, almost a quarter of the conscripts were unfit for service.

In part it was down to industrialisation. Turin's cotton mills were productive and highly lucrative, and the employment of women and children had done wonders for profit margins. However, beneath the gilded baroque surface there was typhus and rampant syphilis, alcoholism and generalised squalor. This city of some 130,000 souls was the European capital of sanatoriums and orphanages, drinking dens and brothels. It was opulent and beautiful, but also fetid.

King Carlo Alberto (reigned 1831–49) had a predilection for young, cerebral, liberal sorts. In 1833 he summoned one of them, a hotshot philosopher from Zurich, to the Royal Palace. Rudolf Obermann was expert in the new-fangled 'gymnastics', which was evidently all the rage across the Alps. He set about explaining it all to Carlo Alberto, to his sickly wife Maria Teresa and to their hangers-on. He convinced them that gymnastics was the future, but that in the wrong hands it tended to have calamitous psychological and spiritual consequences. It was no good for brainy medics, sensitive students or – heaven forbid – women, and under no circumstances should it become competitive.

On the left bank of the river stood Parco Valentino, Europe's most elegant public space, and Carlo Alberto had a spare palace there. Obermann told him he'd convert some of it into a 'gymnasium', and transform the kingdom's infantry into Europe's strongest, bravest, most disciplined fighting force. He'd engender strength and pride in the regiments, but also patriotism and a profound sense of well-being. Strength, pride and discipline – Carlo Alberto liked the sound of that. The palace was duly reconfigured, and his infantry, drilled to within an inch of their lives, improved dramatically.

Obermann stuck around, and by and by the king and his pals joined in. Turin's aristocrats greatly enjoyed their private lessons, and Obermann greatly enjoyed the largesse they bestowed. On 17 March 1844, he and Count Ernesto Ricardi di Netro founded Europe's first sports club, the members-only Reale Società Ginnastica. They made out it was an important scientific/philosophical/ anthropological exercise, told the landed and the titled that it would confer significant health benefits, and invited them to pay an annual subscription.

Word got round, a second site was added, and with it more disciplines. These included fencing and shooting, but also swimming and rowing on the Po, and over time Obermann's non-competitive ideal faded. Gradually (and in the way of these things) shares were issued, and the merely very rich nurdled their way in. Given that membership conferred status and influence, the *Torino bene* – the new-moneyed industrialists – willingly coughed up. By 1861, the year the unification of Italy became a reality, even pallid, delicate, skinny-chested women were joining. Turin, its population now 218,000, was the sporting capital of Europe.

The unification – *il risorgimento* – had been a Turin project ideologically, but also practically. The Savoys had acquiesced in part because, with 70 per cent illiteracy and no common language, Italy was both disparate and inherently unstable. It was inevitable that Rome would eventually become the capital of the new country, so the Savoys' realm would disappear. However, there was a decent chance that no one would chop off their heads and they might even become rulers of the whole peninsula, so it was probably worth it.

In the spring of 1864, as Turin's well-heeled *sportivi* hopped, skipped and preened themselves in Parco Valentino, the onward travel of the city was altered irrevocably. Florence was anointed interim capital of Italy, and the *Torino bene* began to haemorrhage power and prestige, money and intellect. Parliament shipped out, and with it the courts, the central bank and the mint. Next the lawyers and their clerks, the architects and notaries, the lenders, the swindlers and the swindled.

On the morning of 21 September, an orderly crowd gathered before the Royal Palace. By lunchtime its numbers had swelled, and the beer halls were open. By dinner time it had become an angry, braying mob. Most weren't interested in Italy's grand design, but felt cheated. They were hungry and they were angry, and by the following afternoon 52 of them were dead. Turin was in crisis and so the mayor, Emanuele Luserna di Rorà, created an emergency council. They introduced cash incentives for start-ups and tax breaks for businesses prepared to relocate to the city. They dug new canals and insisted the gloating Florentines finance significant extensions to the railway network.

In October 1865, Luserna di Rorà drafted an appeal to foreign business owners. He had it translated into five languages, printed a million copies and dispatched them to Italian consulates abroad with instructions to pay whatever it took to have them stuffed into local papers. The industrialists of Hamburg, London and Paris read that Turin was *the* European centre for business, and was offering land at bargain-basement prices. The appeal also appeared in Zurich, Basel and Vienna.

Luserna di Rorà's initiative was unprecedented, and over time would result in spectacular, unprecedented growth. First came the Remmert family, and then Augusto Abegg took a slug of land at Borgone, transforming it into a factory and ultimately a village. The Gütterman and Ackermann families arrived from Vienna and Alsace respectively. By 1870 the Fréjus rail tunnel was open, and the economy was thriving once more. To the north of Turin, Biella became a centre of the wool trade as the Fila, Zegna and Cerruti families made their fortunes. At Chieri, a thriving mill town fifteen kilometres to the south, they celebrated by building an opulent *arco di trionfo* in the main square. On Turin's western fringes and down into the Susa valley, textiles were king. Italian labour was cheap, so vast quantities of cotton could be spun at low cost and freighted quickly across the Alps. This explains why the city is full of families with Germanic names, why they tend to own the poshest houses and why they're all stinking rich. Napoleone Leumann was the richest of all. In 1876 he built a cotton mill beside the canal at Collegno. He added Italy's first 'workers' village', taught his employees to read and write and took it upon himself to administer to their physical and spiritual well-being. In return they built him a fortune.

Along the valley road from Collegno stood Sant'Ambrogio. There resided the Bosio family and they too were cotton merchants. In 1886 they dispatched 22-year-old Edoardo to Nottingham, and there he got to kicking a bag of wind around with the guys from the silk works. He brought a load of the bags home with him, took them along to his rowing club, and started showing off with them in Parco Valentino. His pals joined in, and soon they had enough for a team. They called themselves Torino Football and Cricket Club, and their first opponents were Nobili Torino. They were a team comprised entirely of young aristos, so right from the outset all the games were class-based derbies.

There were mergers, fusions and new teams, and it's fair to say it developed into a sort of movement. Over in Genoa, a bunch of English sailors, clerks and scoundrels worked on and around the docks. They were quite skilled at the 'football', so the two groups started arranging matches. Then the *milanesi* joined in as well, so I guess that was the start of it all …

At the Massimo d'Azeglio secondary school, with the posh kids

Everyone in Turin knows the Massimo d'Azeglio. It's a secondary school in the heart of the baroque city, and the kids who go there are from 'good' (which is to say wealthy) families. It's synonymous with rigour and achievement, and if you graduate from there there's a decent chance that your folks have a summer house on the Ligurian coast and spend winter weekends skiing at Sestriere. It's also highly likely the job you're handed won't involve you getting too grubby. You'll need to dress and network well, but the chances are you're not going to be lifting heavy things.

In 1897, a bunch of posh kids from Massimo d'Azeglio decided to form a football team. They'd seen all these foreign types playing it in Piazza d'Armi, and it all seemed like a jolly jape. They met in a bike workshop, hummed and hawed over a name, and eventually settled on the Latin word for youth. In the beginning, 'Juventus' didn't have anyone to play against, but that was all right because they didn't know how to play. Eventually they got themselves some kit, and soon 200 were turning out to watch them. Given that they only did one thing, they soon changed their name from Juventus Sport Club to Juventus Football Club.

By now Turin was home to a small community from Nottingham. By all accounts one of them, Tom Gordon 'John' Savage, was a very good player, but he wasn't happy about the club's strip. The shirt was worn with a black bow tie and pantaloons, and there was nothing wrong with that. The issue was that it was pink, the colour of the new-fangled *Gazzetta dello Sport* newspaper. Savage and his mate Goodly thought it all seemed a bit flouncy, so in 1902 they took it upon themselves to order new kit from Blighty. There are any number of theories about what happened next, some fairly persuasive and the majority just plain risible. People get terribly hot under the collar about this sort of thing, so best is probably just to pick one at random and take it with a very large pinch of salt.

Legend has it that Savage sent the order and included one of the existing shirts for reference. The supplier/manufacturer assumed this had been white – because who in their right mind would wear pink to play football? – and that there'd been a washing accident. So, given that the order was urgent, he decided he'd best dispatch the closest thing he had in stock. What he had was a load of red Nottingham Forest shirts and a bunch of black and white Notts County ones. He sent the latter, and the famous *bianconeri* were born.

Six teams contested the Prima Categoria that year: three from Turin, two from Genoa and one from Milan. Juventus reached the final for the first time, but they had to travel to Genoa to play it. They arrived exhausted, and Genoa rolled over them 3–0 to claim their fifth championship in six years.

FIFA was born in 1904, and the following year the Italian federation was affiliated. The game was still strictly amateur, the Juventus players paying subs for the privilege of competing. By now the club had the best players in Turin and, in the Velodromo Umberto I, the best playing facilities. That spring they overcame the other Turin teams to qualify for the finals of the championship. They took on Genoa and UC Milanese in a round robin, remained unbeaten over the four games, and became champions of Italy.

The problem was that their new chairman, a Swiss named Alfred Dick, was pompous and autocratic. That was problematical for the old *Juventini*, for whom the game was just a hobby. It was recreational, and that implied camaraderie and fun. They enjoyed winning, and they *very* much enjoyed the celebrations which followed. For Dick, though, staying up into the small hours to *festeggiare* was unconscionable. They were men of sport, and his interpretation of what that entailed was at variance with theirs. He demanded that they be serious, ascetic and dutiful, and he wasn't interested in partying and infantile gratification. Juventus was a vehicle to confer prestige on him and his shoemaking empire, and the players would do well to comport themselves accordingly. Dick was filling his factories – and his football team – with players from Switzerland and Britain, some of them coarse working-class sorts. He was sucking the fun out of it all, and his proles were uncouth and unworthy.

Matters came to a head at the deciding game of the 1906 championship in Milan. Having inspected the playing surface, Dick proclaimed that it wasn't fit for purpose, and as a consequence Juve wouldn't start the game. The club forfeited the championship, and that turned the majority of the members against him. They sacked him, so he took his money, half the team and the lease he'd signed on the Velodromo, and founded a new club. The players of Torino FC would wear pomegranate-red shirts, and through them Dick vowed to exact his revenge.

Juve went back to scruffy old Piazza d'Armi, their first home. The two sides met there on 13 January 1907, and Hans Kämpfer, one of the defectors, scored the winner for Torino. They say that Dick didn't see it – he'd managed to lock himself in the toilet at half-time – but he was present three weeks later for the return. Kämpfer scored four this time, and one's tempted to think, *He who laughs last* … That, however, would infer that Dick knew how to laugh, and he was barely able to muster a smirk. Dick's new team had beaten the husk of his old one, but still he found no peace. Two years later he'd blow his brains out with a pistol in the bowels of the Velodromo, but the club he'd created – and the metaphor its creation embodied – would endure. Torino would remain the team of the disenfranchised and dispossessed.

Shorn of their best players, their neighbours were for the time being no footballing force. That was regrettable, but at least they had remained true to their ideals. Membership of the club was a status symbol, the preserve of the city's patricians, high rollers and in-crowd. They were reluctant to extend themselves too much in the pursuit of goals, because extending themselves to overcome a bunch of plebeians was beneath their honour. To be seen to be elegant, mannered and well-bred was of much greater importance than winning; football was a game for gentlemen.

No such airs and graces in Vercelli, a town of 30,000 or so set amid the rice fields near the Piedmont–Lombardy border. By then the football craze had spilled over to the toiling classes, and Pro Vercelli was a team full of them. They had no delusions of grandeur, and they loved nothing more than outscoring lily-livered, upper-class twits from Turin. Likewise their compatriots in neighbouring Novara, Casale Monferrato and Alessandria. The area, known as the Piedmontese Quadrangle, was Italian football's epicentre before the First World War. Pro Vercelli – the 'White Jumpers' – would win four national championships on the spin between 1910 and 1913.

Juventus almost folded that year. Football had become so popular that the Prima Categoria comprised three northern sections (Piedmont, Liguria-Lombardy and Veneto-Emilia Romagna) and three southern. The top two from each section qualified for a six-team mini-league, one in the north and one in the south. The respective winners of those played off in a two-leg *finalissima*, a final of finals which the northern champions always won by a cricket score. The chaff would be relegated to make way for new applicants, and that was where chummy old Juve came in. Much the worst side in Piedmont now, they lost the first Turin derby 0–8 and the second 8–6. They were demoted, having won only one game all season, but in Pino Hess they had a young, enthusiastic and brilliant lawyer as chairman. He exploited a legal loophole to gain them a place in the Lombardy section, and the club was saved from extinction.

Two years later, with Italy on the brink of war, the club launched a radical new magazine. The aim of *Hurrà* was to keep members abreast of club news regardless of where the conflict took them. In a country still 40 per cent illiterate, that was indicative. Turin was once more Italy's wealthiest city, and the *Juventini* were the wealthiest of the wealthy. They were the best-read and the best-bred, but the following year their football team entered a three-year hiatus.

On Giovanni Agnelli's doorstep, with Sandro Zambelli

Despite all the privations and death it had visited upon ordinary folk, the conflict had been good for Giovanni

Agnelli. His company had grown and diversified, and in the process contributed significantly to the war effort. FIAT had produced arms, engines and planes, and the shipbuilding and shipping divisions in particular had been highly lucrative. By the cessation it was Italy's third-largest manufacturer, and Agnelli was an extremely powerful man. In addition to FIAT he owned RIV, a ball-bearing company he'd founded in 1906, and part of the Turin daily *La Stampa*. He also had significant interests in textiles and cement, steel and aviation, and even in retail. Rinascente was Italy's first department store, and is still today her most famous.

Agnelli had made a lot of money relaying American aid to a devastated continent, and in the USA he'd visited the Ford plant in Michigan. He'd seen an automated 'production line' and been astonished by the speed and efficiency of it. At FIAT they'd been manufacturing a handful of cars each day, but Ford were making hundreds. The production time of a Model T was 90 minutes, and the build quality and precision were extraordinary. Agnelli resolved to build a line of his own in Turin, but for that he needed new money and new premises. His old headquarters in Corso Dante weren't big enough, and having workshops, offices and factories dotted hither and thither was inefficient, expensive and cumbersome. FIAT needed one large, fully automated, homogenous plant, and so he acquired a number of fields on the south-eastern edge of the city at Lingotto. He had the great rationalist engineer Giacomo Mattè-Trucco design a factory, and by 1922 it was almost ready.

Six kilometres north-west of Lingotto, another Giovanni Agnelli project was in the works. A director of Juventus, Sandro Zambelli, had been peeved because one of his players, Antonio Bruna, kept missing training. Bruna worked at FIAT, but his bosses were forever refusing him time off to train. This was having a negative impact on the team, so Zambelli cycled to Agnelli's house, knocked on his door and asked him to make an exception.

Agnelli was a rather cold, rather austere man but he appreciated Zambelli's candour. He agreed that Bruna could be released as the need arose, accepted an invitation to watch the team play and started going along with his son, 33-year-old Edoardo. Hitherto they hadn't had much in common, but over time they developed a shared passion for the game. When the club president indicated he was ready to stand down, they asked Giovanni whether he fancied replacing him. He was honoured, he said, but what with work and everything he'd struggle to find the time.

Edoardo, on the other hand, had lots of it. He enjoyed travelling, time-wasting and, notwithstanding the ethereal beauty of his red-haired wife Virginia, womanising. Beyond that, though, he hadn't located his métier, and he'd no particular inclination towards heavy industry. Football would at least occupy his time, and better still it would keep his father and the prosaic business of making money at arm's length. Giovanni accepted on his son's behalf, and agreed to chuck in towards a futuristic new stadium. On 24 July 1923 blonde-haired, blue-eyed Edoardo Agnelli was installed as president of Juventus Football Club.

In his acceptance speech, Edoardo told his fellow board members he'd be hands on. His motto was 'Even a good thing can be improved,' and this would inform everything he did. Mostly what he did was what the Agnelli family have been doing for a century since. He threw money – lots of it – at Juventus.

The new stadium, Campo Juventus, was situated close to the FIAT headquarters in Corso Marsiglia. Its design and construction were delegated to one of FIAT's board members, the engineer Pierino Monateri, and it was the first in Italy to be built from reinforced concrete. The stadium included beautiful Liberty-style offices and, for those with the wherewithal to afford the tickets, covered seats. There were tennis courts and gymnasiums – and floodlights, the first to be used in a sporting arena, would be added later. The city built new tramlines to ferry the 'supporters' back and forth, and giant publicity hoardings were installed around the periphery.

Technically, football was still an amateur sport. Players were obliged to prove they lived and worked in the *comune* of their clubs, and ostensibly at least weren't paid. It was increasingly popular though, and clubs were charging to watch matches. Where there's muck there's brass … And vice-versa. Some years earlier, two Genoa players had been suspended for being paid, found guilty of 'professionalism'. The clubs sought to circumvent the rules any way they could. Anonymous 'well-wishers' would bump into players and hand them bulging brown envelopes. Fans would organise whip-rounds, or stars would get prizes which would immediately be sold on their behalf. Ostensibly this was nothing to do with their clubs, but by hook or by crook the more ambitious owners found ways to look after their players.

There was nothing unprofessional about Edoardo's vision for his beloved *bianconeri*. He told Zambelli, Monateri and vice-president Enrico Craveri that together they were going to make Juventus the best team in all Italy. Edoardo Agnelli had a lot of money and a point to prove to his father, and he'd no interest whatsoever in finishing fifth or sixth each year. He started by appointing a coach. Hitherto the players had looked after themselves, but now the Hungarian Jenő Károly would take charge of training and team selection. Like all Agnelli employees he'd receive a salary and a week's paid annual leave. He'd also get a hefty bonus when the team won. The players would get one as well, and they'd drive company vehicles whether they liked it or not.

The new era began with a pre-season double-header against Pro Vercelli, Italian football's most successful team. Pro and Genoa had the best players in Italy, while Agnelli had inherited a group of deadbeats. Reinforcements were being added, but the residency rules meant his options were limited. On the surface the game was an innocuous pre-season friendly between the great of Vercelli and the not terribly good of Turin; in practice it would convulse Italian football, and its repercussions are still felt to this day.

Pro took the field without two of their best players. The reason for this is open to interpretation, and that partly explains why it's been interpreted, reinterpreted and misinterpreted for almost a century since. Everyone *thinks* they know what happened, but nobody *really* does. Broadly speaking, two wildly contrasting narratives have emerged. Football, particularly Italian football, is essentially binary, so there's a Juventus version and an anti-Juventus version. They exist in distinct geostationary orbits, and they are the history of the institution in microcosm.

In the context of the debilitating controversy around money, Pro Vercelli had informed their players that there wasn't any. Football remained an amateur sport, and the club would continue accordingly until further notice. Anyone who was uncomfortable with the idea was free to go, and evidently two of them *were* uncomfortable with it. Striker Gustavo Gay and full-back Virginio Rosetta told the founder and co-chairman, Luigi Bozino, that they wanted out. Gay said he'd had enough of provincial, one-eyed Vercelli. He wanted to move to Milan, and asked that he be deregistered and placed on the mandatory transfer list. That left him in a sort of limbo, because the residency laws stated that he couldn't play for Milan until such time as he could prove he lived there. Step forward the estimable Ulisse Baruffini, director of AC Milan and president of the Northern League.

Baruffini was in possession of a letter from one of his mates which attested that Gay was already resident in Milan and worked in a porcelain factory; it must have just slipped the player's mind to update his residency papers. Baruffini convinced the rest of the Northern League board members, among them his pal Bozino, that it was all perfectly plausible, and so Gay's transfer to Milan was expedited. Bozino, believed by some to be in financial difficulty, declared himself satisfied with the outcome, and Gustavo Gay started the new season a Milan player.

The good people of Vercelli found all this bewildering. How had Gay found time to train and play while simultaneously holding down jobs in both Milan and Vercelli? What's more, if he'd been living in Milan and working at the porcelain factory, then by definition he'd been playing for Pro illegally. Why, that being the case, had nobody reported it? Why hadn't the league sanctioned him then, and why weren't they stripping him of his playing licence now? It stank.

Rosetta's case was the same, but completely different. The Juventus version has it that Pierino Monateri had asked why the full-back was absent for the friendly and been told he'd asked for a transfer. Monateri had subsequently explained to Rosetta that there was a place for him in Turin, and with it a 'displacement' fee of 45,000 lire. Rosetta was an accountant by trade, and as chance would have it Sandro Ajmone Marsan, one of the Juve directors, was in need of one of those. Rosetta said he liked the sound of that very much indeed. Obviously he'd been tapped up, just as Gay had been tapped up by Milan. Everyone knew the game they'd been playing, but the system was predisposed to hypocrisy and technically at least they hadn't broken any rules. If, therefore, Rosetta could provide proof of residency, the way would be clear for him to sign for Juve.

Juventus, though, were a different kettle of fish to AC Milan. Monateri and Craveri understood that Agnelli's presence represented a clear and present danger to the old cabal who ran football in the north. They viewed Edoardo's arrival as a declaration of war, and would fight tooth and nail to derail the Rosetta transfer in the first instance and neuter Juve's influence in the long term.

The case would evolve into a battle of wills and ultimately a contest for political primacy. Numerically at least, the league were in the ascendancy, but Edoardo very well understood that numbers were just numbers. If being an Agnelli had taught him anything, it was that people were for sale. The likes of Bozino and Baruffini were corrupt, and so with time, patience and above all money, they were bound to come round.

On 16 November 1923, Rosetta attended a meeting of the FIGC, the governing body of Italian football. He provided evidence of his job and lodgings in Turin, and they confirmed that they'd sanction his move on condition that it was rubber-stamped by the Northern League. The problem there was that the *milanese* Baruffini was the league's president, and he and his lackeys were making it their business to obstruct the transfer in any way they could.

Their reasons were clear. They're as salient today as in 1923, and in many ways are the story of Italian football. Juventus was being bankrolled by the Agnelli family, rich industrialists from haughty, almost-French Turin. They had a swanky new stadium and fancy new ideas, and if left unchecked they'd use their riches to take over. The clubs of the quadrangle were much closer to Milan than to Turin geographically, linguistically and culturally. Novara is 15 kilometres from the Ticino, the river which divides Piedmont and Lombardy, and 40 kilometres from Milan itself. Priggish, holier-than-thou Turin, 100 kilometres to the west, was further away in every sense. Moreover the league had a lot to lose collectively as well as individually, so it made sense to hold firm and knock Agnelli down a peg or two. They therefore claimed that

Pro Vercelli had failed to circulate Rosetta's availability to all the clubs. Thus his registration as a Pro Vercelli player couldn't after all be rescinded, and he couldn't join Juventus.

Agnelli refused to be drawn into a public slanging match, but instead wrote to the FIGC. After a great deal of toing and froing, they overruled the Northern League and decreed that the transfer could go ahead. On 25 November, 'Viri' Rosetta made his debut for his new club, at home against Modena. Juve won the match 1–0, but Modena appealed to the league (effectively themselves) and were awarded a 2–0 victory. Juve were now at war with the other clubs and with the press. This turned the public sentiment against them, a development which was (and remains) key to the evolution of the club.

The following week, the mighty Genoa came to town. With the result in the balance at 1–1, the ball fell to … Rosetta. He smashed home the winner, but once more the result was overturned. Once more a counter-appeal was lodged with the FIGC, a battle for the moral and political high ground, the two sides still more intractable. Ditto the following week at Padova, and now rival league tables emerged. The FIGC *classifica*, the one endorsed by the International Olympic Committee, had Juve clear at the top. The league, however, had penalised them six points, so on 30 December the FIGC declared its board of directors – specifically the owners of Milan, Modena, Genoa and Internazionale – illegal. In response the league convened a meeting of their own and, by 156 votes to 1 (the 1 being Juventus) told the governing body of Italian football to take a running jump.

Eventually Juve were stripped of the player, the points and a championship they'd started to dominate. Technically at least Rosetta was returned to Pro Vercelli's roster, though as a Turin resident he wouldn't and couldn't play for them again.

The old guard had won the battle, but Agnelli was damned if they were going to win the war. From the outset, Craveri and Monateri had warned him that there would be resistance. He hadn't really grasped that at first, because he'd lead a cosseted life. Football, though, had acquainted him with the tactics of people who wished him ill. He'd been naive, but now he understood that sport and politics were indivisible. He and Juventus would only be successful on the pitch if they were clever off it. They'd need to deploy diplomacy, strategy and political brinkmanship, and from here on in they'd be doing just that. How best, therefore, to exact their revenge?

Italian club sides never ventured abroad. Transport was complicated, time-consuming and uncomfortable, and the players couldn't afford the time off. In April, however, Juve accepted an invitation from (of all places) Germany. They'd play six matches over twelve days and see to it that the players' employers were adequately compensated. They'd have to deploy their second string for the final league game against Inter, but in so doing they'd remind the sporting public of The Northern League's duplicity.

The German adventure was both quixotic and controversial, so it elicited considerable interest at home. That mattered a great deal, and it followed that if Juve performed well they'd augment not only their own prestige but that of Italy. They drew the first game in Berlin, and lost the second in Hamburg. Then, however, they walloped Hannover 6–0, and beat Bremen, Leipzig and Dresden. It was a fantastic return, and it played extremely well with the folks back home. It made them proud to be Italian, and when the players got back they were fêted as conquering heroes. Nothing like it had ever been attempted before, and the symbolism of defeating the Germans, the old foe, was lost on nobody. They'd been successful on the pitch, but more importantly in the circumstances, their victories constituted a political triumph for the country and Italy's ruling Fascist party.

The 1924 Paris Olympics were around the corner, and Italy had high hopes in the football. Rosetta was one of the stars of the national team, but Bozio, his erstwhile chairman at Pro Vercelli, would be in charge. He'd been the author of the whole sorry saga, and his depiction of Rosetta as a mercenary had been a low blow in the war against Juventus. Rosetta loved his country, but when the team departed for Paris on 20 May he stayed at home. Then, following advice from the Juve board, he wrote to the FIGC. Cleverly he stated that he couldn't go to France because his boss in Turin was unwilling to grant him the time off work. This confirmed the legitimacy of Juve's position, and further exposed the hypocrisy of his registration having been returned to Vercelli. It laid the blame fairly and squarely at the respective doors of Bozino and Baruffini, by extension Pro Vercelli and AC Milan.

Italy's Olympic dream was under threat now, so the case assumed national significance. In an attempt to break the impasse, CONI, the Italian Olympic Committee, beseeched Agnelli to intercede on their behalf. Notwithstanding the fact that Rosetta wasn't his player, he was apparently able to convince Ajmone Marsan, his boss, to let him fulfil his patriotic duty to his country. Ajmone Marsan was seen to agree, and Rosetta boarded a train to Paris on the eve of the opening match against Spain. At Juve's behest (as distinct to Pro Vercelli's) he was seen to play his part as the *Azzurri* won 1–0, and then again when they beat Luxembourg to reach the quarter-final.

It was absolutely masterful, and Rosetta came home a hero. He was 22, had a long career ahead of him, and the vicissitudes of the preceding months had convinced him that Turin was his home. It was inconceivable he'd be moving back to Vercelli, but he remained, absurdly, a Pro player. That being the case, it was up to them to decide: either they lost him with no recompense whatsoever, or they did some sort of a deal with Juve.

In the event, outsmarted old Bozio accepted a cheque for 50,000 lire. Agnelli didn't specify what the money was for, but he didn't need to. Juventus had broken the back of shamateurism, and transformed football into a market.

At the training ground, with four-year-old Gianni Agnelli

Italy was a new country, but also a disparate one. It was possessed of a common language, but hardly anybody used it. Rather its peoples spoke (and still largely speak) a myriad of local dialects. Their climates and customs differed greatly and so, as a consequence, did their foods, their cultures and the ways in which they perceived the world. The north had infrastructure, industry and, it could be argued, the beginnings of a homogenous culture. Cities like Milan and Turin were relatively wealthy and quite evolved. They were 'European', while the brigand south, the old kingdom of Naples, was a long way from Berlin, Paris and Geneva literally and figuratively. The *Mezzogiorno*, broadly speaking everywhere south of Rome, was agrarian, poor and illiterate. It had been haemorrhaging people to the Americas and northern Europe for decades, as had the eastern seaboard regions of Romagna, Marche and Abruzzo. They were impoverished economically and socially, and they were deeply disenfranchised from Rome.

Unification had been all well and good, but national unity never was built by decree. It evolves from shared values and experiences, and prior to the war the denizens of Piedmont and, say, Puglia, had neither. Any ideas they had about nation were theoretical, and they were united only in their antipathy towards and distrust of the capital.

Italy's war had been truly apocalyptic. She'd lost 1.2 million sons, and a further million had been maimed. However, the Austro-Hungarian empire had been defeated, Trentino and Trieste gained. Furthermore, for all the carnage and all the privations, Italians the length of the peninsula had experienced the conflict *together*. A literacy programme had enabled citizens to read about life at the front, and by extension to assimilate and disseminate the propaganda. From Venice down to Vesuvius, Milan to Messina, they'd been united in loss, in suffering and ultimately in a victory of sorts.

Young Italian males had fought and died side by side, and through the misery of it all they'd discovered that they weren't so different after all. They were all flesh and blood, they were all fighting for the same cause, and that cause was their country.

Following the armistice, a diplomatic row had developed over the status of an ethnically mixed city on Italy's north-eastern border. Italians believed that Fiume (now Rijeka in Croatia) was rightfully theirs, because Britain, France and Russia had signed an agreement to that effect in London back in 1915. Instead it had been designated a free state after the war. The Italians had been hoodwinked by perfidious Albion and the arrogant French, and worse still their own government, headed by the liberal Vittorio Emanuele Orlando, had caved in.

The Italian war hero Gabriele D'Annunzio had railed against Italy's 'mutilated victory'. He'd gathered together a band of nationalist irregulars and in September 1919 they'd occupied Fiume and demanded it be ceded to Italy. This had provoked a surge in virulent Italian nationalism led by one Benito Mussolini, and like all populists he'd been adept at exploiting grievances for political gain. This had fuelled the ascent of Fascism, and ultimately the March on Rome, which had seen him seize power in 1922.

In the summer of 1924, the great and the good of Italian football had a brainwave. During the occupation of Fiume, D'Annunzio had organised a football match between Italian troops and a group of local civilians. To distinguish themselves, the soldiers had sewn a small Italian tricolour – a *scudetto* – onto their shirts. This had proved highly popular, so now the FIGC decreed that

Italy's national football champions would henceforth get to do likewise.

With the residency rules relaxed following the Rosetta case, Juve made further signings in advance of the new season. The most significant was a foreigner, the first to play for the club post-war. Károly's fellow Hungarian, József Viola, was a good though by no means great midfielder, but in time he'd become a legend. The team led the championship heading into April 1925, but defeats against Pro Vercelli and Padova put paid to their title aspirations. Ultimately they finished third as Bologna, the regime's favourites, qualified from Northern League Group B. Elsewhere Genoa won Group A, and the two played off over two legs for a place in the national final. They drew 3–3 on aggregate, and then decamped to a neutral venue, Milan, for a play-off on 7 June.

By now the clubs had seen the value of having fans travel away from home, and Bologna were subsidising train fares and ticket prices. Thousands of their supporters descended on Viale Lombardia, Milan's home ground, but amid the various pitch invasions, punch-ups, police baton charges and generalised mayhem, Genoa led 2–0 at half-time.

Referee Gianni Mauro tried to abandon the match at this point, but was persuaded to run the gauntlet once more. On the hour he disallowed a Bologna goal and then, in the vernacular, it all went off. Mauro found himself encircled by rabid Bologna fans. Unconfirmed legend has it that a certain Leandro Arpinati, prominent Fascist and future mayor of the city, was among them. Accounts of what happened next vary, but the long and the short of it was that Mauro was effectively taken hostage on the pitch and told he wasn't going anywhere until he awarded the goal. He agreed and they carried on the game, but evidently Mauro told the Genoa captain not to worry. The goal would be subsequently disallowed, and the victory awarded to them regardless. Best, therefore, to play out the final 30 minutes and make the swiftest exit possible. On that basis the Genoa players agreed that it was probably in everyone's interest to finish the game and get the hell out of there. The problem was that Bologna equalised, and now the *genovesi* refused to countenance extra time. They didn't trust the ref after all, and figured that if Bologna won he'd renege on his promise. That being the case they'd be hung out to dry, so no extra time and another draw.

It seems that they were right. Mauro forgot the deal he'd made over the goal/non-goal, and the league threw out Genoa's appeal. To be fair they also threw one out from Bologna, who demanded that Genoa be disqualified for having refused to play extra time. This was no way of carrying on, so they put it down to experience and agreed to try again at another neutral venue.

That venue was Turin. The game itself ended 1–1, but then the directors of the respective clubs came to blows at the train station. The violence escalated, and two Genoa fans were shot in the ensuing riot. Bologna were invited to deliver the culprits to the *questura*, the police station, and informed that failure to do so would result in Genoa being awarded the win. Produce them – or someone not unlike them – they duly did, and it was agreed they'd give it yet another go at Campo Juventus on 19 July.

Problem now was that the authorities refused to host the game on public order grounds, and they finished up playing it behind closed doors on a mud heap somewhere south of Milan at 7.30 in the morning. Bologna finished with nine men, but managed to put everyone out of their misery with a 2–0 victory. They then beat Roma Alba, the southern champions, 6–1 on aggregate, to claim their first *Scudetto*. It was all highly prophetic; Italian football was shambolic, anarchic and corrupt, but also utterly compelling.

Over the season Juve had been very good at the back, with Rosetta in particular outstanding. In Gianpiero Combi they had the best goalkeeper in Italy, but the team was short of creativity. Thus, when Agnelli et al. convened to plan the season ahead, it wasn't difficult to figure out what was needed. Three years earlier, Juventus had played a Christmas Eve friendly against a travelling Hungarian side. Törekvés had beaten them 4–3, and one player in particular had been sensational. His name was Ferenc Hirzer, and although still a teenager, he'd been unstoppable. He'd scored two and made another one, and he'd been just about the fastest thing on two legs. Now Károly made contact, and Hirzer became the fifth of ten new *Juventini* to sign on.

Predictably enough they nicknamed him the Gazelle, and during pre-season training he received a very special visitor. Edoardo Agnelli's boy, four-year-old Gianni, loved football, the two of them had a heart-warming little kickabout, and apparently it did Hirzer the power of good. He scored a hat-trick in the opening game against Parma, and thereafter just kept going. He just kept scoring, Juventus just kept winning, and there was not a thing anybody could do about it. They beat Genoa home and away, and between January and April won an unprecedented nine games in succession. In the home fixture against poor Mantova, Hirzer scored five times in six first-half minutes, and he'd finish the season with a (still) record 35 goals.

Juve galloped away with Group B. They scored 68 goals in 22 games, and Combi famously went for 934 minutes without conceding. It earned them a two-legged final against Bologna, the first Italian city to have been taken by the Fascists and the party's spiritual home. There a new stadium, said to be the greatest of its kind in Europe, was under construction. Commissioned by Leandro Arpinati, it would be Fascist sport's first great amphitheatre. Externally it would resemble the Colosseum, while inside it would feature a giant bronze statue of Mussolini, resplendent on horseback. There would also be a 42-metre tower symbolising the ardour and spirit of the Fascist athlete, built on the very spot where the nationalist martyr Ugo Bassi had been executed in 1849.

More new stadiums would follow. The old national stadium in Rome would be tarted up and renamed the Stadio del Partito Nazionale Fascista. In Milan Piero Pirelli, tyre magnate and owner of AC Milan, would build a new ground at San Siro. It would be inaugurated on 19 September 1926, and a month later Torino would move into their new home. Their owner, Count Enrico Marone di Cinzano, was a distant cousin of Agnelli, but also something of a rival. He'd acquire a large plot in Via Filadelfia, on the western edge of the city, and on it he'd build a dreamy, opulent, red-brick art deco masterpiece. Though it would hold only 15,000, the Filadelfia would be much more beautiful than Campo Juventus, and infinitely more sophisticated. My stadium's better than your stadium …

The 1926 grand final would pit the Hungarian Károly against Hermann Felsner, his Austrian counterpart over in Bologna. Central European soccer was by a distance the best, and Hungarian and Austrian players and coaches proliferated across the continent. Bologna had placed an advertisement in a Viennese newspaper for a manager, and then interviewed the applicants. Felsner, apparently possessed of a 'football degree' from England, had got the job.

On the pitch, Hirzer would go toe to toe with Angelo Schiavio. Between them they'd netted 60 times in the regular season, and Hirzer added two more as the first leg was drawn 2–2 in Bologna. The second game was 0–0, so they reconvened for a play-off in Milan the following weekend.

What with the political climate and the pressure of the job, Jenő Károly had been operating under a great deal of stress. Now, on the Tuesday morning before the play-off, he began to feel unwell. He went home to Rivoli, west of Turin, but by lunchtime he'd died of a suspected heart attack. With the city in mourning, József Viola, his erstwhile translator, friend and confidant, was placed in temporary charge of the team. On a white-hot afternoon in Milan, Juventus honoured Károly's memory. Before the party bigwigs – Arpinati included – they won 2–1 to claim their first championship since 1905.

In two seasons, Edoardo Agnelli had first challenged the old cabal, and then upended Italian football's apple cart. Things, however, were about to become still more complicated. The very next day a new structure would be unveiled, and with it a completely a new footballing *realpolitik*. It would reward Agnelli's perspicacity on the one hand, but acquaint him with a foe infinitely more pernicious than the old guard of the Northern League on the other.

At Viareggio, with the Fascists

Prior to the Fascist accession, cycling had been the most popular sport for the man in the Italian street. Only a tiny majority could afford the modernist wonders being produced at Lingotto, and absent a public transport network, ordinary Italians had moved hither and thither on bikes. The sport of long-distance cycling was an extension of that fact, and the Giro d'Italia held Italy in its thrall each May. Now, though, cycling's pre-eminence was under threat.

Mussolini understood the political value of sports. He loved to be photographed doing them, and he'd particular penchants for tennis and fencing. He also enjoyed being photographed with a horse between his legs or strutting around bare-chested by the swimming pool. He carefully cultivated the image of a consummate *sportivo*, but he was no lover of bike racing. Its technology was primitive, and its protagonists were overwhelmingly working class. As a populist, Mussolini was obliged to pay lip service to it, but deliberately and famously he described its champions as 'proletarian'. By deploying the communist term he was deriding them as old-fashioned and unenlightened, and suggesting that their sport was the antithesis of Fascist modernity. The regime viewed motor sport – faster, more dangerous, technically cutting edge – as ideologically superior. It promoted its practitioners as Fascist exemplars, because they were pushing the boundaries of technology and bravery, and their exploits served the national interest. The drivers were sporting visionaries: swashbuckling, buccaneering daredevils who risked their lives to advance Italian values and virtues.

Football was more challenging ideologically, and Mussolini wasn't much interested in it per se. That said, huge crowds gathered in large, enclosed spaces to watch it, and as a vehicle for disseminating propaganda it was unrivalled. So popular was it that a successful national team could inspire all social classes, and so the regime focused on its collective, all-for-one nature. Like everything else in Mussolini's Italy it became a political construct, bent to Fascist will.

Football mattered a lot, then, but its officialdom was strictly amateur. The referees were volunteering former players and directors, and remained affiliated to their old clubs. The inevitable consequence, among a populace given at the best of times to controversy and conspiracy theories, was an endless slew of rows about officials' neutrality. The clubs were invited to specify those they felt were unsuited to officiate at their matches, a recipe for disaster if ever there was one. In theory all clubs got to choose, but in practice the bigger, wealthier ones seemed always to get the referees they wanted, and those lower down the food chain were often disadvantaged by contentious decisions. The whole thing came to a head following a disallowed goal during a game between Casale and Torino. The ref, Guido Sanguinetti, was accused by Toro of having officiated 'without the requisite serenity of spirit'. That was code for cheating, so the refs went on strike.

Next, amid rumours (later confirmed) of a 150,000 lire 'loan' provided by Juventus to the FIGC, ten of the smaller, provincial clubs formed an ad hoc association. By way of a riposte, the owners of ten of the more moneyed clubs convened a meeting of their own. In the normal course of events most of them couldn't stand one another, but they held it together long enough to declare, somewhat euphemistically, that football needed to be made more 'meritocratic'. They were no longer willing to underwrite the Northern League's debts and pronounced themselves heartily sick of the regionalised system. It compelled them to prop up clubs with whom they'd no affinity and also, in the case of their southern cousins, against whom they never even played. The two groups agreed that the current structure was no longer fit for purpose but had no common view as to what would replace it. So the Italian Olympic Committee – in effect the regime – delegated that decision to three 'experts' under the leadership of the former sports journalist Lando Ferretti.

Rumours had been circulating that non-Italians were to be barred from the game. Fascist rhetoric was designed to engender xenophobia among ordinary Italians, and foreign nationals were increasingly under attack. Slavic and French-sounding place and family names were Italianised, among them that of Juve's Italian midfielder Antonio Vojak. He became Vogliani, while József Viola morphed into Giuseppe. Agnelli resolved to keep him if at all possible, and likewise Hirzer.

Privately, Juventus argued that to kick out the *stranieri* would be a geopolitical own goal. It would mark Italy as myopic and unenlightened, the opposite of the modernist ideal Mussolini and his henchmen were so keen to promote. They were entirely right but also, as ever in their dealings with the party, entirely expedient. Edoardo Agnelli and his father understood that public criticism of the regime would be at best counterproductive, at worst catastrophic.

On 2 August 1926, the three wise men of Italian football emerged from a hotel on the Tuscan coast. The document they were clasping, later dubbed the Viareggio Charter, simultaneously nationalised football under fascism and recognised it for what it was – a market.

First the north–south divide, anathema to Fascist ideology and identity, would disappear. Truth be told, it had been nothing but trouble anyway. Such was the weakness of the game in the south that the grand final had become a farce. The southern champions had been routinely humiliated by their northern cousins on the pitch, and age-old regional prejudices had rendered it a public order liability off it. The new structure, the Divisione Nazionale, would instead divide twenty teams into two sections. Given the disparity in abilities, the old Southern League would provide only three of them. The Roman outfits Alba and Fortitudo were in, while the various clubs in Naples would be consolidated into a single entity. Initially at least, they would be whipping boys for the northern clubs.

The regime loved to promote strength and ardour, and all the usual blood and soil tropes. That said, they resolved to stamp out some of the more 'impulsive' behaviours the sport seemed to provoke among its supporters. Thus, Juve and Toro would each have to finish in the top three of their respective sections in order to play one another. If they did so they'd progress to a six-team mini-league, whose winner would claim the *Scudetto*.

A 'non-amateur' categorisation was to be introduced, as expected. The wording was a sop – players would be professional in all but name – but it provided a legal framework within which to address the old loss-of-earnings chestnut. Players could henceforth be paid, would be free to seek a transfer if they felt 'morally distressed', and the residency nonsense was swept away.

Despite Juve's pleas, Hirzer and Viola would be invited to leave Italy along with the other *extracomunitari*. They'd be afforded a season's grace, though only one would be allowed to take part in any given match. Viola, redeployed now as player-coach, would sit out most of the season.

All club directors would be vetted for their ideological suitability. Those who didn't come up to scratch would be replaced, and the FIGC would relocate to Arpinati's Bologna. As the party tightened its grip on the daily life of ordinary Italians, he would assume the stewardship of the national game. With the newspapers strictly censored and with radio now at its disposal, the party would portray the star players –particularly Bologna's – as model citizens at home and the very best Italian diplomats abroad. The club's new stadium was *the* symbol of fascism's sporting excellence, and so, by hook or by crook, Bologna would have a team worthy of it.

In downtown Turin, with Luigi Allemandi

The big cities dominated the 1926–27 season. Toro and Juve were joined in the final round of six by the two Milan clubs, by Genoa and by Arpinati's Bologna. The pioneering age of Pro Vercelli, of provincial football and of *dilettantismo* was thus consigned to the dustbin of history.

The two Turin clubs had generally rubbed along reasonably well. Their players had been part-time football enthusiasts, and many of them had grown up playing together. The Torino players and officials had attended Károly's funeral not through duty or political expedience, but because their friends were suffering. Though the oldest of all the derbies (not that the term had yet permeated Italian football), the matches between them hadn't been any more malevolent than, say, those between Bologna and Genoa. Nor had there been any thought of segregating those attending according to allegiance. Most *torinesi* thought nothing of watching Juve one Sunday and Toro the next, and indeed the practice had been quite commonplace. Blokes would go to church, eat lunch with the family and then toddle off to the match. Turin had its fair share of idiots, but many of those who attended matches were non-aligned – enthusiasts but not fanatics.

Football, however, increasingly captivated Italy and the Italians. Like the country itself it was provincial by nature and increasingly beset by a particularly virulent form of what Italians call *campanilismo*. For every parish there's a church, and for every church a *campanile*, a bell tower. *Campanilismo* is a pejorative term which denotes the excessive parochialism which has defined – or disfigured – the country for 150 years.

Italy is no more than a cobbled-together collection of city states and fortified villages, and its history is characterised by continual bloodletting. Fascism's great objective – and for a while it seemed its greatest achievement – was to mobilise *campanilismo* and to corral it into a coherent form of nationalism. Arpinati was committed to ensuring that football would play its part, and nobody doubted that a successful national team could contribute. The problem was that all the nationalist tub-thumping was diametrically opposed to the precepts of club football. Thus, given that Italians were a) crazy for club football, b) increasingly bellicose and c) sectarian by nature, there was bound to be trouble.

In the half-dozen years preceding Agnelli's intervention, Torino had been the better Turin side. They'd never won the national championship, but they'd invariably finished runners-up in their section. They were the workers' team, Juventus were the bosses', and so, regardless of the fact that Juve were the older club, they were never going to be more popular locally.

While Bologna was fascism's great bulwark, industrial, left-leaning Turin was reckoned to be the Italian city least predisposed to buy into Mussolini's project. Call it *vittimismo* or what you will, but many *torinesi* were uncomfortable with the idea that the fruits of their labour were being spent on a game. The Agnellis were using their profits to build a new stadium and a team of pampered athletes, openly blending football with commerce. Some were fine with it and many vehemently opposed, but hardly anyone was indifferent.

Juve won the first derby 1–0, courtesy of a header from one of Italian football's more flamboyant individuals. Born in Padua in 1903, Piero 'Cicca' Pastore had made his debut for his local club aged 15. He'd scored twice that day, and hadn't stopped scoring since. He'd moved to Turin when the residency laws had been relaxed, and had formed a cracking partnership with Hirzer. His great passion, however, lay elsewhere. He'd pretensions to be an actor, and following his Juve stint he'd move to Lazio to be near Rome's famous film studios. By then he'd developed a reputation as a gigolo, but he also built himself a half-decent acting career. Look carefully and you'll see him in *Roman Holiday*, among others.

On 5 June, Turin's two football clubs met again, this time at the Filadelfia. In Gino Rossetti, Adolfo Baloncieri and the Italian-naturalised Argentinian Julio Libonatti, Toro had a front three to die for. The so-called *trio delle meraviglie* were too good and too clever, and the fact that Juve were trailing only 2–1 with ten minutes left was due principally to Combi's heroics in goal. Then Pastore got himself sent off for a horrendous tackle on Enrico Colombari. Given that sendings-off were generally only handed out for common assault, it's safe to assume it was quite some challenge. Anyway, that was pretty much that. Juve, unusually bereft of fighting spirit, went down without so much as a whimper, and Toro went on to clinch their first championship.

Or so it seemed …

In downtown Turin lived a Sicilian student named Francesco Gaudioso. He was a football fan, and as chance would have it he shared his lodgings with a famous player. Luigi Allemandi was a highly promising young left-back, and he played for Juventus. It seems that prior to the derby, young Gaudioso had been in dialogue with Guido Nani. He did the books for Enrico Marone di Cinzano, owner of Torino and head of the eponymous vermouth dynasty. Gaudioso told Nani that with Allemandi's help he could see to it that Toro would win the match. The up-front fee would be 25,000 lire, with a further 10,000 in the event – highly probable – that Torino went on to win the championship.

Nani stumped up 5000, and for the rest he turned to Toro vice-president Eugenio Vogliotti. Gaudioso got his 25,000, and Toro beat a subdued Juve. They subsequently wrapped up the title with a game to spare, whereupon Gaudioso approached Nani for the outstanding 10,000 lire. Here, though, the story becomes somewhat opaque, complicated and (it must be said) *extremely* Italian. The broad and the short of it is that Nani told Gaudioso he wasn't getting another lira. The pretext was that Allemandi had been one of the better Juve players on the day so must have welshed on the deal and tried to win. Nani probably figured that Gaudioso wouldn't make a fuss. He already had 25,000 lire, and if he told anyone his own criminality would be exposed. Gaudioso, however, *did* make a fuss. He made the mother of all fusses, and in so doing scandalised Italian society.

He and Allemandi shared their lodgings with a journalist. Renato Ferminelli reported on Turin sport for Milanese and Roman newspapers, but he'd fallen out with Toro over his accreditation for their games. Ferminelli was a journalist with an axe to grind and now he had a major scoop. He wrote the whole thing up and published it in a series of sensationalist articles. One was headlined

SOMETHING IS ROTTEN IN THE STATE OF DENMARK, and although names were redacted, the message was abundantly clear: football in general and Toro in particular were institutionally corrupt.

In his role as president of Bologna and of the FIGC, Arpinati had a lot riding on football. He'd convinced Il Duce (as they were now obliged to call Mussolini) that in his hands the sport would become an asset to the regime, and he needed to make good on his promise. He had no choice but to be seen to intervene, and so intervene, in the form of an inquiry, he did.

Gaudioso had been a nondescript, indeterminate sort of a bloke. Of late, however, he'd become quite the man about town. He'd acquired all manner of fancy clobber and started eating in the best restaurants. Summoned to appear before the investigating commission, he first denied all knowledge of any wrongdoing and then, presumably having been acquainted with what lay in wait if he didn't cooperate, implicated two more Juve players. The 25,000, he said, had been split between Allemandi, Federico Munerati and Pastore, sent off during the match for his assault on Colombari.

Munerati denied involvement, though he did admit to receiving a case of plonk from the Toro directors in advance of the match. That wasn't so very unusual, though Pastore having placed a bet on his own team to lose seemed a bit odd. Technically, though, neither had broken any rules. There was no paper trail and no conclusive evidence, so they each got off scot-free.

That November, Arpinati issued his verdict. He stripped Toro of the championship and banned Allemandi for life. A torn-up letter he'd written to Gaudioso demanding payment had been pieced together, so he was bang to rights. Moreover, 23 Toro shareholders and members were barred from holding sporting office. Marone was among them, and, given that the Cinzano dynasty was a Turin institution and he regularly broke bread with European royalty, nobility and high society, this was a shocking turn of events. Still more shocking, however, was Arpinati's refusal to award the *Scudetto* to second-placed Bologna, his own team. In the normal course of events that ought to have been case closed. However because this is Italy and this is football, that was never going to happen.

The *Caso Allemandi*, it soon became apparent, was the tip of the iceberg. A consequence of the new money flooding into football was that matches were routinely being bought and sold, and the sport – Arpinati's great unifying project – was lousy with cheats, spivs and ne'er-do-wells. Alessandria's goalie was widely believed to have thrown a game against Toro, and the more they dug the more they found. Conspiracy theorists, crackpots and behavioural psychologists still pore over the minutiae of it all, and there's little likelihood they're going to stop any time soon. Over the decades it's assumed the characteristics of a *giallo* – a yellow – the term Italians use to describe the most intricate of mysteries.

Allemandi denied ever having received money from Gaudioso, much less having shared it with Pastore and Munerati. In point of fact that was pretty much his last public utterance, as he lay on his deathbed in 1978. If that seems extraordinary, it's because the *Caso Allemandi* was and still is. Everyone agrees that he was a decent chap, and he always claimed the letter he was alleged to have written was a forgery. Regardless, he found himself in a catch–22. Logic suggested that if he *had* received the cash from Gaudioso, he'd have been pretty dumb to draw attention to himself by playing badly. Better, surely, for him to be seen to carry on as normal, and newspaper reports suggest he played out of his skin. Without his heroics and those of 'rubber man' Combi, Juve would have been on the receiving end of a tonking. It's also a matter of record that Munerati and Pastore, his alleged co-conspirators, who had had no *direct* contact with Gaudioso, underperformed. What's more, hadn't the entire team seemed lethargic that afternoon?

Some hypothesise that Allemandi, a junior member of the team, was simply a mule. Though he *received* the envelope from Gaudioso, he knew not what was in it or what it was for. He simply handed it over to Pastore and/or Munerati as he had been told, and as a consequence made himself a patsy. Uniquely among the Juve players, Allemandi wasn't a member of the Fascist party. Moreover, by the time the inquiry had run its course he'd been sold to Inter, a club with less money and political clout than Agnelli's Juventus. Who better than a nonbeliever to carry the can, and who better to demonstrate the moral delinquency of those who opposed the regime's ideology than a crooked footballer?

Suspicion also began to hover around Rosetta – that's right, him again. He was a champion, and yet his error in letting an innocuous free kick through his legs for the first of the Toro goals that afternoon was so uncharacteristic it was bound to cause comment. Then weren't Marone and Agnelli as thick as thieves anyway? Weren't they all in it together, these millionaire industrialists, and wasn't football mutating into just another shady private members' club? Wasn't Agnelli a major shareholder in *Il Resto del Carlino*, Bologna's favourite paper, and wasn't he negotiating with Arpinati to divest himself of those shares? Wasn't the deal that if he relinquished them to the party then FIAT (and by extension Juventus) would be taken care of when the public works contracts were handed out? Yes, yes and categorically yes …

Then what, amid all this sleaze, of Arpinati himself? The party propagandists claimed that writing off a season's football, while undesirable, was both sensible and fair. So widespread was the corruption that to award the title to Bologna would be to open Pandora's box. As more dodgy refereeing decisions came under the spotlight, there was speculation that he and Marone had been engaged in a sort of match-fixing tug-of-war. Some were convinced that while Arpinati (or more likely his former associates) threatened the refs, the Toro president was attempting to buy them. Arpinati couldn't award the title to Bologna, because to do so would simply confirm to the Italian public that the sport was institutionally corrupt.

Arpinati had been a Fascist vigilante, and a pretty brutal one at that. His rise had been meteoric, and he'd been adept at currying favour with Mussolini. Everything he did was self-serving, rooted in political expediency. Many thought that he couldn't have cared less about fairness per se, because like most career politicians his sole objective was to be *seen* to be doing the right thing. Everyone knew Bologna was his team, but it was also Mussolini's town. Awarding them the championship would be perceived as pure *campanilismo*, and that, in the long run, would be counter-productive both for Arpinati and for Il Duce.

The 1927 championship has never been assigned, and everyone except the small-fry Nani received an amnesty. Allemandi would win the World Cup with Italy in 1934, which of course made him untouchable. Italy was indivisible from fascism by then, and Fascists didn't cheat. His stock has risen further still since the Second World War. The revised version has it that he, a non-Fascist, had been a convenient scapegoat for the regime. The point here is that fascism's great victory had been but a mirage, and that 500,000 Italians died in the conflict. In postwar, revisionist Italy, hardly anyone admitted to having been a card-carrying party member. In Allemandi's case there was demonstrable *proof* that he wasn't, so the former pariah was perceived as a great patriot. All this, of course, because history will have its way ...

The *Caso Allemandi* has never truly been resolved, and over the years there have been repeated calls for it to be reopened. That's partly because, if there's one thing Italians love more than football, it's a good old-fashioned *giallo*. As recently as 2015 the Toro owner, Urbano Cairo, demanded that it be re-examined. Cairo owns RCS, a media conglomerate which publishes *La Gazzetta dello Sport*. He's a very powerful man, and he's made it his project to have the 1927 championship restored to Toro. They haven't won one since 1976 and nor, given that Cairo will probably neither bankrupt nor sell the club, are they likely to any time soon. Watch this space ...

Allemandi happened almost a century ago, and of course there have been countless football scandals since. Virtually without exception they've been good for business in the long term, because outrage, faux-outrage and tittle-tattle are the lifeblood of the sport in Italy. In that respect *Allemandi* is both the prototype and the archetype, a mirror on the way Italians view sport, institutions and the world in general. They don't trust politicians, they *certainly* don't trust power and, outside their own kith and kin, don't particularly trust one another. They generally like one another and even respect one another, but that's another matter entirely.

Not for nothing are there more lawyers in Italy than anywhere else in Europe, and not for nothing do Italians have a perception of sport which is the antithesis of their northern European cousins'. To thrive in the Italian Republic (or even to *survive* it), you need to be smart and resourceful, and even cunning. If Italians have a reputation for the latter it's because everyday life on occasion resembles a competition between the state and its citizens. It's a giant intellectual, bureaucratic and fiscal chess match in which everyone is obliged to take part, and this explains why they admire stealth as much as strength. They understand that sport doesn't exist in a vacuum, and they're not so deluded as to believe that it operates according to some dim-witted Corinthian ideal. The latter-day Juventus mission statement – that the only important thing is winning – is a natural extension of a mindset which recognises that results on the pitch are conditioned by politics and statecraft off it. By commercial acumen and diplomacy, subterfuge, artifice and guile.

Eleven against eleven it may be, but there's infinitely more to Italian football than Italian football.

Chapter 2

The Best of Times,
the Worst of Times ...

> For fascism the state is absolute, individuals and groups
> relative.
>
> Benito Mussolini

At the Amsterdam Olympics, with
Raimundo Orsi

Inspired by the Libonatti–Rossetti–Baloncieri *trio delle meraviglie*, Toro finally had their day in the sun the following season. During the opening phase they won 14–0 at Reggiana, and scored 11 against both Brescia and hapless Napoli. 'Matador' Libonatti and Baloncieri scored 66 goals between them, more than their neighbours' team tally for the entire season. Deprived of the talisman Hirzer, Juve finished a distant third.

Juventus needed goals, and goals were football's most expensive commodity in 1928, just as they are today. The question was where to find them? In Angelo Schiavio, Bologna had a young, rapier-quick, natural goalscorer, but no amount of money would prise him away. Nor were Genoa likely to part with the splendidly nicknamed

Felice 'Net Ripper' Levratto. The day-to-day management of clubs like Bologna and Genoa had been taken over by the party. Mussolini had installed his flunkeys, and the sport's mutation into a scene of internecine party squabbling compromised Agnelli's ability to buy the players he wanted.

That summer, Juve's Combi and Rosetta represented their country at the Amsterdam Olympics. The tournament was won by Uruguay (Italy finished third), but the undisputed star was a brilliant little Argentine, a left-sided Hirzer facsimile named Raimundo Orsi.

Shortly after the release of the Viareggio Charter, Agnelli had dined with Arpinati on the banks of the Po. He'd wanted to find a way to keep Hirzer, but in the event had to settle for a single year's grace. However Arpinati had intimated that he wasn't averse to the idea that footballing sons of the Italian diaspora might return. Hungry Italians had been emigrating to the Americas for the thick end of 70 years now. Vast numbers of them, particularly from the desolate south, had made their way to Argentina, and their national team was full of Italian surnames. How better to demonstrate Italian modernity and excellence than by enticing them back? They'd escaped the poverty of the old regime, but now there was political and sporting capital to be gained by their repatriation.

Some years earlier, Toro's Libonatti had been granted citizenship. Though brought up in Argentina, he'd grown up speaking Italian and *feeling* Italian, and he'd gone on to play in the Italian national team with distinction. While the notion that European non-Fascists might despoil Italy's gleaming new stadiums was abhorrent, these 'unredeemed' Italians, the so-called *oriundi*, might be a useful propaganda tool. They might also improve the national team, and Arpinati had staked his political future on precisely that.

With Combi and Rosetta waxing lyrical about Orsi, Agnelli sat down with his right-hand man. Giovanni Mazzonis had been born into a family of Turin nobles, and like many young men of breeding had played football for Juventus. He was a stern man and a wealthy man, but also a brilliant one. The players had nicknamed him Stalin on account of a distinct physical similarity, and it's fair to say that he brooked no nonsense. Agnelli, on the other hand, was collegiate by nature. Though born into privilege he wasn't dogmatic, and he delegated much of the decision-making to Mazzonis. It's to his credit that he viewed him as an equal, and to Mazzonis' that he respected Agnelli's judgement.

The two of them drew up a shortlist of the positions they needed to fill, and the players they wanted to do the filling. They then assembled a transfer committee and dispatched a secret emissary to Buenos Aires. He tracked Orsi down – probably not difficult given he was a sporting deity – and immediately agreed to pay him 100,000 lire up front with a further 100,000 per year in salary. In a single month he'd earn a FIAT *operaio*'s annual wages, and there'd be a top-of-the-range FIAT 509 Sport to boot.

None of which cut any ice with the Argentine footballing authorities. They refused to release the player, in part because they understood Italy represented a dream ticket not only for Orsi, but for all their best players. It meant Europe, but also football as a career and a life less ordinary. Orsi was the jewel in their crown, and if they allowed him to leave then others would surely follow. Argentina's talent pool would be decimated, and with it the national team, so they dug their heels in.

The problem was that Agnelli dug his in as well. He knew that if Orsi simply downed tools and left he'd be suspended for a year under FIFA rules. That said, he'd only be 27 at the end of his suspension, so in principle he'd still have a few good years ahead of him. The money was neither here nor there, because Agnelli and Mazzonis would cover half of it. The rest would be underwritten by Monateri and the other board members, wealthy men all. The club was in need of new blood and a new impetus, so they agreed to pay Orsi's wages while he was suspended and to organise as many friendlies as possible to keep him ticking over for a year.

Raimundo 'Mumo' Orsi packed his bags and crossed the Atlantic.

Agnelli appointed a 32-year-old Scot as team coach. Willy Aitken was an advocate of the fashionable new 'method' formation, and that was great in theory. Unfortunately, though, the group of players he inherited was ill-equipped to master it. The strikers were ordinary, and there was a distinct lack of authority among the halfbacks. Rosetta was Rosetta, but having failed to adequately replace Allemandi they were short of a left-back. Time, therefore, for the transfer committee to earn its corn.

Another of the Olympic team, Umberto 'Berto' Caligaris, had grown up a stone's throw from Rosetta in Casale Monferrato. Alongside Combi, the two of them had been the backbone of the side in Holland. Their excellence had enabled the *Azzurri* to punch above their weight, and when he got home Caligaris was informed that Juve wanted him. He'd only ever played for his home-town club, but with the best will in the world there was no way Casale were going to be competitive in the new football. It was nice, Casale Monferrato – elegant and comely and surrounded by glorious, verdant, pin-cushion vineyards. It was *tranquillo*, and it was home, but Juventus were offering a mind-boggling amount of money, and those new FIATs were lovely. Caligaris started looking for lodgings in Turin.

It could be argued that there were two 1928–29 seasons in Italian football. The first, and simultaneously the last of the Divisione Nazionale, was only ever going to result in a head-to-head between Toro and Bologna, the irresistible force and the immovable object. The other was a de facto play-off for places in the new Serie A. The first eight sides from each of the two groups would make it, while the rest, the old-world amateurs and the provincial have-nots, would be condemned to the below-stairs of Serie B.

While Juve were reconfiguring football off the pitch, Toro were doing hitherto unimaginable things on it. They scored 115 goals in 30 Group A games, 31 more than Bologna, the runaway winners of Group B. A two-legged final couldn't separate them, so on 9 July they each made for the cauldron of Rome. There, in the stadium renamed in his honour, Il Duce and his serfs settled in for 90 minutes of madness.

The game back then was unvarnished at the best of times. Italy was a nation heading deliberately and inexorably to war because, quite simply, Fascist ideology glorified death. Football has always been but a mirror on everyday life, and in Mussolini's Italy daily life was more brawn than brain. The players kicked lumps out of one another in the first instance because they could, and in the second because to do otherwise would have been derelict. If they maimed the opponents' better players they were more likely to win, and with the refs having been issued newer, tougher guidelines games routinely finished ten against ten, eleven against nine or whatever. This one finished nine against nine, the *bolognesi* winning with a late winner from another iconic figure.

Italians always did love a nickname, and during fascism they tended to be macho and quite gladiatorial. Local-boy-made-good Giuseppe 'Teresina' Muzzioli, however, was very much the exception to the rule. He was a cracking left winger, but he'd inherited some sort of glandular condition which had visited upon him what can only be described as small breasts, a marked tendency towards bloat and, as a consequence, the least flattering appellation in Italian football. The Italian suffix *ina* (or, when appended to a masculine noun, *ino*) is a diminutive. 'Teresina' therefore meant 'Little Teresa'. It was a reference – not *entirely* flattering – to the self-proclaimed fattest woman of all of Italy, Teresa Polsini. So now you know.

Aitken's Combi–Caligaris–Rosetta axis was the best defence in the league, but the Juventus attack was another story. Once more the goals dried up when the going got tough and the playing surfaces deteriorated. They failed to win any of their last eight games and finished second – again – seven points behind Bologna. They did beat Inter to qualify for the Central European Cup, though they were beaten over two legs by Slavia Prague. The real story of their season, however, lay elsewhere.

Agnelli had promised Orsi there'd be matches for him to play in, so Juventus embarked on a tour of the provinces. Everywhere they went he wowed the locals, who couldn't get enough of his dribbling, his pace and – wonder of wonders – his ability to *bend* a football. The guy could score direct from a corner kick, and that had never been done before. There was also a highly symbolic Christmas Day friendly with a Hungarian national side, the great Hirzer pitted against his heir apparent Orsi. The *transalpini* of Marseilles were beaten in their own back-yard, and Buenos Aires' Barracas Central embarrassed at Campo Juventus. As the anticipation of his competitive debut grew, all of Italy seemed in the grip of *Orsimania*. There were no points at stake, but they queued round the block all the same. The friendlies were very important historically, because they marked an evolution of the philosophy which had informed the Germany trip in 1924.

Like many of the 'second' clubs of big cities, Torino prides itself on being the locals' choice. Though demographic changes and Juve's hegemony have challenged that conceit, it still just about rings true; among the older Turin families at least, there are still more *granata* fans than *Juventini*.

There are a great many reasons for this, but chief among them is the fact that Agnelli's Juventus never set out to represent the city or its occupants. Juventus are probably unique in world football because they've always made it their business to represent their country rather than their home city. That distinction has underpinned their success for the best part of a century. These days it goes without saying that the most successful football clubs are global brands by design. That's a relative novelty though. Shirt sponsorship didn't arrive until the early 80s, and prior to that Italian clubs derived almost all of their income from transfers, benefactors and Sunday-afternoon bums on seats.

Prior to the Agnelli family intervening in 1923, football had been an amateur sport. *Campanilismo* was more or less congenital, and nobody had given much thought to abstracts like marketing and demographics. That was because, for all that some of the clubs were patronised by wealthy industrialists, football and business were two entirely distinct entities. FIAT had no *direct* way of monetising the sport's popularity with Sicilian bank clerks and Tuscan factory workers. That said, the directors understood that they wanted to own things, and the things they wanted to own most of all were the things being made at Lingotto. The motor car was already *the* symbol of social status, and everyone dreamed of owning one. Turin constituted less than 10 per cent of the Italian market, so the trick was to win over ordinary folk all over the country. That was where Juve came in.

Giovanni Agnelli, in common with all Italian industrialists under fascism, also had a lot to lose. There's a school of thought, propagated mainly by modern Juve historians, that he had no interest in ideology one way or the other. They would have us believe that his one true faith was FIAT, and he simply did whatever it took to avoid falling out with the party. Supposedly the Agnelli family merely paid lip service to fascism, understanding that in order to thrive they needed to exploit both its populist tendencies and its insecurities. If Juventus could become Italy's favourite team, the regime would be less inclined to move against FIAT.

Of course in a society in which everything is politicised, everybody needs to adapt. However it's also a matter of record that Toro fans started turning up to games wearing scarves the scarlet of communism. They became extremely fashionable at the Filadelfia, and a caustic rivalry developed between their team and 'Fascist' Bologna. Obviously both sides were competing towards the top of the league, but then so were Inter, Roma and Genoa. The press was censored, but there's plenty of empirical evidence suggesting that Toro was the closest thing to an anti-Fascist club in Italy. Walk around Turin, and you're pushed to find anyone over the age of seventy who would claim to be both *Juventino* and socialist. You're hard-pushed because the old *socialisti* all support Toro.

Mussolini relied on popular support, and he'd identified football as a means of gaining it. More and more Italians were falling in love with it, but most clubs were parochial in their outlook. While they were minding their own guileless businesses, Juventus were busy co-opting journalists and politicians, showbiz sorts and opinion formers. The more of them they won over, the more the team strengthened FIAT's hand in dealing with Rome and the more the family business was indemnified against Mussolini's idiocy and the ideology's worst excesses. In political acumen, strategy and image management, the Agnellis were already streets ahead.

Giovanni Agnelli probably wasn't a convinced Fascist ideologue, but he collaborated with and benefited from the regime. He was also a senator; for that you had to be a party member, and membership was obligatory when tendering for public works. He won lots of them, and made gargantuan sums of money from projects like the construction of the Milan–Turin motorway. Later, during the Nazi occupation of Turin between 1943 and 1945, he happily broke bread with the *Wehrmacht*. If anyone was being played, therefore, it was the people whose efforts filled the Agnelli coffers, those subsequently deported to Auschwitz and the resistance fighters his Nazi dinner-party guests would routinely butcher in cold blood.

Back in 1929, by the time the all-new Serie A began in September, the English term 'football' had been proscribed in favour of *gioco di calcio* – 'kicking game'. In common with all sporting bodies the FIGC had been relocated to the capital, while Triestina, the team of the disputed north-eastern city of Trieste, had been shoe-horned in for political reasons. Most people couldn't have cared less about all that though, because they only had eyes for Orsi. In addition to him, Juve had acquired a tall, elegant young half-back named Giovanni 'Nini' Varglien. His older brother Mario had been a mainstay of the team the previous season, and both would enjoy successful careers in black and white. Juventus were improving, but for all Orsi's brilliance the endless friendlies caught up with them. They were lucrative, these extra games, and as PR exercises they were priceless. They came at a price though, and by the spring the players were out on their feet. They lost three of the last six, and Inter, renamed Ambrosiana because the party couldn't stomach the 'Internazionale' tag, galloped away to claim the title.

Ambrosiana were managed by Árpád Weisz, a Hungarian Jew believed by many to be the most astute football man of his time. For now there were no restrictions on foreigners coaching in Italy, just playing. Eventually, though, Weisz would fall victim to the racial laws enacted following Hitler's visit in 1938. He'd be deported with his wife and kids, and would die in Auschwitz in 1944.

During Orsi's 'gap year', he'd been tasked by the board with identifying and tapping up other high-class *oriundi*. He'd made overtures to Renato Cesarini, a striker born in central Italy but whose family had emigrated when he was a toddler. When, at the end of the season, Cesarini disembarked at Genoa, his ship had come in figuratively and literally. He was as mad as a box of frogs, and his nocturnal comings and goings are legion. Mazzonis was forever fining him, but he'd a great physique and an even better technique.

The board at Juve liked big ideas and critical thinkers, and Aitken, nice chap or otherwise, hadn't been convincing. Nobody doubted his decency, but there was something one-dimensional about him, something pedestrian and uninspiring. They made it clear they wouldn't be renewing his contract, and it would be the best decision Agnelli and Mazzonis ever made.

At Corso Marsiglia, with Carlo Carcano

In common with most of the provincial clubs, Alessandria had been hit hard by the move to professionalism. They'd been flirting with relegation, but in 1926 a returning son had rescued them from footballing oblivion. Carlo 'Carlin' Carcano had spent his playing career at the club, and as a coach he'd made them a force once more. Though Alessandria were still ostensibly amateur, he had them doing all manner of cutting-edge stuff. There were post-game debriefs, psychological profiling, 'scouting' trips to watch forthcoming opponents ...

Carcano was just different to normal football people. He dressed differently, moved differently and, above all *thought* differently. He had a slightly ethereal quality about him, but also an understanding of the footballer's psyche. Under his tutelage, Alessandria had finished the inaugural Serie A season joint sixth with Roma and Bologna. In modern football that was miraculous, because they were a team of part-timers in a provincial town of 80,000. Vittorio Pozzo, simultaneously national team manager, *La Stampa* journalist and godfather of Italian football, reckoned Carcano was a prophet.

Carcano joined Juventus for the 1930–31 season. With him came a wonderful inside left named Giovanni Ferrari, and the combination with Orsi was a mouth-watering prospect. Throw in the striker Giovanni Vecchina and Cesarini, and, five years on from the last championship, *la vecchia signora* seemed finally to have a team capable of sustaining a challenge. They confirmed it by winning eleven of their first twelve games.

On 15 March 1931, Juve travelled to Roma, finished with nine men, and got thumped 5–0. You can see highlights on YouTube, and they're worth a watch. The players don't shake hands like namby-pamby liberals, but rather give a full-blooded and by now mandatory Fascist salute.

The spectators are suited and booted and still in their Sunday best, and the tackling is probably best described as robust. The result was unexpected and highly unusual, but what followed was instructive. By then, Italy was a country obsessed by *calcio*. No stadium sport had ever resonated quite so much, and through radio broadcasts and newspapers people were able to consume it remotely. Sunday afternoons at the football weren't quite as ubiquitous as Sunday mornings in church, but even the more modern stadiums were struggling to cope with the numbers. Football was becoming what football, for millions of Italians, would remain. Not so much a way of life as the prism – one-eyed, delusional or otherwise – through which they viewed the world.

The Roma match is a case in point. It became so famous that they made a movie about it, or at least around it. Appropriately enough it was called *Cinque a Zero*; it came out at Christmas and, despite competition from Joan Crawford and Greta Garbo, it was a huge hit. It filled cinemas not because it was any good – by all accounts it was garbage – but because it ticked all the boxes. A load of old nonsense perhaps, but nonsense about the holy trinity of love, life and football. The runaway success of a new magazine, the weekly *Calcio Illustrato*, simply underscored the fact that Italians were hooked on the game.

It turned out the Roma debacle was just a blip. Despite its limitations, Campo Juventus was a fortress. Juve dropped only three points there, and ran away with the *Scudetto*. They were good, but under Carcano they were about to get a whole lot better. The *quinquennio d'oro* – five golden years – had begun ...

Another brilliant *alessandrino*, Luigi Bertolini, joined in summer 1931. A right-sided midfielder capable of covering prodigious distances, he was reckoned to be the best header of a ball in Italy. He loved heading it, Bertolini, and he loved to bandage his head, rugby lock-forward style, in readiness for the heading. They were heavy, those old balls, and quite percussive. They had laces on the outside. Bertolini's regular midfield partners would be Ferrari, Varglien and another Argentine son of Italian parents. Luis Monti had been the scorer of the Argentinian national team's first ever goal, and he'd played in that 1930 World Cup final alongside Orsi. Given his nickname back home had been 'the butcher', it's not hard to deduce what kind of midfielder he was. It's true to say he was a tackler like no other, though he was also a very tidy passer of the ball.

After the World Cup, Monti had decided to call it a day. Though only 29, he'd won three championships with his club side, San Lorenzo, and said there was nothing more he could achieve as a player. He was going to take time out and think about his next move, but then a letter arrived from Turin. Orsi had convinced Juve's directors that Monti was the best defensive shield in the business. He'd told them he was precisely the player they needed in front of Caligaris and Rosetta, and they took him at his word. However, when he stepped off the train at Porta Nuova he weighed 92 kilos, and that was about 15 too many.

The press had a field day. They applied the epithet 'double wardrobe', and he responded by refusing to talk to them. Instead he set about proving that he was a serious athlete, and in tandem with Juve's fitness coach

Guido Angeli did precisely that. He'd be up at six, and begin the day with a run to Stupinigi, the great Savoy hunting lodge to the south of the city. Out-and-back and out-and-back, and all this wearing three great sweaty woollen jumpers. Then the medicine ball, a slab of beef for lunch and repeat ad infinitum. They'd thought it hilarious when he'd shown up with all that ballast, but he who laughs last . . .

By December, the *bianconeri* in general and the three *oriundi* in particular were tearing it up. Orsi was the magic, Cesarini the craft, Monti the destroyer-in-chief, crowd favourite and talisman. Off the pitch he was a very private man, but on it he was a winner, a scrapper and a bit of a nutter. That, for football fans, has always been a winning combination, and with him as the fulcrum Juve won and won again.

The Italians were smitten by the *oriundi*, and the more successful they became the more they were deployed as political pawns. Initially there had been controversy around their arrival, particularly in light of the treatment meted out to other foreigners. The difference, the party maintained, was that these sons of Italians were repatriating their genetic superiority. They'd *chosen* Italian citizenship, and in so doing sacrificed friends, family and in most instances the country of their birth. Besides, if they were prepared to die for Italy – and it was implicit that they were – then nobody could deny them the right to represent it on the football pitch.

Sport was absolute, easy for the man in the Italian street to understand, and easy for the propaganda machine to spin. Each win by boxer Primo Carnera, racing driver Tazio Nuvolari and cyclist Learco Guerra was portrayed as a great patriotic act. Italy's sporting champions were bigger than what they did, and what they did transcended mere sport. It legitimised Fascist ideology, and by now the ideology was indivisible from the flag. So when the *Azzurri* won, it induced still more loyalty and still more patriotism. That largely explains why they played more friendlies than other European sides, and why they took part in as many international tournaments as they could. They played eight times in all in 1931, and remained unbeaten throughout. In Giuseppe Meazza, Ambrosiana-Inter had Italy's pre-eminent footballer, but the backbone of the side was cast-iron black and white. Combi, Caligaris and Rosetta were the shield, Ferrari, Orsi and Cesarini the sword. *Forza Italia, e forza Juve ...*

The final game of the year, against Hungary at the Filadelfia, looms large in Italian sporting lore. As usual Pozzo selected his six *Juventini*, and one of them, Cesarini, scored a historic injury-time winner. Italy had finally toppled one of the central European leviathans, and the country went berserk. Injury time became the 'Cesarini Zone'. The term was immediately hardwired into Italian footballing argot, and there it remains.

The 1931–32 domestic season developed into another battle of wills with Arpinati's Bologna, but they blinked in the spring. In one catastrophic month they lost to Milan, Genoa and Inter, as Juve kicked on to a second successive title. Bologna were a good side, but in the battle for Italian sporting primacy Arpinati was outthought, outspent and ultimately outplayed. Agnelli, Mazzonis and Carcano had outmanoeuvred him, and made their football club *la fidanzata d'Italia* – Italy's sweetheart.

By the time the 1932–33 season began, Mussolini had imposed punitive tariffs on imported vehicles; from here on in Italian people would be driving Italian cars. Ownership had previously been the preserve of the wealthy, but the FIAT 508 Balilla turned that on its head. Produced at Lingotto, it cost just over half as much as its predecessor, and would sell in unprecedented quantities. It was to middle-class Italians what the Model T Ford had been to middle-class Americans – a new way of life and a dream come true. Little wonder Il Duce chose to celebrate the tenth anniversary of the March on Rome with a visit to the FIAT factory and a speech which was prolix even by his standards.

Once they hit their stride, Juve ran away with it. They dropped only one point at home, and in 19-year-old Felice Borel discovered a goal-scoring meteor. They called him *il farfallino*, 'the bow tie', because of his lightness and grace, but also because his hands flapped by his side as he ran. Inter's Meazza was all bustling purpose and brute strength; Bologna's Schiavio speed and sinew; Borel was 60 kilos of something else altogether. Where others laboured he seemed to glide. Where they trudged through the February mud, he skated over it. He had neither the power nor the pace of Meazza and Schiavio, and yet for two years he was unplayable. He scored 61 goals in 60 games, and he did so with astonishing facility. He'd receive the ball and then, seemingly irrespective of where he was on the pitch, slalom to within shooting range. Then – and this was the most astonishing thing of all – he'd *place* the thing, ever so carefully, out of the keeper's reach and into the corner of the goal.

Italy had secured the 1934 World Cup Finals at vast expense. Obviously it needed the very best, most advanced stadiums, and obviously Juventus would do their bit. Built in just six months, The Stadio Mussolini featured the obligatory Fascist tower (still standing), and Carcano's side debuted there against Hungarian side Újpest on 29 June 1933. In time, the stadium would be re-imagined, renamed and rebuilt. Juve would share it with Toro, with the Italian Automobile Association, with athletes, rock bands and politicians. By hook or by crook, though, it would be home for nearly 60 years.

Three weeks into the season, Borel scored a sensational hat-trick as Juve came from behind at Roma to win 3–2. He scored again the following week in a 4–0 demolition of Toro, and then grabbed the winner in Palermo. His appearance and character flew in the face of all accepted Fascist sporting tropes, but Pozzo had been charged with winning the World Cup on home soil. Mussolini's infamous 'win or die' proclamation would come later, but Italy's investment was huge geopolitically as well as financially. Pozzo understood that failure would be catastrophic on just about every level, and that the upcoming visit to Budapest to take on the favourites was an important staging post. It mattered within the context of preparing for the World Cup, but also because Fascist Italy was increasingly perceived as a pariah state. Ever the pragmatist, Pozzo handed Borel his first start.

The match, like all the big matches now, was broadcast live on the radio. The *radiocronista* was a young Sicilian named Nicolò Carosio, and no journalist was ever so instrumental in the dissemination of a sporting legend. Borel's winning goal had him in something approaching paroxysm, and nine of the starters that evening were from Juve. As such, paradoxically, one of the defining moments of this great team – and by extension one of the defining moments in Italians' relationship with the sport – was a match they played not in black and white, but in *azzurro*. A match they played not in Turin, but a thousand kilometres east in Budapest.

That same evening, 22 October 1933, man-mountain Carnera retained his World Heavyweight Championship in Rome. Like Juve, Carnera authenticated the regime, but unlike Juve he did so as an individual. The *Azzurri* belonged to and had been created by the towering cultural, social and political edifice which was fascism.

The year ended with Italy once more unbeaten, but on 11 February they took on Austria, the old enemy, in Turin's new stadium. The visitors scored three times in eight first-half minutes and ran out 4–2 winners. Now anyone can lose a football match, and even the most finely honed tactical plans can unravel. This, however, was no ten-minute aberration. Rather the '*Juve-Nazionale*' were eviscerated by a really, *really* good side, and Berto Caligaris in particular was embarrassed. For over a decade, Caligaris had been a mainstay of club and country. He'd played for Italy an astonishing 59 times, and it would be fully 40 years before anyone would break that record. Now, though, he was 33. There'd been a sense he was running out of steam for a while, and he was destroyed by Austria's flying winger Karl Zischek. He scored three of the Austrian goals, and Pozzo felt compelled to act. Caligaris would be an unused sub throughout the World Cup, and his replacement – irony of ironies – would be Luigi Allemandi.

Combi too had been less than his old self against Austria. He was replaced by the Inter keeper Carlo Ceresoli for the final warm-up match against Greece, but then providence had its way. On 15 April, the day they entertained Brescia, Juve trailed Inter by a single point. Though they prevailed 2–1, Combi played the second half with a broken rib. Inter were overhauled, but when Juve celebrated a fourth consecutive *Scudetto* on 4 May, the rubber man announced that his playing days were over. He'd 'taken a wife' and so that was apparently that. However, ten days before the beginning of the World Cup, Ceresoli hurt his elbow in training. He was taken to hospital, and the worst fears of the nation were confirmed. He'd need 20 days of total rest and so Gianpiero Combi would be pressed into service one last time.

Pressed into service and, when he lifted the Jules Rimet Trophy in Rome on 10 June, pressed into Italian football immortality …

What a guy. What a team.

At Forte dei Marmi, with Edoardo Agnelli and his flock

In winning the World Cup, the *Juve-Nazionale* had performed their duty not only to their country, but to their paymaster as well. Agnelli's objective had been for them to become Italy's team, and in cementing their legend they'd done just that. However, he knew, just as everyone knew, that this great team's time was nearly up. Of Juve's nine World Cup winners, six were the wrong side of 30.

Combi had retired in a blaze of glory, while Caligaris and Rosetta were 33 and 32 respectively. Monti had agreed to stay on, but with Italy on the verge of a war in Ethiopia, the most emblematic of all the *oriundi* had decided he wanted out. Amid an almighty stink, Orsi told the Juve board he'd be going home to Argentina at the end of the season, Cesarini too. They'd loved their time in Italy, but on reflection it wasn't *really* their country. *Grazie mille* and all that, but they'd rather rejoin their loved ones than risk being conscripted to some east African hellhole.

On the afternoon of 2 December 1934, Turin's trademark fog enveloped the Stadio Mussolini. Thus, in advance of the kick-off of the game between Juventus and Triestina, thousands of those seated behind the goals migrated across the running track to the side of the pitch. They stood there quite peaceably, but referee Camillo Cairoli wasn't having it. He said the game wouldn't be kicking off until they retreated, and retreat they duly did. Then, as the game started, they emerged once more from the gloom. Cairoli went with the flow.

In attempting to write it up for *La Stampa*, Vittorio Pozzo noted that 'from time to time ghostly figures emerged, and then disappeared from view. For a while, 15 minutes or so from the finish, you could barely see your neighbour in the stand, let alone the ball.' He deduced quite correctly that it had ended goalless, and that Serantoni had been dismissed ten minutes from time for persistently berating the ref. By then most of the crowd had given up the ghost (so to speak), and made for the exits.

As metaphors went it was pretty good. As free-scoring, table-topping Fiorentina thumped Toro 4–0, Juve's season was lurching joylessly and nebulously towards the Christmas recess. The team was still in contention, and the football they played was still by and large effective. The style and swagger of the recent past was entirely absent though, and so too was the energy. The Juventus mania which had swept the team to four championships and, de facto, the World Cup, had peaked. The sublime passing game which had been Carcano's calling card had evaporated, and in its place came ugly, mealy-mouthed professionalism.

Ten days on from the Triestina game a small, almost perfunctory announcement appeared in *La Stampa della Sera*, Agnelli's evening paper. Carlo Carcano, it stated, had left his post at Juventus the previous week. No explanation was offered as to why, but eventually the club conceded that Carcano's departure wasn't directly related to his management of the team. That went without saying – the guy had built the most successful side in Italian history – so what was going on? Carcano had been a visionary. Under him and because of him, good players had literally become world beaters, and that, they always claimed, was because he'd had them take responsibility for their own performances. They were never browbeaten, and there were no dressing-room histrionics. Instead there was an understanding of the game, a unique intensity and a profound sense of duty. The question, therefore, was why, with a new era beginning and a new team to be built, would they fire a guy who'd delivered four straight championships?

According to the Fascists, homosexuality wasn't a crime as such. It *had* been a crime prior to 1927, but then they'd reclassified it as a disease. There may have been the odd foreigner practising it here and there, and isolated outbreaks among feeble-minded Italians. Those afflicted, however, were generally rounded up and dispatched to the Tremiti Islands, an archipelago in the Adriatic Sea. The regime boasted that statistically as well as actually, Italian manhood was 100 per cent heterosexual, disease-free, incorruptible.

Everyone knew this was a big lie, but then everything the party did and said amounted to monumental self-deceit. Homosexuality didn't exist in precisely the same way that prostitution didn't exist. But Italians were flesh and blood, and while the country was profoundly Catholic, it was hardly puritanical.

Within the club, Carcano's preferences had been an open secret for a while. It's not clear whether someone had threatened to out him, but now the rumours spread like wildfire. Suggestions that he'd 'sodomised' (in Fascist terminology) Borel on the club premises were unconscionable, but then why had Juan José Maglio, the Argentine striker earmarked to replace Cesarini, shipped out so suddenly? Some even speculated that the dressing room was lousy with it, that Mario Varglien was involved and that Monti, the great barrel-chested infantryman of the team, was one of the worst culprits! Monti! The iron man of *calcio*! It didn't bear thinking about.

In some respects, the sordid details didn't matter. Once the rumours had found their way into the public domain, the board had been left with no choice but to act. The Agnellis had always been at pains to portray their employees as ambassadors for decency, transparency and above all discipline. Some among the parochial old *torinesi* reckoned this was all management-speak and PR mumbo-jumbo, and truth be told they still do. Back then, however, company policy was to characterise Juventus players as the sporting epitome of honest, homespun FIAT values.

Italy was a new country. It had only been unified in 1861 and was struggling to define a coherent national identity. FIAT – and Juventus – had positioned themselves front and centre of that struggle, exemplars of a shared vision. That's why Juve had become Italy's team, and that, in large measure, had been down to Carcano. He'd been charged with instilling Agnelli's philosophy of *semplicita, serieta, sobrieta*. Juventus had been telling anyone who'd listen that simplicity, seriousness and sobriety were the three pillars of the club, but now Carcano's depravity had besmirched their good name. They'd mitigated the disaster as best they could, but it was a disaster all the same.

Old Juve stalwart Carlo Bigatto took over the team, and at first glance that seemed a smart move. He was a thoroughgoing *bianconero* legend, and he'd captained them to the championship eight years before. More importantly, his morals were unimpeachable. However Bigatto, good egg or otherwise, was no Carcano. He had neither the intellect nor the charisma to galvanise the team, and under him the football became even worse. Juventus scored just four goals in seven league matches, and so, new man at the helm or otherwise, the whole thing felt decidedly *fin de siècle*. Orsi boarding a ship bound for Buenos Aires suddenly seemed even more prophetic, but later the same day his erstwhile team-mates chiselled out a 2–1 home win against Livorno. As such they began the final day of the season level on points at the top of Serie

A with Weisz's Ambrosiana-Inter, runners-up the previous two seasons. Each would travel south, the *milanesi* to Lazio and Juve to Fiorentina, third in the league and all but invincible at home.

Fiorentina dominated possession, but by now that wasn't unusual. Juve were increasingly a counter-attacking side anyway and, marshalled by curmudgeon Rosetta and wrecking ball Monti, they held firm. Then, with seven minutes remaining and Inter 3–2 down to Lazio, Ferrari broke Iniesta-style on the left. He cut inside and beat two defenders, rounded Fiorentina keeper Amoretti and tapped in. Juve had been a shadow of their former selves, and the Carcano sacking had shaken the club to its very core. Somehow though they'd hauled themselves over the line. One last great hurrah for a great team, and five *Scudetti* one after the other. Astonishing.

Regardless, Carcano's golden years were over, and now Edoardo Agnelli faced a steepling new challenge. Somehow he had not only to replace poor, put-upon Bigatto, but also to construct a completely new team. Replete with cash or otherwise, that would be very far from easy. Juventus had lost their back three to retirement, and now Borel to military service. Orsi and Cesarini had upped sticks, and Ferrari decided he didn't want to stay without Carcano. Their replacements would need to embrace and assimilate the Juve philosophy, but more importantly be capable of winning football matches from the get-go.

Part one, the managerial-philosophical stuff, required a big decision. As kids, Caligaris and Rosetta had rubbed up against one another in youth games. They both hailed from the Monferrato, and between them they'd played over 500 games in the black and white. With Combi they'd comprised the celebrated 'three accountants', the meanest back line in the sport, but with Combi retired that was all finished. Rosetta and Caligaris were also friends, but their partnership, like many great footballing double acts, was underpinned by a definite if unvoiced rivalry. They'd grown up wanting to be the best and, as the most talented in the Monferrato, wanting to be *seen* to be the best. Thus, their combined excellence had been rooted in a desire to outperform one another. Rosetta was a *Juventino* to his core. He was the natural choice to replace Carcano, but Caligaris would struggle to subjugate himself to his leadership. Something had to give, and the consensus was Caligaris. He was shipped out to Brescia for his footballing dotage, and Rosetta installed at Juve's helm.

Carcano's team would be a very tough act to follow, but Agnelli was convinced that he and Rosetta would author another glorious chapter of the Juve story. It might take a season or two, but in time they'd build a younger, faster and still more dazzling team. However nobody, not even Italy's burgeoning film industry, could have imagined what would befall Juventus Football Club next.

On 13 July 1935, Edoardo Agnelli waved his players off at Porta Nuova station. They were bound for Prague and a meeting with Sparta in the semi-final of the Central Europe Cup. It was a big match, and when they came back they'd assemble again for a great reception at the Agnelli family mansion south-west of Turin at Villar Perosa.

In the meantime, Edoardo and his family headed off to the exclusive seaside resort of Forte dei Marmi, on the Tuscan coast. On the Sunday they all went to mass, and then 14-year-old Gianni went for a brief ride in his dad's seaplane with the aviator Arturo Ferrarin. Gianni then got out of the plane, and his father took his place alongside Ferrarin. Gianni, his mother and his siblings would take a train to Genoa, while his father would fly. They'd meet up at the train station there later, and the whole family would travel on to Turin.

Edoardo's wife and kids alighted at Genoa and waited for *Papa* to arrive. They waited and waited and then, anxious now, they waited some more. Anxiety gave way to desperation and then, when the news came, to utter desolation

Papa wasn't coming, and he never would.

As it taxied towards the jetty, the float of Edoardo Agnelli's seaplane had hit a drifting tree trunk. The plane had overturned, and Agnelli had been struck on the head by the revolving propeller.

In twelve months Juve had lost Carcano and Orsi, Cesarini, Combi and Caligaris. The club had lost its manager and most of its team, and now it had lost its figurehead and benefactor.

Juve had lost everything, and for the Agnelli family everything was lost.

Everything. It was over.

Everywhere and nowhere, with Virginia Bourbon del Monte

Shortly after Edoardo's death (or, if unsubstantiated legend is to believed, some considerable time before) his wife Virginia fell head over heels for a very famous, very brilliant writer and social commentator. Curzio Malaparte had taken part in the March on Rome and been editor of *La Stampa*, but then he'd been to Russia and met Stalin. On his return, he'd published a book apparently advocating the overthrow of the state. He'd been placed under house arrest, but was pardoned on the intervention of Mussolini's daughter and her husband.

The affair scandalised and titillated the *Torino bene* in equal measure. There were even suggestions that little Umberto Agnelli, born nine months before the tragedy in Genoa, was in fact Umberto Malaparte. His grandfather wasn't much interested in gossip, but when he learned that the couple intended to wed he instigated court proceedings against them. Virginia was at liberty to *marry* Malaparte, but under no circumstances whatsoever were her children going to be *brought up* by him. He was a narcissist and a dandy, but his character wasn't the issue. The issue was that he was a famous communist sympathiser, and his presence in the Agnelli family would represent a real danger to the delicate, highly profitable relationship the company had cultivated with the party. That couldn't be allowed to happen.

Giovanni Agnelli was a powerful man, and he could be a ruthless one. Virginia would have known she'd have had no chance whatsoever in a Turin court. She moved her flock – all seven of them – to Rome, but only when she renounced Malaparte did Agnelli renounce any claim on the kids. Giovanni Agnelli had actually quite liked his daughter-in-law back in the day, and he'd *really* liked the fact that his son had married her. That was because he was a terrible snob, and she had something even his money couldn't buy. She looked, moved and spoke like a noble, but most importantly she had a title like one. At the beginning she'd ticked all the boxes, but then one by one she'd started unticking them.

Freed from the Agnelli yoke and separated from Malaparte, she embarked upon a rackety, bohemian and ultimately tragic second life. She became a voracious collector of art and also, evidently, of lovers. She flitted between the Côte d'Azur, Forte dei Marmi, Rome and Turin, searching for the peace of mind which would always elude her. She was wealthy, loveless and powerless, and she oscillated between hedonism and self-loathing, its alter ego. Her mothering was probably best described as unorthodox. She wasn't equipped to deal with responsibility and snot-nosed mundanity, so childcare was delegated to Agnelli functionaries.

While her lifestyle was complete anathema to her father-in-law, they had one thing in common. Virginia had always loved Juventus, and so it was agreed that her oldest son, football-mad Gianni, would start attending Juve board meetings. Obviously his presence would be symbolic, but everyone remembered the day his dad had taken him along to meet the great Hirzer, the sheer joy of it. His father had been the making of Juve and the king of Juve, so it was only natural that his heir got involved.

Gianni liked football a lot, but he wasn't interested in listening to a bunch of middle-aged men dripping on about politics, money and business. Football was supposed to be fun, and besides he was discovering that he liked other things as well. Specifically he liked girls, and they seemed to like him back. In that respect he was a chip off the old block, and like his father before him he needed to be doing stuff, not sitting around in some stuffy old boardroom with Mazzonis, Craveri and Monateri.

Meanwhile, with Edoardo gone, Juventus was becoming a football club not unlike its rivals. The family retained a shareholding, but day-to-day running passed to Mazzonis and Craveri. The heart had been ripped out of the team, but Ferrari and Borel were still there, and in Alfredo Foni and Pietro Rava they'd unearthed replacements to Rosetta and Caligaris. Handsome, blond-haired Rava had been born in Alessandria. His family had moved to Turin, though, and he'd grown up kicking a ball around 200 metres from Corso Marsiglia. He'd seemed destined for greatness from a young age, and so it was. Pozzo once claimed that he was the most powerful left-back in the world, and he probably had that about right.

In 2006, the *comune* of Turin inaugurated a public space, the Giardino Pietro Rava, in his honour. That was because he was a great player, but also because he volunteered to go to the Russian front during the Second World War. He said he wasn't prepared to hang about in Turin while his friends were fighting and dying for their country; he wanted to contribute. As a player, 'Pietrone' Rava is probably most famous for an away match at Modena. Juve lost it 2–0 and he more than anyone was responsible for the defeat. His intention at the outset had been for Juventus to lose, and as usual with Italian football it was all to do with money. This, however, was no *Caso Allemandi* ...

Turin was his city, and Juventus wasn't so much his club as his very being. It was inconceivable he would represent anybody else, and like thousands of hometown players down the years, his wage packet reflected the fact. In 1938, though, he became a World Cup winner and Italy's blue-eyed boy. He was one of the players of the tournament, and Mussolini received him in Rome. He was the only player to have won the Olympics *and* the World Cup, and people kept telling him he was the best in the world in his position. He felt he deserved a salary increase at this point, but he'd signed a two-year deal the previous summer. The club was under no obligation to improve it, and nor was it in a position to. If the board acquiesced to his demands others would likely follow suit, and post-Edoardo there was no magic money tree.

The row rumbled on. Rava insisted the club had promised him a new deal, the board that he was deluded. They advised him to keep his head down and see the season out. He was 23 years of age, he had a long career in front of him, and his achievements would be reflected if and when they renewed his contract. At this point it became a battle of wills, and on 5 February 1939, it came to a very, very public head.

Juve travelled to bottom club Modena, but when the game kicked off Rava simply folded his arms and stood where he was. This was novel even by Italian standards, and despite his team-mates' imprecations he point-blank refused to budge. Juve went in 1–0 down, and Mazzonis steamed into the dressing room demanding an explanation. He stated – quite correctly – that regardless of his beef with the club, Rava had agreed to start the game. He'd therefore an obligation to his team-mates and the Juventus fans to participate, and if he didn't he was a fraud. Rava threw his boots at Mazzonis at this point and invited him to play himself. The other players tried to intercede, but when Rava came out for the second half he just stood there again. Modena won 2–0, Rava was fined and suspended, and it would be a month before the two parties reached a settlement.

Rava was forever falling in and out with the club, most probably because he loved it too much for his own good. When he turned 30, they signed a putative replacement in Oscar Vicich. Pietrone never could cope with rejection, and he was heartbroken by this. Newly promoted Alessandria offered him a shoulder to cry on, and to win back Juve's affection he accepted and kept them up virtually single-handed. That won him his place back in the national side, and Juve realised they still loved him after all. Having sold him for 4 million lire, they paid 14 million to get him back, and the most tempestuous relationship in football carried on. And off. And on again ...

Famously and gloriously, Rava once knocked out the Inter centre forward Bruno Quaresima with a right cross. He was suspended for three games, but Rava maintained it had been a case of mistaken identity. He'd meant to hit Lorenzi, Quaresima's team-mate, because he'd seen him spitting at the Juve striker Giampiero Boniperti.

Rava's counterpart, Foni, was a yeoman footballer. He never boycotted a game in which he was supposed to be participating, and as a consequence still holds the club record for consecutive appearances. He started 229 in a row, and he and Rava would accumulate over 600 for Juve and 50 for their country. Rosetta and Caligaris had been great full-backs, but they'd played in a great team. These two never enjoyed that luxury, but there's a body of opinion that they were the better pairing.

However they couldn't do it on their own, and assembling a top team required cash. Under Edoardo's stewardship, Juve had had oodles of it, and they'd deliberately and systematically transformed football into a market. Then the Carcano scandal, the break-up of the squad and, finally and decisively, the crash at Genoa, had constituted the perfect storm. Without the family's munificence, the club could no longer afford top salaries or transfer fees and would have to live within its means. As a result Serie A became more equal, and Bologna and Inter, perennial bridesmaids during the Carcano era, seized the initiative.

Roma came to town in March 1936 and, in winning 3–1, inflicted Juve's first home defeat in four years. This extinguished any lingering pretensions the *bianconeri* had of retaining the championship and acquainted their fans with a new reality. Ultimately Juve finished fifth as Bologna pipped Roma and a resurgent Torino for the title. Having not won a derby since 1928, Toro won two in 1936 alone.

On 4 September, the Italian Olympic Committee appointed Juve's new chairman. Emilio de la Forest de Divonne was an Italian war hero and Turin's deputy mayor. He was also an associate of Giovanni Agnelli and a disciple of Mussolini. In practical terms his appointment was nominal. Craveri and Mazzonis carried on at the coal face, and another old *Juventino*, the textile magnate Andrea Remmert, joined them. The five-year interregnum over which they presided would be fallow on the field, and horrendous off it. As the Fascists saw it, sporting institutions needed to advance the regime's values. Following a sealed-bids ballot, they'd installed Renato

Dall'Ara, a wealthy clothing manufacturer and true believer, as the chairman of Bologna. Dall'Ara had two great attackers in Carlo Reguzzoni and the Uruguyan *oriundo* Héctor 'golden head' Puricelli, and their goals would fire the club to three titles in four years.

In May 1939, Mussolini came back to Turin for the inauguration of FIAT's new Mirafiori plant. Seven years earlier he'd been well received, but that was then and this, categorically, was not. Not only did he turn up two hours late but did so, very deliberately, in an Alfa Romeo. Though their alliance had been mutually beneficial, he'd never much liked Agnelli. Mussolini had reason to believe that the FIAT factory floor was jumping with communists, and his own inadequacies had seen to it that he wasn't far wrong. Il Duce had fallen into a trap entirely of his own making. He needed FIAT planes, trains and automobiles and, having signed a pact with Hitler, he needed them yesterday. The issue was that even his own minister for production had said the military wouldn't be equipped for war before autumn 1942. Industrial workers were toiling harder but earning less in the rush to Armageddon.

Il Duce had never been much of a strategist, nor much of a listener. In his arrogance he'd made himself a hostage not only to fortune, but also to Agnelli. The marriage of convenience would hold for now, but FIAT had all the cards. Mussolini's tardiness that afternoon was essentially an act of petulance, because he knew he'd been outwitted. He left that day muttering about 'Piedmontese swine', and would never again set foot in Turin.

By June 1940, when Italy declared war, Juve's hegemony on the field was but a distant memory. They were a shadow of the side that had bossed football under Carcano, and the more they lost, the more they lost their identity. With the club struggling for money, Mazzonis ploughed on as best he could. He helped to organise an exhibition game featuring the old guard, as Combi, Caligaris and Rosetta rolled up their sleeves once more. Some minutes into the game, 39-year-old Berto Caligaris took himself off and sat down on a bench. He said he felt poorly, but by the time they got him to hospital it was too late. Six weeks later Mazzonis was dismissed by party decree. He hadn't displayed sufficient enthusiasm for the national psychosis, which by now consumed any semblance of reason.

The party had decided it needed one of its own at the helm, and that was Piero Dusio. A one-time Juve player and racing driver, he was the owner of the Cisitalia sports club just up the road from the stadium. He also owned a textiles business, and had made his fortune supplying oilskin to the military. He'd become extremely rich extremely quickly, and they said that if it moved in Turin and Agnelli didn't own it, you could bet your life he did.

The players were reassigned, at least ostensibly, to his factory. All of life was subordinated to the war effort now, and by putting them on the shop floor and renaming the club Juventus-Cisitalia, Dusio was seen to be fulfilling his patriotic obligations. Meanwhile – with mind-bending irony – Toro became Torino FIAT.

Lingotto and Mirafiori had been bombed and bombed again, and vast areas of the city flattened. The party felt the need to keep sport going, however, because it needed ways to distract the plebs from the real-time catastrophe which was unfolding around them. Mussolini needed the carnage, the hunger and the destruction of their city to seem, well ... normal, and for the nation's athletes not to be blown to bits. Pozzo urged a friendly personnel officer at FIAT to offer the Toro players work in one of the armaments factories. That indemnified them against conscription, and as a consequence Torino FIAT became the club to play for during the war. Not only was it sustained by Agnelli money, but its players weren't sent to the front. The regime's propaganda machine spun the idea that this was a great example of a company doing its bit, but Juventus-Cisitalia and Torino FIAT were symptomatic of a world gone mad. Nothing made sense any more, and everything was spinning out of control.

By 1943 Italy was breaking apart. The North African campaign had been a disaster, the tide had turned in Russia, and Mussolini was everybody's favourite imbecile. Ordinary Italians were bewildered, but most of all they were angry, tired and hungry. On 1 March, workers at Mirafiori downed tools, and it quickly escalated into a general strike. In July Il Duce was dismissed by the king, and by September Turin was under German occupation.

Football continued piecemeal, but with the country torn asunder there was no Serie A; in fact there was no meaningful championship at all. However, Torino FIAT and Juventus-Cisitalia took part in a Piedmontese-Ligurian mini-league. Toro qualified from it, and then from another involving the Milanese clubs. They then contrived to lose to the La Spezia fire brigade (you read that correctly). La Spezia is a lovely town on the Ligurian coast. Its population back then was only about 100,000, but its fire brigade was happy to provide board, lodging and a place to train for talented *sportivi* displaced by the war. As a result they progressed to a two-legged semi-final against mighty Bologna, but the first game was suspended because of crowd trouble and the firemen were awarded a 2–0 win. The second never took place because of bombing, so La Spezia progressed, without having completed a match, to the final round of three with Toro and Venezia.

To cut a long and scarcely believable story short, they won it, but that championship exists in a state of limbo. The good people of La Spezia are convinced their boys were the 1944 Italian champions, and they're right after a fashion. The problem is, nobody outside La Spezia cares, and so, all these years on, they still haven't got their blessed *Scudetto*.

Drat and double drat.

Chapter 3

From the Ashes

Poor footballers are certainly overpaid. The good ones
never earn enough.

Gianni Agnelli

At the stadium formerly known as the Mussolini, with Guglielmo 'the baron' Gabetto

In March 1945, the National Liberation Committee
formally indicted 78-year-old Giovanni Agnelli as
a Fascist collaborator. They sequestered the company
he'd built, placed it into public ownership, and broke
him completely. Without FIAT and his two kids, his life
was utterly meaningless. Later that year, Virginia, his
estranged daughter-in-law, lost hers. On 21 November
she was being driven from Rome to Turin when her car
collided with an oncoming American military truck
near Pisa. The details of the crash remain unclear, but
while her driver escaped with minor injuries, she was
killed outright. The passenger side of the car seems to
have taken the impact, so it's assumed that either the car

was out of control on the wrong side of the road or had spun to a standstill there.

That's all supposition, but supposition and the Agnellis tend to go hand in hand. In his book *Agnelli – FIAT and the Network of Italian Power* the American journalist Alan Friedman asserts that she was 'seated next to her trouserless driver, when her neck was broken'. That may or may not be true, though its having got past the lawyers suggests it probably is. Then again it's also true that Virginia had written a letter to her children some weeks earlier. We don't know the exact content of the letter, but we do know that she'd placed it an envelope on which she'd written, 'To be opened after my death.' We also know that she was 46, lonely and depressed.

Giovanni Agnelli had lost his son, his daughter-in-law and, worst of all, his business. His health was failing, and he was telling anyone who would listen that he had 'got everything wrong'. He shut himself away at home, cared for by a small army of nurses and by his wife, Clara. A week after Virginia's death he fell and broke his arm. He contracted pneumonia shortly afterwards, and passed away on 16 December.

By then a new paper had appeared on Turin's news stands. Milan and Rome had *Gazzetta dello Sport* and *Corriere dello Sport* respectively, and now the *sportivi* of Piedmont had their own daily. The first edition of *Tuttosport* had focused on the Milan–Turin bike race, but in October football started again as something resembling normal service was resumed. While the cyclists Coppi and Bartali would dominate the front pages during the summer months, *Tuttosport* concerned itself with soccer when the nights drew in.

With the nation's infrastructure in ruins, the FIGC reprised the old north-south format. The opening game of season 1945–46 was a Turin derby at the renamed Stadio Comunale, the Stadio Mussolini as was. Juve won 2–1, but it was false dawn. Toro overhauled them soon enough and, inspired by the striker Guglielmo Gabetto, headed the section. Nicknamed 'the baron' and born in Turin, Gabetto had begun his career with Juve. However in 1941 they'd been forced to sell him and Borel, probably their two greatest assets, to their neighbours. Borel's career had pretty much fizzled out at the Filadelfia, but not so that of *il barone*. He'd become a big star and the scorer of miraculous goals. Moreover each time he scored one, he reminded both sets of fans that the force, post-Agnelli, was with Toro.

Both clubs advanced to a final group of eight. They were joined by the two Milan clubs and four no-hopers from the south, but it quickly became apparent that this was a two-horse Turin race. On 21 July 1946 they met at the Fila in what amounted to a championship decider, and Gabetto scored a late winner. Of course, that cemented his legend because this was the derby (or *la Stracittadina* as it was known back then) and it was ever thus. This particular one, however, resonated more than most.

In the collective imagination, VE Day evokes delirious throngs in Trafalgar Square, demobbed sailor boys embracing all-American beauties in Times Square, multitudes marching arm-in-arm along the Champs-Elysées. Of course Turin revelled in its *Festa della Liberazione* as well, but the Italian war didn't end on 8 May 1945. On 2 June, a national plebiscite banished the Savoys. They'd been complicit in Mussolini's accession, and Italy needed a scapegoat. In washing their hands of them, Italians deluded themselves that they'd drawn a line in the sand, and that everything was now fine. However everything *wasn't* fine, because all over the country battles still raged. Communist militia squads and former partisans sought out and butchered Nazi collaborators; trials for wartime treachery and atrocities continued; communities torn apart by the conflict and ideology failed to come together.

Old man Agnelli had famously glad-handed the Fascists, and FIAT had been one of the regime's biggest suppliers of arms. It was true that the canteen at Lingotto had provided food for the poor (it's reckoned it fed 11,000 a day), but the factory had also fed the German war machine. The city had been targeted by Allied bombers as a result, and the civilian population had suffered terribly. It was inevitable, therefore, that the Turin derby would accumulate still more ideological baggage.

Obviously Juve was in the blue corner, while Toro stood four-square in the red. Football matches weren't ideological battlegrounds in themselves, but nor did they exist in a vacuum. Though the two clubs took pains to distance themselves from politics, whichever way they spun it and whichever way you looked at it, their respective fan bases were different. Juve *were* the team of the bosses, and the workers *did* gravitate towards Toro.

While Gabetto's exploits still resonate in one half of one city, the legend of Toro's captain that afternoon is boundless. One may legitimately argue that Italy has produced better players than Valentino Mazzola – his own son, Sandro, springs to mind – but one is hard pushed to identify one who so personified a footballing era. Nobody was more resourceful, nobody more inspirational, and few if any have had the ability to determine the narrative arc of a football match so completely. Post-war Torino would become a truly great football team, and Mazzola would be its captain, fulcrum and heartbeat.

Someone once asked Giampiero Boniperti, arguably Juve's greatest player, to name his all-time favourite footballer. Boniperti replied, 'If I had to name the player most useful to the team, the one I'd absolutely want to sign, I wouldn't think of Pelé, De Stéfano or Cruyff. I wouldn't think of Platini, and nor even of Maradona. Actually I would think about all of them, but only having first thought about Mazzola.'

Valentino Mazzola began his career with the Alfa Romeo factory team near Milan. He was a major talent, however, and in 1939 he moved to Venezia. They were newly promoted to Serie A, and in Mazzola and Ezio Loik, they chanced upon a pairing which would power them to an unprecedented run of success. Wing-half Loik combined industry and strength, inside forward Mazzola, leadership and extravagant talent. On 31 May 1942 they thumped an excellent Torino side 3–1, simultaneously ensuring a third-place finish for their team and depriving Toro of the title. At the conclusion of the match, Ferruccio Novo, the Toro president, made directly for the Venezia changing room and told Mazzola and Loik that he wanted to buy them. He was informed that negotiations were already well advanced with another club, but Novo immediately offered Venezia 1.4 million lire in cash, two squad players and a firm handshake. It was take-it-or-leave-it, and Venezia, saddled by crippling debts, accepted on the spot. Torino galloped to the championship the following year, as Juventus-Cisitalia finished third.

Mazzola formed an extraordinary double act with one of the fans. Oreste Bolmida worked as a guard at Porta Nuova, and used a bugle to coral slow-moving passengers onto departing trains. The station is a 20-minute tram ride from the Filadelfia, and it seems that one afternoon he left work and made straight for the ground. Once there he pulled out his horn and gave it a blow, and it struck a bit of a chord. Bolmida and his bugle would become a Sunday-afternoon fixture at the Fila, and one of the symbols of post-war Italy. If Toro found themselves in difficulty on their home turf, Mazzola would wait for the ball to go dead and very deliberately roll up his sleeves, and Bolmida would blow a clarion call on his bugle. Thus began the legendary 'quarter of an hour of Toro', 15 minutes of high-intensity pressing which seems to have induced psychological paralysis in opposition sides.

Evidently this 1940s Fergie-time precursor worked because Toro became invincible. Between January 1943 and 1948 they were unbeaten at Filadelfia, and would win four consecutive championships.

At a crossroads, with Gianni Agnelli

Dusio had charted a course through some extremely choppy waters, but by 1947 he wanted out. He was busy with his sports-car factory; as he saw it he'd done his bit, and the club belonged to the Agnellis. In winning the league, Toro had amassed 10 points more than second-placed Juve. It had been their third *Scudetto* in succession if you discounted the La Spezia blip and the lost season, and they seemed to be getting better and better. Torino looked unassailable, and Dusio had neither the time nor the inclination to try to catch them. There weren't enough hours in the day, and it would take years.

It had been 12 years since Edoardo Agnelli's death, and eighteen months since his father breathed his last. Ownership of FIAT had reverted to the family, but it was being run by Vittorio Valletta, a meticulous Genovese known as 'the professor'. Valletta had been with the business for 25 years, and he was every inch an Agnelli man. That said, Giovanni Agnelli had always assumed that Gianni would take over. He'd chosen him principally because he was his eldest grandson, but also because Gianni was funny, smart and eminently likeable.

Agnelli legend has it that Gianni had distinguished himself during the war, though the details are somewhat opaque. We know he was a second lieutenant, that he spent a brief period at the front in Russia and served for three months in a (FIAT) armoured-car division in Libya. There's also a story that when Italy changed sides in 1943, he'd gone into hiding down in Tuscany. He and older sister Susanna ('Suni') had been escorted to one of the family holdings by a German officer who'd been promised a nice new FIAT for his trouble. However there was a crash during the journey, and Gianni was hospitalised in Florence with a broken leg. Subsequent to that he's believed to have made himself useful to the Allies, deploying his near-perfect English to liaise between the American forces and the resistance movement.

At the end of the war he travelled to the States on at least two occasions. He did so ostensibly as president of the family ball-bearing company but also because, like many Italians back then, he was fascinated by all things Yankee. He fell in love with New York, but we also know he spent time with his old regiment pals in Bergamo. While there he busied himself organising sports events and socialising, and reacquainting himself with football. He began to follow Atalanta, and Gianni being Gianni became friendly with some of the players. It was now two years since the German surrender, and there was nothing to suggest he was interested in managing FIAT. The business was in flux as a consequence, and the staff and directors needed both answers and direction. Valletta famously sat him down and explained that the possibilities were two – either Gianni became president of FIAT or he did. Gianni said, 'Professor, you do it,' and that, for the next 20 years, would be that.

In the circumstances, Gianni's reluctance was perfectly understandable. At a time when the average wage of a guy on the factory floor was under 200,000 lire a year, he had an annual stipend of over a million to get through. Spending that lot was quite an undertaking, and quite time-consuming. Endless days spent twiddling his thumbs at Lingotto would have been a bit of an impediment and also, for somebody like him, a lot of a bore.

Gianni Agnelli was 26 now. He had a degree in law – he was nicknamed *l'Avvocato* – 'the lawyer' – and he had the financial wherewithal to do whatever he wanted.

What he did wasn't particularly the issue, just so long as he was seen to be knuckling down to something which wasn't partying. He'd always loved Juve, so what better way to honour his dad's memory than by taking the reins there? Hadn't it been the glue that had bound three generations of Agnelli men together, and wouldn't both his father and his grandfather have been proud? Hadn't he met Hirzer that afternoon as a four-year-old? Hadn't Juventus been the first great love of his life, and wasn't it time somebody knocked Toro off their perch?

At the board meeting of Juventus Football Club on 22 July 1947, Gianni Agnelli became its president. The side he inherited was decent, but decent didn't begin to cut it in the age of the *Grande Torino*. Like his father before him he arrived with money to spend, but the situation in Italy was completely different. The country had been brutalised economically as well as psychologically and physically, so everybody, young or old, rich or poor, needed to roll up their sleeves and get stuck in. People needed calories, clean water and a roof over their heads, and paying vast sums of money for or to footballers was seen as vulgar in the circumstances.

Juve would finish Gianni's first season joint second with Milan and Trieste, 16 points behind Torino. Though way off Toro's pace, they did boast Serie A's *capocannoniere* – top scorer. Giampiero Boniperti was a blond-haired, blue-eyed teenager from the rice fields of Novara, Italy's football factory. He was a cracking centre forward and in time would become the most famous of all the *Juventini*. Still today, over 70 years since he first appeared for the club, he ranks alongside Michel Platini and Alessandro Del Piero as its most celebrated player.

He played over 450 competitive games long before any meaningful international competition existed, and his association with the club as player, administrator, president and fan spans nine decades.

Boniperti is well into his nineties now, but they still venerate his name. He once said that Juve 'isn't *in* my heart. Juve *is* my heart.' He was one of the first to be inducted into the Italian Football Hall of Fame, and he was awarded the Order of Merit of the Italian Republic. Those honours, however, are of secondary importance to him. What matters – still – is Juventus. Through all its triumphs, its tragedies and its scandals, he goes on. The club motto is, 'Winning isn't important – it's the only thing that matters,' and no one has embodied it quite like Boniperti. He's always been witty, affable and intelligent, but also, when the need arises, quite ruthless.

Stories of his playing exploits are legion, and also those of his *furbizia*, his cleverness. Much of what passes for the law in Italy is advisory, and most rules have workarounds. If they didn't then nothing would function because the bureaucracy is measured in layers. There's a good yarn about Boniperti's goals incentive which illustrates that pretty well, but which also says a lot about his character. If, as they say, a man is known by the company he keeps, it probably tells us quite a lot about Gianni Agnelli as well.

Boniperti came from Barengo, a small farming community. Livestock was an important commodity there, and Gianni Agnelli liked nothing more than a deal. So, with the wage cap in place, he and Boniperti came up with one. It stipulated that Boniperti would earn a cow for each goal he scored. He'd be at liberty to choose which one he wanted, and Gianni would settle up with the *contadino*, the farmer, later on. After some time, the farmer rang *l'Avvocato* and complained that Boniperti was stripping him bare. Gianni told him he didn't understand. Boniperti insisted on selecting the animals in person but was under strict instructions to take only one cow per goal, and Gianni knew exactly how many he'd scored.

The farmer said he knew as well, because he'd been keeping count. The problem was that Boniperti insisted *absolutely* on taking only pregnant cows, so he always got two for the price of one. Gianni laughed. He laughed because of all Italians the *contadino* is probably the most revered. He's considered the smartest, the most difficult to outwit. Gianni laughed because he respected Boniperti. He liked guile, and Boniperti had it in spades.

In 1993, 18-year-old Alessandro Del Piero was the hottest prospect in football. He'd grown up in Padua; his debut season there had gone really well, and he was probably a genius. Like millions of Italians, Del Piero had grown up supporting *la vecchia signora*. Now they wanted to buy him, and that was a dream come true. He and his agent, Gastone Rizzato, met in advance of their appointment with Boniperti, the Juve chairman. They devised a strategy, honed it and then honed it some more. By the time Del Piero walked into Boniperti's office he knew *precisely* what he was worth, what the other clubs were prepared to offer, and what, given Juve's status, he was prepared to accept. He had the answers to all the questions Boniperti was likely to ask, and he knew precisely the questions he was going to be asking himself. Five minutes later he walked out again, having signed a blank contract. Boniperti had 'told him not to worry' just as, over the years, he'd told dozens of Juve legends not to worry. First you signed and then Boniperti calculated what you were worth.

Upon signing for Juve, the teenage Boniperti had taken a flat close to three of Toro's superstars. The keeper Valerio Bacigalupo and the defenders Danilo Martelli and Mario Rigamonti were collectively known as the *trio Nizza* on account of their sharing a bachelor pad in Via Nizza, directly behind Porta Nuova. As footballers they were well known around town, and still more so in San Salvario, their *quartiere*. Nothing unusual in that nor, at that time, in them knocking around with a player from a rival team. Boniperti was decent company; he was new in town, and like them he fancied his chances with the girls.

Heading into the Turin derby of March 1948, Toro were level with Milan in the race for the championship. Boniperti was scoring prolifically, but Juve were seven points adrift and effectively out of it. Toro were a much better side, and as established professionals and Serie A winners, the *trio* were earning much more than him. Somehow he persuaded them to bet 30,000 lire – two months wages for him – that Toro would win by two clear goals.

Toro had identified Carlo Parola as the *Juventino* to stop. At the start of the match he was the recipient of a flying elbow from Gabetto, his former team-mate, and what's best described as a karate kick to the right knee from Menti. That virtually immobilised him, and with no substitutes Juve shunted him out to the left wing and got on with it as best they could. Franco Ossola put Toro in front after 35 minutes, and Juve went in at half-time

1–0 down. They'd barely been out of their own half, and now they were up the proverbial creek.

We don't know what was said in the dressing room, but we do know that Parola ingested a gob full of Simpamina, a brand of amphetamine. It's not entirely clear whether he knowingly took it, but the net result was that he came out for the second half not a little agitated. Just after the hour Toro had a goal disallowed, and Martelli, one of Boniperti's Toro mates, squared up to the Juventus midfielder Sentimenti. The usual name-calling and general petulance ensued, and amid the ruckus Boniperti was seen to have words with Parola. Martelli, he told him, had been throwing his weight around all game, one insult and one gratuitous foul after another. Someone bigger than him needed to put him back in his box, and so Parola hobbled over like a three-legged bull in a china shop. Foaming at the mouth and generally off his rocker, he threw an absolute haymaker at Martelli, who promptly larruped him back just as Boniperti had known he would. Both were promptly sent off, just as Boni had known they'd be.

Juve had begun the half 1–0 down and they'd been 10¼ to Toro's 11. Now clever Boniperti had seen to that it would be 10 against 10, and in the process got right under Torino's skin. They lost their heads, and Juve salvaged both a point and a slightly immoral victory. In its (Italian) way it was genius. Boniperti had set the trap and known that Martelli was the Toro player most likely to fall into it.

That evening, he and the *trio Nizza* bumped into one another, and the row continued. Martelli was still apoplectic, but Giampiero Boniperti was never one to take a backward step. Seemingly it was handbags, but it was public handbags following a derby *La Stampa* stated had 'shamed the sport, the city and the country'. News of the incident spread like wildfire first through Turin and then, inevitably, the length of the peninsula. In Sicily they heard that Boniperti, his dad and his brother had taken the three of them on, in Abruzzo that Martelli had chased him down the street screaming blue murder. In Tuscany they reckoned there had been a full-scale riot, and so on and so feverishly forth. It's not clear whether the *trio Nizza* paid out on the bet, but the whole episode was classic Boniperti.

That summer the Italian amateur side were on the receiving end of a pasting at the London Olympics. In the quarter-final they met Denmark at Highbury, and were undone by a strapping inside forward from Copenhagen. John Hansen was 23 and worked at the Carlsberg brewery. He scored four times against Italy, and two more as the Danes beat the hosts in the bronze-medal match.

Hansen's coach had dealings with a vermouth company south of Turin. The owner was a Toro fan, and he politely enquired what it might cost to sign the player. The Danish guy said he didn't understand the question, because football was an amateur pastime in Denmark and Hansen was free to come and go as he pleased. Toro sent a delegation to meet him, but while they shilly-shallied Juve stepped in. With the wage restrictions lifted and no fee payable to Hansen's club, Gianni instructed FIAT's Danish distributor to offer a signing-on fee of 12 million lire and a salary of 120,000, bonuses contingent, per month. Once he'd picked himself up off the floor,

John Hansen said he more or less understood. Then he signed on very, very quickly indeed.

So too did Johnny Jordan, an inside forward from Spurs. At Juve he joined the Glaswegian coach Billy Chalmers, one of 45 British trainers working 'overseas'. Inter's Dai Astley and Toro's Les Lievesley were highly regarded, and Gianni believed Chalmers' appointment would send a signal that Juve were a serious club.

Hansen struggled initially. He didn't understand the language, the customs or the Italian style of play, and he wasn't used to professional football. The games were too tactical, the defenders too dirty, the pressure of it all just too much. Gradually, though, he found his feet, and by Christmas he was something like the player Juve had hoped they'd signed. He would become a majestic number 10 and score over 120 goals for the club.

Jordan, on the other hand, was the archetypal English footballer abroad. He'd limp back across the Channel at the season's end, as would the oddball Chalmers, whose training methods were unusual and at times just plain bizarre. He'd haul the players back in after lunch if he wasn't satisfied they'd sufficiently applied themselves in the morning. He'd also have them running up and down the train carriages on the way to away games, which may well explain why their away form was so utterly hopeless.

On the morning of 30 April 1949, the *trio Nizza* met up with Mazzola, Loik, Gabetto and the rest of Toro's superstars. They took a coach ride to Milan, and the 0–0 draw they played out with Inter virtually cemented yet another *Scudetto*. Next they boarded a flight to Lisbon, where they played Benfica in a friendly. The Portuguese champions were honouring Chico Ferreira, their retiring captain. He was a great friend of Mazzola, and a visit from Toro, the greatest club of all, seemed a fitting farewell. So, for the players a touch of celebratory jet-setting off the pitch, and business as usual on it in the shape of a comfortable 4–1 win.

At 9.40 a.m. on 4 May 1949, a three-engined FIAT G.212 airliner departed from Lisbon. In addition to its four-man crew it carried eighteen footballers, six staff and three journalists. It refuelled in Barcelona, crossed the Pyrenees and set a course for the Ligurian coast. At Savona it turned sharp north and made for Turin Collegno airport. The pilot, Pierluigi Meroni, was advised that dense fog had descended upon the city. With visibility reduced to about 40 metres, he'd do well to delay landing, or better still divert to Milan. Meroni was an experienced flyer though, and he knew the approach like the back of his hand. At 4.59 p.m. he informed the tower that they were south-east of Turin, altitude 2000 metres. All was in order, and he was about to commence his descent.

Commissioned by the House of Savoy to celebrate victory over the French at the siege of Turin in 1706, the magnificent Basilica Superga was – and indeed remains – one of *the* enduring symbols of the city. It sits 670 metres above sea level at Pino Torinese, houses the tombs of the Savoy and is visible, on a clear day, up to 40 kilometres away. However this was not a clear day. Not a clear day at all.

At 5.04 p.m. Don Ricca, chaplain of the Basilica, was reading in his study. He heard a 'mighty rumble, like thunder, and then a deafening roar'. At 180 kph the plane had crashed into a retaining wall metres behind the basilica. There were no survivors.

They estimate that one million attended the funerals, amid speculation that the plane's altimeter had jammed at 2000 metres. Four days of national mourning, the *Grande Torino* wiped out at a stroke.

The skies above Turin had fallen in.

At Lingotto, with Carlo 'Nuccio' Parola

On 5 May 1949, Gianni Agnelli proclaimed, well-meaningly though clumsily, 'From the ashes, Turin will see the birth of a team worthy of their memory.' Then, by way of adding insult to this most grievous injury, he set about acquiring one right under *granata* noses. He assumed sole ownership of Juventus, transforming it into a private limited company, then started spending American taxpayers' money on it.

In immediate post-war Italy, GDP was half its 1938 level. The trains didn't run, the agricultural sector had been decimated and large swathes of the country lacked clean water. Sugar and meat production were 10 and 25 per cent respectively of pre-war levels. There was real hunger, and Capitalism PLC very well understood that all this represented a communist disaster waiting to happen. The Americans chose to mitigate this the only way they could – with cash. The European Recovery Program, better known as the Marshall Plan, would transform the continent's economy, and ultimately its society. In the process it would turn Europe into a collection of client states, but their beleaguered denizens didn't give a fig about that. They weren't interested in economic modelling and ideological imperatives; they needed work, shelter and food for their kids.

Italy was one of Europe's most impoverished countries and, in consequence, one of the most at risk of communist contagion. Stalin couldn't be allowed to gain a foothold there, and so $1.2 billion was earmarked. Disbursed over four years, pretty soon it started sloshing around the boardrooms of the industrial triangle of Genoa, Turin and Milan. The cornerstone of the plan to improve living standards was the 'motorisation' of the country. FIAT, Pirelli, the petrol company Eni and the Milanese construction firm Italcementi would work together to realise it and would be the plan's principle beneficiaries.

From the age of 13, Gianni Agnelli had been brought up by his half-American mother and a plummy British governess, so he was fluent in English at a time when very few Italians, businesspeople or otherwise, had even the most basic command of it. He was also young, wealthy and extremely personable, and his lifestyle was enchanting. He flitted here, there and first-class everywhere: now in Cannes, now in London, now in Milan and now in New York. He was always impeccably dressed and mannered, and American diplomats couldn't get enough of him, his lavish parties and his oh-so-European sophistication.

Gianni became friendly with James Clement Dunn, the American ambassador in Rome, and later with his successor Clare Boothe Luce. Defeating communism was a major part of their brief, and they had money – oodles of it – to spend on accomplishing it. As a major employer, *bon viveur extraordinaire* and owner of an important daily newspaper, Gianni ticked all the Americans' boxes. While Russian money sustained *l'Unità*, the communist daily newspaper, the Agnelli-owned *La Stampa* became an organ of the Italian centre right tacitly if not overtly. Gianni was somewhat frivolous, but his sidekick Valletta was serious, practical and rock-solid dependable. They were the dream ticket, and they saw to it that FIAT got 20 per cent of Italy's Marshall Plan cash. Valletta spent it on rebuilding the railway network, constructing new motorways and ramping up production at the factories.

The Iron Curtain existed, and Uncle Sam knew that factory floors like those at Lingotto and Mirafiori were fertile recruiting grounds for the commies. Gianni and Valletta promised to do whatever it took to root them out, and that kind of thing was highly bankable for foreign diplomats. It amounted to tangible proof that they were effective in their role; just what Washington ordered. In time, FIAT employees would be subject to a covert surveillance operation not dissimilar to those operated by the communist regimes of eastern Europe. Tens of thousands would be vetted for their ideological, political and behavioural orientations, and even for their sexual proclivities. It was highly illegal, but the CIA weren't much interested in details like that.

The English national team had visited Turin the previous autumn. They'd walloped the hosts 4–0, and afterwards a chastened Agnelli had been in conversation with the secretary of the FA. Stanley Rous agreed with him that Toro had been perspicacious in hiring Lievesley, the English fitness expert who'd lost his life at Superga. Agnelli made no secret of the fact that he was an admirer of all things British, and English coaches were now de rigueur across the continent. Rous recommended the

Scouser Jesse Carver, and told Gianni he was the coming man. Juve, he said, would do well to keep an eye on him.

The war had ended Carver's playing career, and in 1946 he'd taken a coaching job at Xerxes, Rotterdam's least-successful club. Dutch football was strictly amateur, but Carver had done amazing things there. The Dutch national team had been without a manager following the death of the previous incumbent, the Wearsider Bob Glendenning. Impressed by Carver's methods, they'd approached him in January 1947. He'd accepted, and four months later been charged with preparing a team of Europeans to play a Great Britain XI in Glasgow. The Brits had won 6–1, but to a man the 'Intercontinentals' had been bowled over by Carver's innovative methods. One of their number was the Juve stalwart Carlo Parola, and upon returning home he'd confirmed Carver's excellence to the board.

The following year, Carver's Dutch amateurs had almost caused the mother of all upsets at the London Olympics. They'd taken the hosts to extra time, and by common consent had been the better side. Carver had then quit Holland, and spent a season coaching down-at-heel Millwall in England's Division 3 South.

Undeterred by the Chalmers debacle, Agnelli sent for Carver. Impressed by his manners, pipe and tweeds, Anglophile Gianni had him sign a contract straight away. By the time the season began on 11 September 1949, the two of them had an interpreter, a new keeper, a new midfield, a gifted new forward line and the chance of Juve's first championship in 15 years. Another Danish Olympian, the mazy left winger Karl Aage Præst, had been added to the payroll, while *oriundo* inside right

Rinaldo 'velvet paws' Martino arrived from the Argentine club San Lorenzo. Throw in Hansen, Boniperti and the clever winger Ermes Muccinelli and, on paper at least, Juve had a devastating front five. Agnelli had been naive in his choice of words in the aftermath of Superga, but he was a young man in a hurry. As he saw it, someone had to fill the void, so why not Juventus?

Carver's interpreter was 24-year-old Gigi Peronace, from down in Calabria. As a teenager during the war he'd organised football matches between Allied troops and locals. His English had stood him in good stead when he'd moved to Turin to study. Now he was Carver's dressing-room translator, and in time he'd become one of the most influential fixers in the transfer market. He'd broker one of the greatest transfer deals the club ever did, but more of that later ...

The proof of the pudding would arrive in pretty short order. In thumping Fiorentina, Lazio and Bari in the opening three games, Juve scored twelve goals and, courtesy of Carver's radical new zonal marking system, conceded only three. By Christmas they were six points clear. Not only were they unbeaten but also, seemingly, unbeatable. However, on New Year's Day, Juve reject Mihály Kincses scored a dramatic late winner for Lucchese at the Comunale. Most assumed it was a blip, but it heralded a slump. The goalless draw with Fiorentina was particularly dreadful, but it's immortal all the same. That's because it featured perhaps the most famous scissor kick in the history of football, and certainly its most reproduced photograph.

Carlo Parola had been born in Turin in 1921. His father died when he was seven, and he and his mother moved to Cuneo, a sub-Alpine city known as Little Turin close to the French border. He was good with his hands, little Carlino, and just as well. He wanted a football and had no money to buy one, so he made his own from bits of old shoe leather, cloth, rope and whatever else he could lay his hands on. Once he'd made one he made more, and evidently he was skilled in their use as well. As a teenager he moved back to Turin, got a job as a fitter at FIAT and started turning out – and turning heads – for the *dopolavoro*, the factory team of his section. He began as a centre forward but, graceful, athletic and perceptive, evolved into a fantastic *centromediano*, a ball-playing centre half.

Urged by Juve to sign a professional contract, Parola insisted that he be allowed to combine his football career with his 'real' job at the factory. His ambition, he said, had always been to become one of the test drivers on the roof at Lingotto. That marked him down as the classic Juve player, and in many respects he remains the archetype. Though its players are extremely wealthy, the club still likes to portray them as blue-collared grafters. It's quite a stretch, but if nothing else the club is a masterpiece of sports branding. It purports to value collective graft over individual virtuosity, natural ability in tandem with (not as a substitute for) hard work.

Anyway Gianni Agnelli had it right when he said Parola was 'the sort a player who made you love football'. He soon became a Juve fixture, and one of the few non-Toro players to appear regularly in the post-war national side. He'd been the best player on the pitch when that Intercontinental side had played the British in Glasgow, and evidently Chelsea had offered him an eye-watering contract there and then. Parola was a FIAT man to his marrow though, and wouldn't countenance leaving old Piedmont. His name still inspires awe among the octogenarians who saw him play. Most agree that the Toro captain Mazzola was the best, most influential player in post-war Italy, but Parola wasn't so very far behind. He was Juve's leader and captain, and quite rightly the club portrayed him as a working-class hero and a local boy made good.

Curiously, he was criticised for his smoking habits. About half the Juve squad smoked back then and, given that the whole continent resembled a giant ashtray, the fans thought nothing of the habit. Boniperti and Piccinini preferred Laurens ('light and aromatic'), while keeper Giovanni Viola puffed away on North State. Parola's brand of choice was Gauloises. Nobody minded that they were poisonous, revolting and injurious to his health, but they minded a lot that they were *French*. We digress. His legacy endures in popular footballing culture because of that awful 0–0 draw with Fiorentina. During it, a freelance photographer named Corrado Bianchi shot him performing his trademark scissor kick. It was a cracking picture, but it was archived like the rest and nobody thought anything more of it.

However, in 1965 Panini selected it as their album cover picture. That presented a number of issues, not least the fact that Parola's kit is unmistakable. It made no commercial sense for the Panini brothers to be seen to favour one team over the others, so they recoloured his shirt red and, for good measure, his socks black. Apparently, no team anywhere wore that combination, and so Parola's scissor kick – his *rovesciata* – took its place on the cover. It's been there on and off ever since, and they reckon it's been reproduced over 200 million times. Looking at it, one automatically assumes it's a striker scoring a spectacular goal, but in reality it was a clearance in a lousy goalless draw. It happened on a freezing Turin afternoon, on a quagmire of a pitch, and Carlo Parola never got a penny for it. Neither did poor Bianchi, who sold it to the agency for the price of 200 Gauloises. You live and learn ...

Parola, whom I'm supposing many of you grew up with but have never heard of, cemented his legend during another seminal game at the Comunale the following month. By then Juve were *in crisi*, and Milan, their visitors, had closed to within three points.

RAI had built Italy's first bespoke TV studio in Via Verdi, just off Piazza Castello. It transmitted to (almost) the entire city, but televisions cost 12 months' wages for the average FIAT *operaio*. Hardly anyone in Turin owned one, but on his frequent visits to America Gianni had been wowed by the possibilities the technology offered. He'd lobbied for the match to be broadcast, and had contributed financially to the installation of repeaters in the hills above the city in readiness. The superstars of Italian cinema were invited, and so too the cyclist Fausto Coppi and the racing driver Alberto Ascari. In the event, however, the match was a traumatic experience for just about everyone. The commentator, Carlo Bacarelli, had to contend with thick fog, viewers with the fact that as yet camera lenses weren't able to cover such a large area. Moreover for Carver's side in general and Parola in particular, the whole thing was a Calvary.

Following Sweden's stunning victory at the London Olympics, her champions had been scattered to the four winds. Milan had acquired three of the most gifted, forwards Gunnar Gren and Gunnar Nordahl, and midfielder Nils Liedholm. Collectively they were known as Gre-No-Li, and between them they'd amass over 750 appearances for the *rossoneri*. Nordahl, who remains the club's record goalscorer, was a singular talent. On this occasion he cancelled out Hansen's opener after a quarter of an hour and then, horror of all *Juventino* horrors, Carver's zonal marking system disintegrated completely. Each of the Swedes scored within the space of four apocalyptic minutes, at which point Parola lost the plot completely. In fact he lost the plot, the subplot, his lines and even the screenplay, lashing out at Nordahl, having lost a 50–50 on the edge of the centre circle.

Mortified by what he'd done, Juve's captain and spiritual leader implored the referee to send him off and, before a stadium stunned into silence, he obliged. Milan went on to win 7–1, and a country of football fans contemplated its collective navel. *What madness was this? What moral torpor? What was the point of calcio when it provoked behaviour like this in decent men like Parola?* Interviewed afterwards, he apologised to everyone he could think of, and anyone he couldn't. He said nothing like that had ever happened to him before, excepting that time during the Turin derby of 1948 when he'd overdone it with the amphetamine and had the punch-up with Martelli.

It's not clear what happened at the post-mortem, but whatever it was Carver said or did, it worked. Normal service was resumed as his team won eight games on the spin, scoring 32 goals. They won the league at a canter, and some maintain that, their dreadful January aside, they were the greatest of all Juventus sides.

In Brazil with the *Juventini*

In the summer of 1950 Italy – and her four *Juventini* – set sail for the World Cup in Brazil. In light of the Superga tragedy, the delegation eschewed air travel and took a marathon 15-day boat trip instead. By the time they arrived their footballs had all been booted overboard, and they were bored witless, seasick and exhausted. Little wonder the Swedes, their Milan contingent included, beat them 3–2 in San Paolo.

Pozzo's side overcame Paraguay, but it was too little too late. Having been in possession of the trophy for 16 years either side of the war, they came home with their tails between their sea legs. So did Carver's countrymen, beaten 1–0 by the United States in *the* greatest upset in the history of the game.

Agnelli took it upon himself to install one of Carcano's golden boys, Luigi Bertolini, as joint coach alongside Carver. However, their footballing philosophies were poles apart. Bertolini had been a striker, Carver a stopper. Bertolini favoured Italian artistry, Carver English control and defensive rigour. Bertolini's arrival undermined Carver, because the players found it easier to talk and identify with him, although by now Carver was speaking pidgin Italian. He informed the directors, in no uncertain terms, that he wasn't happy.

By November, when the Turin derby came around, the shape of the title race had been established. So had the long-term future of Italian football, and it amounted to a three-horse race. Ferruccio Novo had tried to rebuild Toro in the image of those lost at Superga, but had failed. In the immediate wake of the tragedy there'd been a groundswell of support for Toro, but promises of financial assistance hadn't materialised and they were languishing in the bottom half. Their fans were in open revolt, and at the Filadelfia, formerly a fortress, Juventus steamrollered them 4–1. They'd fold again in the return fixture, this time 5–1, and would wait 27 years to win another title. The balance of Turin power had shifted conclusively and definitively away from them.

As poor, beleaguered Toro flirted with relegation, Milan, Inter and Juve disappeared off into football's sun-lit uplands. Ever more ambitious and still more high-minded, Juve in particular were perceived by those who wished them ill to be profiteering from the tragedy. They claimed deference to the memory of Mazzola and his team-mates, but to the heartbroken, the vanquished and disenfranchised of Turin, their new-found pre-eminence smacked of rank opportunism. Football was becoming more radicalised and, while Toro had been universally admired, no team divided opinion like Juve.

When they suffered shock losses to Como and Novara, Toro fans had something to crow about, if not exactly to cheer. It was all their own team could do to save themselves from the drop, but at least Juve came up short. Their fate was sealed by defeats against both Milan clubs, and Milan won their first title in 44 years. Fourth-placed Lazio trailed Juventus by eight points, and the rest

– the southern clubs and those from elsewhere – were nowhere. (By and large they've remained nowhere ever since. Post-Superga, Italy's big three have won 54 Serie A titles at the time of writing; the rest have 13, and precisely none for 18 years.)

Jesse Carver had been increasingly irritable as the season had progressed. His love-in with Gianni had run its course, and he'd fall on his sword in the most extraordinary circumstances that summer.

Superga notwithstanding, commercial air travel was expanding. Agnelli, the great globalist-modernist, had accepted an invitation for his team to fly to Brazil for the Copa Rio. A prototype world club championship, it featured five European sides and three South American. A second Brazilian sojourn within 12 months for Boniperti and Parola and, ultimately, a second complete debacle …

The great Italian diaspora had uprooted millions to the Americas, and many of them were excited to see Juve, but the locals – and consequently the local press – found the tactics of the Italian players shocking. They berated the match officials constantly; they fouled cynically and dived on the slightest contact, and their games were blighted by acts of psychological and physical violence. One way or another they were lousy house guests, and the whole thing reached its nadir one calamitous evening in San Paolo.

In the dying seconds of their semi-final clash with Austria Vienna, Juventus led 3–2. An innocuous cross was slung into their box, and by all (Italian) accounts Sergio Manente chested it down and passed it back to Giovanni Viola, his keeper. However, the ref blew up for handball against Manente, the penalty was converted, and all hell broke loose. Fighting broke out between the expatriate Italian fans and the locals, Juve players shoved the referee, and the police came onto the pitch. Blows were landed, and things escalated further still in the changing rooms. Viola and Ermes Muccinelli were arrested for assaulting a police officer, hauled off to the cells still wearing their kit, and detained until the small hours.

Still more ignominy the following day, as the entire Juve delegation was invited to vacate Rio's Hotel Palasanda. The management claimed there had been a 'series of incidents', and the party left under armed guard. Juve would eventually lose a bad-tempered final to Palmeiras. One of the Brazilians blatted Muccinelli after the half-time whistle, as things went from bad to unthinkably bad, and then to worse.

Carver was livid. When he got back he took himself off to the coast to unwind and to enjoy a few days of peace and quiet before pre-season training. One day he walked into a bar and, because his Italian was passable by now, got talking to a bloke. The bloke asked him about the Brazil trip, whereupon the balloon went up. Carver's interlocutor, it transpired, was a journalist from *La Gazzetta dello Sport*. Very obviously he went away and wrote it all up, and when his piece came out it was sensational, incendiary stuff. Carver had railed against Agnelli's absenteeism, and against the inertia it created within the club. He criticised Juve's Danish contingent, whined that the grass hadn't been cut all summer and complained that the directors were 'incompetent'.

Some of it was probably true, but the last bit was sacrilege. Guys like Pierino Monateri had given their lives to

Juventus, and their love for it was profound and unconditional. Monateri had been the driving force behind the
construction of Campo Juventus and one of the architects of the five golden years. He was a Juve legend, and
what's more he'd known the Agnellis all his life. He'd been
present the very first time Gianni had visited Campo
Juventus as a toddler, and extremely present in the aftermath of his father's death. His character was beyond
reproach, his knowledge of football second to none, his
belief in Juventus ecclesiastical.

With no actual football being played, the 'Carver
Scandal' became front-page news. Agnelli put him on
garden leave, and Gianpiero Combi was drafted in to
help prepare the players pre-season. They enjoyed having him around, and he and Bertolini agreed to take
charge until a new trainer could be found. That, as far as
Carver was concerned, was that. The players didn't want
him back anyway, and so, five days before the opening
game, Gianni sacked him. Typically witty, he said, 'I told
him not to learn Italian, but he didn't listen, and it seems
he's gone and learned too much of it.'

With Carver out of the way, Juventus began the season
with renewed vigour. By Christmas they'd installed the
Hungarian György Sárosi as coach, and by June had run
away with their second *Scudetto* in three years. Agnelli
had been as good as his word. From the wreckage of
Superga he'd built a team that Turin – at least the black
and white bits – could be proud of ... And the black and
white bits were expanding. By now the IRI, the official
body for the reconstruction of Italy, had approved the
so-called Sinigaglia Plan. During the war, Italy's factories had necessarily been reconfigured to produce

armaments. Now they needed to be reconverted, and what's more the country required new railway lines and rolling stock, machinery and low-cost housing. It needed vast quantities of steel, and so did FIAT.

As manufacturing output increased, so, exponentially, did the need for workers. Meanwhile in southern and central Italy, traditionally the bread basket of the peninsula, farming was modernised as steel machines replaced flesh and blood human beings. With less work in the south and loads of it in the north, a new wave of migration began. In times past, the *disoccupati* of the south had sought their fortunes in Europe and the Americas. Now, as production doubled at FIAT, they were relocated to public housing projects on the fringes of the city. In the ten years from 1950, Turin's population would increase by some 300,000 people. It would become home to over a million, a modern European metropolis.

Italy, hitherto the financial basket case of Europe, was becoming an industrial powerhouse. The economic miracle saw millions desert the arid, feckless south. One-way tickets in hand, they made gleefully for the burgeoning cities of the north. Enticed by the easy money and the *dolce vita*, they alighted at Porta Nuova and drank from the intoxicating fountain of consumerism. Here was a nation of peasant farmers and economic parasites systematically demobbed, scrubbed clean and uprooted to shiny new, edge-of-town tenement communities. They made directly for Lingotto and Mirafiori, and waited for the great leap forward. Once that came they were delivered, pockets bulging, to the neon glow of the city centre. So progressive were the new communities and so purposeful the factory floors that, the more they came the more cars they produced, and the more they produced the more the company earned. The more it earned the more it invested in new staff, and with labour and steel costs halved, overall production costs were reduced. Now even the ant people working at Lingotto could aspire to own the cars they built. The *boom economico* of post-war Italy had begun, and with it the inexorable, unstoppable rise of the Fabbrica Italiana Automobili Torino.

Those who didn't work for FIAT worked for its subsidiaries and suppliers, or for the suppliers of its suppliers. There were dozens of them, and then there were hundreds. By 1956, a million cars would be in circulation in Italy, and by 1965 there'd be five million. Here and there you'd see a Lancia, from time to time an Alfa, very occasionally a Peugeot or a Renault. For every ten cars on the road, however, nine were made by FIAT.

The company had taken the Yankee dollar, expanded its empire exponentially, and re-engineered both Piedmont and the Piedmontese. Its white-collar staff dreamed of winters skiing in Sestriere, the Alpine playground Edoardo had constructed near the French border. The blue collars read the Agnelli newspaper, built cars in Agnelli factories (over 85,000 toiled at Lingotto and Mirafiori alone), lived in low-rent, Agnelli-built apartments on the outskirts of the city. On sweaty Friday evenings in the summer, they piled into their staff-discounted Agnelli cars, drove south out of the city and, via the Agnelli-built Turin–Savona motorway, made for the Ligurian coast, stopping only to pay tolls to its Agnelli-owned management company. And on a Sunday? On a Sunday they watched the Agnelli-owned football team.

The thing with Juventus, Edoardo Agnelli had always claimed, was that it never claimed to represent the city of Turin. Rather it was the team of all of Italy – north, south, east and west. While Milan and Inter squabbled for local primacy 90 miles to the east, Juventus studiously avoided association with Piedmontese cultures and values, Piedmontese identity and *vittimismo*. It became the club of small-town Italy, and of Italy's small-town mentality.

FIAT was the engine room of a bold, dynamic and successful new country, and its resurgence was absolutely indivisible from that of Juventus FC. Each and every car rolling off its production lines constituted a down payment on another star player, a tiny cog in the Agnelli money machine. And so, *ad infinitum*, it rolled on.

The point was that in supporting Juventus and not Torino – an idea and not a place name – Agnelli's toiling masses reasserted their own regional identities. Allegiance to Juve suggested that while they were resident *in* Piedmont, they were not *of* Piedmont. Neither were they of the left, and so, by definition, they were a mirror of the loyal, hard-working Italian patriots who wore the black and white.

FIAT provided its employees with their identity, but also an extended family and an ideology which aimed to keep out the unions. The 'FIAT way of life' was a catchy motto but also a financial and social safety blanket. Company doctors took care of the workers' health, company crèches their toddlers, the travel section their holidays. FIAT provided access to lawyers, classes, cultural events and social services. There were clubs for reading, for sports, for lectures and for days out. For Italian wives and mothers, hanging a FIAT overall on the washing line was a dream come true in the most literal sense. FIAT jobs were the best jobs, and they were jobs for life. To have a son or a husband on the payroll was the best thing that could happen to any working-class family.

As Turin's demography altered, so too did its cultures and behaviours. Delivered from the back-breaking, seven-day toil of farming, the incomers were replete not only with cash, but with myriad ways to spend it. Electronic consumer goods, icons of modernity, became their must-have status symbols. Washing machines and fridges spewed from Milan's factories, and television began to replace radio as the opiate of the post-Catholic masses. Cocksure southern migrant boys splashed out on Vespas, their parents on the discounted FIATs they'd built themselves. Hardly believing their good luck, they took photos (of the car, the oven, the electric shaver, the week by the seaside ...) with their new cameras and mailed them to those kicking their heels in the stagnant, malaria-infested south. Subliminally, each and every letter carried the same postmark, and the postmark was FIAT.

FIAT provided *pane e salame*, but with strings attached. The changes were seismic socially as well as architectur-ally, and the old *torinesi* believed themselves to be pick-ing up the tab. Social cohesion was compromised, and with it their sense of self. Unused to and ill-prepared for the invasion, they felt themselves besieged. They labelled their new, olive-skinned neighbours *terroni* – 'dirt people' – and derided them as ignorant and feckless. The usual urban myths emerged around them: they slept five to a bed, utilised their baths not to wash but to cultivate vegetables, and didn't know how to use an indoor lavatory. They couldn't read or write, they spoke incomprehensible dialects and tended towards criminality. Their culinary habits were horrendous. They added spicy *pepperoncino* to everything, and if it moved they fried it. Most *torinesi* had never heard of their 'pizza', let alone eaten it. Still today some of the old guard recoil at the very idea of it. They still perceive it as a mongrel food and associate it, unwittingly or otherwise, with the invasion of their city. Food matters *a lot* in Italy, more than any foreigner can possibly imagine. Theirs was a city invaded by a bunch of southern degenerates who had never eaten risotto and – God forgive them – never even *heard* of agnolotti or polenta. NO SOUTHERNERS signs began to appear on rental properties and boarding houses across the city. Many *torinesi* blamed the Agnellis for all the upheaval, and for better or for worse they weren't wrong.

On the Côte d'Azur with Pamela Churchill, the daughter-in-law of the British prime minister

Aside from his role as mayor of Villar Perosa and a largely ambassadorial post with the family ball-bearing company, Gianni's only true job of work was Juventus. Insofar as he was able, he took it seriously, and he'd a pretty good understanding of the game. Some argued that he was away too often to be an effective president, but there's little doubt that he was an enthusiastic one.

Not being much for sitting still, he tended not to watch the matches in their entirety. Rather he'd crack a few gags and throw the assembled journalists a few scraps, then settle down as best he could to watch and shove off ten minutes before the finish. That's not to say he didn't love footy, because he most certainly did. It was just that spectating is by definition passive, and Gianni had the attention span of a five-year-old.

He had no clear role in FIAT and, ostensibly at least, no brief. That said, he was highly effective in diplomatic circles, probably because his approach – such as it was – was so unorthodox. Beyond schmoozing, gossiping and seducing beautiful women, you'd be hard pushed to define his methodology, and therein lay his great gift. People liked him a very great deal, and women in particular adored him. The story went that he treated ladies like whores and whores like ladies, and he pursued them all with equal vigour. Ultimately he possessed one of the greatest talents of all – he made everyone feel good about themselves, and his presence *always* constituted a happening.

The legends built around him speak not only of a style icon, but also of a brilliant, erudite man – a charmer, yes, but also a doer. It's a very seductive narrative, but it suggests a depth of character at variance with who the young Gianni was. He was courteous, faultlessly mannered and socially adroit, but he owed his popularity not to any great political or ideological heft. Rather it was his superficiality which enamoured him to the great and the good. Fundamentally, he was shallow. He was intelligent but almost completely devoid of philosophical and emotional substance. His role in high society was as a courier

of transatlantic tittle-tattle, the crown prince of everything and nothing. He never read books – he couldn't sit
still long enough – and famously stated that he 'preferred
footballers to intellectuals'.

Gianni increasingly eschewed the family residence
at dreary old Villar Perosa; instead he availed himself
of Villa la Leopolda, the grandest mansion on the Côte
d'Azur. There he and his friends had the very best of
everything, including the best yacht in Cap Ferrat.
Though he'd been instrumental in securing the Marshall
Plan money, he wasn't interested in matter-of-fact car
manufacturing. He *liked* cars a very great deal, but only
the fast, expensive ones he used to hurtle along the coast
road at insane speeds. He couldn't have cared less for
the low-cost models being churned out of Lingotto and
Mirafiori and nor, truth be told, for the proles who did
the churning. Delegating the running of the family business to Vittorio Valletta had been, by some considerable
distance, the smartest thing he'd ever done.

He revelled in the absence of anything resembling
responsibility, in the trappings of his wealth and in a
social circle which included Prince Rainier of Monaco,
Errol Flynn and Rita Hayworth. Gianni was a raconteur,
a party animal and an incorrigible philanderer, but his
predilection for the high life would almost kill him on
22 August 1952.

Stories of his womanising are legion, but one recur-
ring name is that of an Englishwoman named Pamela
Digby. Aged 19 she'd famously married Randolph,
Winston Churchill's blithering-idiot son. They'd split
soon after, but she made good use of his surname and her

new-found celebrity. She'd developed a reputation as a bit of a laugh and a lot of a goer, and by and by had begun a relationship with Prince Aly Khan. Like Gianni he was *torinese* by birth, and just like Gianni he was rich, handsome and unencumbered by any sense of duty. Khan's problem was that he'd fallen in love with Hayworth, so he needed to shake Pam off. He asked Gianni to help him out by taking her out on his boat and seducing her. Gianni agreed, though evidently Pam didn't need a great deal of seducing.

Gianni appreciated her savvy and her decadence, and they both understood the mutual benefits of an alliance. Her erstwhile father-in-law was a political colossus, and Gianni understood that made her a conduit to Anglo-Saxon power. In Gianni she saw the most eligible bachelor in all of Europe, the biggest fish in a massive sea. Pam convinced herself he'd make her an Italian princess and, although the child they are believed to have conceived together was aborted in Switzerland, had him procure a magnificent Parisian apartment for her to live in. She even converted to Catholicism, but it was all wishful thinking on her part. Gianni's sisters thought her a trollop, and marriage was out of the question. She and *l'Avvocato* were together (after a fashion) for getting on for five years, and family aside she was the closest thing in his life to real, lasting companionship at that time. However neither was much for monogamy, and their break-up was prompted by a classic jet-set scene on the Côte d'Azur.

The story goes that she decided to surprise him at Villa la Leopolda. When she arrived, however, she found him *in flagrante* with a 17-year-old girl named Anne-Marie d'Estainville. She blew her top, supposedly threw him out of his own house, and he sped off some time around 4 a.m. He entered a tunnel on the Lower Corniche at breakneck speed, lost control and crashed head-on into a truck carrying a gang of workers. He smashed his leg so badly that there was talk of amputation, and he'd walk with a pronounced limp for the rest of his life.

Reports in *La Stampa*, the newspaper he owned, stated that he was in the company not of the girl, but of a Belgian friend. That's possible (he may have already dropped her off), but *La Stampa* also maintained he was behind the wheel of a mid-range FIAT 1400 when it happened. The paper made scant reference to the fact that three people in the other vehicle were gravely injured, and neglected to mention they had been in a truck. It simply stated that they were in a Lancia, which suggests a car. Quite why isn't entirely clear, but the tone of the article implied that Gianni was blameless. That may very well be true, but he'd a reputation as a mad driver at the best of times.

FIAT liked to pretend Gianni was a model of probity. This didn't remotely correspond with the truth, but it played well with the snooty old *Torino bene* and with the blue-collared multitudes who bankrolled his lifestyle. Regardless, it's almost inconceivable that he was driving a stodgy old 1400, and all the anecdotal evidence points to him having been with the girl, in a Ferrari and out of his mind on his drug of choice. The 'white nights' of Leopolda are the stuff of legend, and not without reason ...

At the San Siro, with Alfredo Foni

Gianni's crown had slipped that night on the Lower Corniche, and his football club would stumble the following season. Pierino Monateri had been 42 years on the Juve board, 13 of them as vice-president. He'd been overseeing the day-to-day running of the club since Gianni's father died in 1935. He dealt with all the bread-and-butter stuff which kept the thing ticking along, and he ate, drank and slept football. Furthermore he wasn't perceived as an Agnelli stooge, because his presence at Juventus predated theirs. His longevity and decency transcended the tribalism and myopia which increasingly characterised the sport, and he was universally liked and respected. People will always do business with people they like, and so when he died on 1 October 1952, the loss was incalculable.

The previous season had seen four clubs relegated, as Serie A was reduced from 20 teams to 18. Toro had survived again, but only by the skin of their teeth. They desperately needed a new team but needed to sell in order to buy. The two Turin clubs had always traded players, but the sale of the 'Italian Matthews' Riccardo Carapellese to Juventus seemed to crystalise the new reality. Carapellese was a mazy, goal-scoring winger capable of playing on either side. He was an Italian international and, by a distance, Toro's best player. For three years he'd been their captain and crowd-pleaser-in-chief, and yet Juve signed him as a backup in the event that Muccinelli and/or Præst got injured.

In a practical sense the move worked for Toro. They spent the money well and finished comfortably mid-table. Carapellese scored nine goals in sixteen games for his new club, but without Monateri the whole thing felt a little bit hollow and a little bit rudderless. The net result was that Inter, thirteen years without a *Scudetto*, finally reached the promised land. The irony was that the architect of their success was a *bianconero* legend. Alfredo Foni had spent the best years of his playing career in Turin, thirteen of them all told. He'd been a natural-born defender – quick-witted, rugged and iron-willed. As a coach he was more of the same, and what he created at Inter was a new, totally different kind of *calcio*.

Unusually for a modern footballer, Foni boasted a university degree. He was highly intelligent, and he'd been a qualified success in his previous job at Sampdoria. Having flirted with relegation for two seasons, they'd finished a commendable seventh principally because they'd stopped conceding stupid goals. Now he took a call from Carlo Masseroni, Inter's corpulent, rubber-baron president. Masseroni charged him with breaking the post-Superga duopoly of Juventus and Milan, and Foni came with a ready-made plan.

He inherited three very gifted forward players. Benito 'the poison' Lorenzi was an outstanding number 9, and he had an absolute stonker of a nickname. The Swedish winger Lennart 'Nacka' Skoglund possessed a beauty-queen wife, an alcohol problem which would kill him before his 50th birthday and a wand of a left foot. Completing the trio was the Hungarian István Nyvers, scorer of 110 goals in 141 games over the four previous seasons. Nyvers' strike rate was outstanding, though not unique. John Hansen, Juve's great Dane, had been equally prolific, and Gunnar Nordahl still more so for Milan. Goals scored, however, weren't the issue as Foni saw it; goals *conceded* was the issue, and Nyvers' excellence would count for nothing until he addressed it and resolved it.

Foni understood that defensive cohesion was much more coachable than attacking flair, and that there was no value per se in scoring shedloads of goals. Inter had been outscoring sides for years, and it had won them precisely zero *Scudetti*. The way to win, therefore, was to out-defend Juve and Milan, and if that meant sacrificing goals and style on the altar of points, then so be it.

He therefore packed the midfield with stoppers and, critically, had his strikers contemplate the idea that they might contribute defensively as well. They bought into the idea, and Foni redeployed veteran full-back Ivano Blason as a sweeper, or *libero*. Inter brought sides onto them, and then broke quickly and decisively. Invariably one quick long ball over the top would suffice, and once they had the lead they'd shut up shop for the duration.

This was the first true iteration of *catenaccio* – deadlock – the anti-football which scandalised Italy but which proved extraordinarily effective. Juve had scored 98 goals in winning the league the previous season. This time they scored 73 to Inter's 46, and yet still conceded the title with three games left to play. While Juve's buccaneers won one game, against Fiorentina 8–0, Foni's misers won eight games 1–0. No champions had ever scored or conceded fewer goals, and none were ever so unloved. Inter parked the bus even at home. The more they did so the more opposing fans complained, but

Foni wasn't in the business of winning popularity contests. He'd scratched a 13-year itch, and he couldn't have cared less for the aesthetes, the purists or the naysayers.

Calcio was becoming more tactical and more professional but much less exciting. The way Inter played it was extremely efficient, but then so was a tin opener. So was a paint brush, but nobody in their right mind would pay to watch paint dry.

Would they?

Chapter 4

Il Boom Economico

Without good men, you're not going anywhere.

Umberto Agnelli

At home, with poor, orphaned Umberto Agnelli

On 13 November 1953, a small sidebar of *La Stampa* stated, 'At a meeting of the board of directors, it was decided to entrust Umberto Agnelli with the role of vice president in place of the deceased Monateri. Umberto, a university student, will collaborate with his older brother Gianni, and will substitute him when he's away from Turin for professional reasons.'

Six days on from the announcement, Italy's most famous gigolo went and got married. Marella Caracciolo di Castagneto was six years Gianni's junior, and like his mother was an Italian-American noblewoman. She was also graceful, feline and highly bred. *La Stampa* neglected to mention that she was highly pregnant, but no matter. Nineteen-year-old Umberto, the youngest of Gianni's siblings, was best man. Gianni had been a brother but also something of an idol to Umberto. Notwithstanding the 13-year age gap, they cared about one another a lot, and they both loved Juve.

By his own admission, Umberto had endured an unhappy, fretful and rather isolated childhood. He'd been a baby when his father's plane had crashed into the Ligurian Sea, and eleven when his mother's car had hit that American army truck. His closest sibling, Giorgio, led a troubled life and ultimately a short one. He studied at Harvard and briefly edited an art magazine, but he never worked in the family business. He seldom appeared in public, struggled to maintain personal relationships, and would die in a Swiss clinic aged 36. The circumstances are still unclear, though it's probable he threw himself out of a window. One former girlfriend claimed he was schizophrenic, though it's also quite possible he suffered from clinical depression. His story is still shrouded in mystery; the family decided, understandably, that it's not for public consumption.

Giorgio was five years older than Umberto, and it's no secret that he and Gianni detested one another. Umberto alluded to having been caught in the crossfire, and he'd had no father to protect him. Malaparte had been a divisive figure among the kids, and following his departure their mother had been constantly on the move. Evidently discipline was in short supply. There's a famous story about the children drinking champagne for breakfast because, quite simply, they wanted to and they could. Following the death of his mother, Umberto spent some time in Rome with his older sister Suni, and it was there that he watched his first football match. Ironically enough he saw the *Grande Torino* thump Roma, but he had *Juventino* DNA.

There was always a certain melancholy in Umberto's smile, and a certain unease in his bearing. Obviously there was wine, women and song, and his profligacy with money is the stuff of Turin legend. However, one associate (who chose not to be named) told me there was also a nagging insecurity, an uncertainty about who he was and what he was supposed to do about it. One always had the sense that, while he loved football, it was also something of a bolt hole for him. It was essentially binary and essentially just a game. As a young man it served to insulate him from the big, scary decisions of the family business, and to insulate the business against him being the one making them.

Foni, previously the chief proponent of *catenaccio*, loosened the Inter shackles somewhat the following season. They destroyed Juve 6–0 in Milan, but with three games left the two of them were neck and neck on 46 points. Then, however, Juve conceded three first-half goals on a mud heap in Bergamo. They rallied after the break as Parola, playing his final game for the club, pulled one back with a volley. Boniperti added a stupendous bicycle kick, but it was too little too late.

That match is legendary, not least because it underscored the new reality. While Rome was Italy's capital, the Turin–Milan corridor was its financial engine room. Milan, Inter and Juve routinely occupied the top three positions, because football was a market and they had the deepest pockets. Provincial clubs like Atalanta were sporting Davids by comparison, and the gap between the haves and the have-nots was widening all the time.

Beating any of the big three was a cause for celebration, but it's unarguable that victory over Juventus was the greatest scalp of all. The question is, why? Why Juve and not Inter, and why does a visit from the *bianconeri* still constitute a major happening in provincial towns up and down the country? Why do they fill so many stadiums, hotel beds and column inches, and why do people love them and loathe them in equal measure? Isn't it, objectively, just another game of footy?

Although Italy is becoming more and more secular, its sporting leitmotifs remain biblical. Faith and hope, blood, sweat and tears are still its foundation stones, still prerequisites for success. God-given talent is necessary as well, but there's no particular virtue in being gifted. Football fans demand that their players apply themselves heart and soul, because that's the currency of the sport. Their vocabulary is a reflection of the fact, so when the *tifosi* – fans – of Toro, Fiorentina and Roma invoke faith (and they constantly do), it's because they genuinely believe that they're the custodians of it. In post-Catholic Italy the stadium is their church and the club their religion. It's pure *campanilismo*, but their football club is as central to their being as it is to their city. It's the vehicle through which they self-identify, and in Turin in particular their connection to it has connotations beyond mere fandom.

While cities like Rome, Florence and Venice constantly evoked the Middle Ages and the Renaissance, Turin was far too busy working to concern itself with its artistic patrimony. Though more beautiful than, say,

Milan, it had never felt the need to promote itself, so the Grand Tourists had bypassed it and made directly for Tuscany, Liguria and the Veneto. That was OK though, because the *torinesi* didn't need them. They were too insular for frilly hospitality, and they didn't much care that their city had developed a reputation for heavy industry, battleship skies and sodden, joyless autumnal afternoons.

In truth it wasn't a good look, but it informed the Juventus philosophy absolutely. Edoardo Agnelli had been at pains to hawk Juve as Italy's club rather than Turin's. The more the *torinesi* insisted on being narrow-minded and inward-looking, the more Juventus would be ecumenical and expansive. It would aspire not to *campanilismo* but to some higher – though in truth ill-defined – worldly principle. Some saw it as a denial of regional identity, the Agnellis as an expansion of it.

People's choice of club is broadly determined by three elements – heritage, success on the pitch and geography. Italian society is much less fluid than, for example, those of its northern European counterparts. Family remains its bedrock, and millions still support the team their father, uncle or grandfather followed. Others attach themselves to whoever happens to be most successful when they become interested, because young people struggle to cope with defeat. There's nothing unusual in any of that, but Juve's apparent denial of anything resembling a Turin character would have been unfathomable to many in this of all countries. Allied to the perceived airs and graces of the owners, it smacked of outrageous conceit, supreme arrogance and a massive superiority complex.

For all that Gianni had delegated the running of the club to Monateri, FIAT owned it and he was its public face. Italy's media paradigm was expanding rapidly, and he was both a celebrity and a fashion icon. Magazine editors couldn't get enough of him, and his lifestyle and personality fired the public imagination. The Italian public was football-mad, so while the other clubs – Milan's clubs included – dripped piously on about faith, Juve cleverly promulgated the notion that he was the embodiment of the *stile Juventino* – the 'Juventus style'.

Lo stile Juventino isn't so difficult to understand, because it's really no more than an idea. There's not much to it, but that's its genius. It's rooted in the fact that Italian behaviours and mentalities have been conditioned for centuries by the Catholic Church, and that as a people they have an absolute need to line up behind things. Style is both a universal construct and a highly seductive one. Nobody can quantify precisely what it is, but everybody wants it.

Cities like Milan and Rome portray themselves as global commercial hubs, but they're the exception and not the rule. Italy, overwhelmingly, is a country of small towns and small businesses. Italians are incredibly provincial, and while there may be more conservative populations in western Europe, none spring to mind. In supporting Juve, even small-town Italians utterly bereft of style feel entitled to claim it. After all, what better than to be associated with style, and who better to support than a winning team which bestows it on its subjects? All of that may appear infantile, but since when has sports branding been anything but?

Juventus fans are often caricatured as bumptious, intellectually challenged potato heads. It's one of the sticks with which they're beaten, but most of them couldn't care less and neither could the club. Juventus sets out its stall to attract precisely that type of customer because they believe them to be the most susceptible to marketing guff like *lo stile Juventino*. While it would be nice if educated, urbane metropolitan sorts from Milan and Rome bought into Juve, they're in the statistical minority. They're also far more difficult to persuade, because they're more likely to support Milan or Roma. Or indeed not to support football at all.

Whatever. The fact is that 14 million Italians claim allegiance to Juventus, and they're spread far and wide. A 2016 poll by Demos suggested that Juventus is the favourite club of 34 per cent (and rising) of all Italians. The two Milan clubs can lay claim to 14 per cent each, but their support is drawn overwhelmingly from in and around the Milanese conurbation. Napoli boasts 13 per cent of the national support, but it's concentrated almost entirely within Campania and the *Mezziogiorno*, the old kingdom of Naples. Likewise Fiorentina and Roma are popular in Tuscany and Lazio respectively, but singularly fail to resonate elsewhere.

Uniquely in European football, there's very little difference in the geographical distribution of Juve's support base. So while the north-west (Piedmont, Valle d'Aosta, Lombardy and Liguria) is 32.5 per cent Juve, the regions of the south and the islands of Sicily and Sardinia are 29.5 per cent. Of the 20 Italian *regioni*,

Juventus is the best-supported club in no fewer than 13. The three central regions of Umbria, Marche and Abruzzo are instructive. Collectively they are home to 3.7 million people, but they have no population centres over 170,000 and only five (Perugia, Ancona, Pescara, Terni and Pesaro) over 70,000. Little wonder, therefore, that they have no major football clubs and that almost 50 per cent of those surveyed expressed a preference for *la Juve-Nazionale*.

Over half of those polled expressed 'strong antipathy' towards Juventus, and that tells its own story. It implies that Italian football fans make binary choices, and that every match Juve play is therefore a derby. Fans of every other club, Milan and Inter included, claimed that Juventus was their least favourite. A whopping 75 per cent of Inter fans disliked Juventus more than Milan, and Juve is public enemy number one for 97 per cent of Napoli fans. That seems extraordinary, but it's illustrative of the prevailing 'anyone but them' attitude towards Juventus.

There's a slightly sugary tradition of *gemellaggio* – twinning between sets of fans – in Italian football. In some instances it's based on old ideological leanings, in others on historical ties. The fans of Toro and Genoa are twinned largely because their respective clubs were among the founding fathers of Italian football. Some derive from shared antipathy, and that, in part, is where Juventus come in. There's only one top-level Italian side which isn't on friendly terms with at least one other. I'll leave you to take a wild guess at who that might be, but the *Juventini* probably wouldn't want it any other way. Most almost certainly view it as a badge of honour, because the last thing they want is to be like the rest.

Prior to his death in 2017, Giorgio Barberi Squarotti was one of Italy's foremost poets, academics and literary critics. In critiquing the Juventus phenomenon, he stated, 'It's implicit that the Juve fan base feels the need to be associated with the sort of wealth and power which, even if it fails to win, will always be a protagonist.' Squarotti's assertion was that Juventus fans delude themselves that they are stakeholders in the Agnelli empire, whereas in reality they are subjects of it.

Others suggest, it must be said rather too simplistically, that the club's great skill is in making its supporters feel like *protagonisti*. The more the team wins the more it's able to perpetuate the deceit, but ultimately the fans are the opposite of important. Supporters of other clubs, for whom winning is less frequent and by extension more valuable, hold the *Juventini* in contempt because they're too stupid and too blind to realise that they're just numbers. The suggestion is that they're merely a means to acquire the money they spend, and that has absolutely nothing to do with the glory of sport.

It's an argument which finds favour in Milan, in Rome and in the *granata* half of Turin, and it's true that Juve sometimes feels like a cult. The evangelical zeal one experiences in the hour preceding kick-off there is unlike anything else I've experienced at a football match, but the argument that the *Juventini* are all mindless, exploited zombies is flawed. While the ownership of Toro, Roma and Milan has at time resembled a revolving door, it's a matter of undeniable fact that one family has been investing billions, literally and continuously, in Juventus since 1923.

Neither here nor there, with Sandro Puppo

Well, more or less continuously.

That defeat in Bergamo was symptomatic of a sport – and a club – in a deep trough. The hosts were awarded a goal for a shot which didn't cross the line, and this became a metaphor for the times. By now allegations of match rigging were almost a weekly occurrence, and Juventus in particular seemed convinced that the rest were conspiring against them. *Catenaccio* was defiling the sport; fans and journalists were increasingly maniacal, and Italian clubs were once more disallowed from signing foreign players.

Monateri was gone and Gianni largely absent, and by now collective responsibility was breaking down in the dressing room. The club had signed Argentinian Eduardo Ricagni, but his colleagues thought him lazy and uncooperative. On the pitch he wasn't bad, but a punch-up with John Hansen would see both of them offloaded at the season's end.

One way or another it was all turning a bit ugly, and Gianni Agnelli had no time for ugly. As usual he was busy doing whatever took his fancy, and as of now that was preparing to be a father. He'd been minded to pack Juve in for a while, and now he informed the board that he'd had enough. He'd never been one for toughing it out, and by the time little Edoardo was born in New York, his father was to all intents and purposes the former president of Juventus FC. When the club formally announced this on the eve of the 1954–55 season, his departure was already the most open of secrets.

Nineteen-year-old Umberto would, however, continue to attend board meetings. It was to be hoped that by the time he completed his military service the club would have rediscovered the unity of purpose missing since Monateri passed away, and that being the case the family might be persuaded to start signing cheques again.

The 1954 World Cup had seen Italy eliminated in embarrassing circumstances, beaten twice by the hosts, Switzerland. The tournament, the highest-scoring and most exciting in history, served to highlight the uncomfortable truth about the Italian game. While the Hungarians, the Austrians and the West Germans scored freely, the Italians were a mirror on Serie A: nasty, cynical and at times just plain neurotic.

Juve was being run by a three-man committee but the consequences, like the team absent the talisman Parola, were shocking. There were dressing-room squabbles, threats of strike action by the players and well-founded rumours of a proposed merger with woebegone Toro. Both sets of fans were vehemently opposed, and they made their feelings known by posting anti-merger posters all over the city. History tells us that did the trick, but with the matches themselves almost incidental, Juventus finished a dismal seventh. Udinese, miraculously second behind Milan, were relegated for match fixing. So were Catania. It was that kind of football and that kind of season.

In the summer of 1955, more of the Juventus old guard shipped out. Keeper Viola stayed alongside Boniperti and Præst, but beyond those three the team was barely recognisable from the championship-winning outfit of two years earlier. Financial necessity being the mother of invention, half a dozen youngsters were drafted into the first team, and so too a new coach.

Sandro Puppo had played for a number of Serie A sides. He'd then managed the Turkish national team for two years, and had performed a footballing miracle in qualifying them for the World Cup. They'd held the mighty Spaniards over two legs, and held them again in the replay at Rome's Olympic Stadium. After the match a blindfolded 13-year-old boy had drawn lots, and the Turks had won. Now, following a successful stint at Barcelona, Puppo returned to his homeland charged with transforming Juve's ailing fortunes.

While Puppo was papering over the cracks at Juve, Inter and Milan each had a new president and new impetus. Inter's Angelo Moratti was a 46-year-old petrochemicals magnate and a rival to Gianni Agnelli in Italy's millionaire club. He possessed none of Gianni's charisma but had a vast fortune, a lifelong devotion to Inter and a winner-takes-all mentality. Andrea Rizzoli, head of the eponymous publishing giant, had spent liberally in his first season as Milan president. He'd smashed the global transfer record in signing Uruguayan 'god of football' Juan 'Pepe' Schiaffino, and they'd run away with the 1955 title. Milan had tended to play second fiddle to Inter, but Rizzoli made no secret of his intention to develop the club into a sporting juggernaut. He had the financial wherewithal to do it as well, so the *nerazzurri* and *bianconeri* needed to look to their laurels.

By now football matches were being screened live in Italy. Televisions were still too expensive for the many, but communities would fund their purchase collectively and install them at the local *osteria*. This was how, on 2 October, millions of Italians watched Juventus capsize to a humiliating 0–4 home defeat against Fiorentina. Worse still, they failed to win any of the opening seven games of the 1955–56 season. They were hovering just above the relegation zone, and financially they were sinking fast.

The truth of the matter was that Gianni had been away from the club for less than two years, and it was already in disarray. He and Umberto had a decision to make – either they abandoned Juve to its fate, or they intervened and went toe to toe with the *milanesi* Moratti and Rizzoli.

There was (and remains) a fierce rivalry between Piedmont and Lombardy. Increasingly it manifested itself through their sporting institutions, and the Agnelli family felt it as keenly as anyone; for all that Juventus sought to transcend local identity, they were bound both to their city and their region. The notion that Juve might become an incidental in a Milanese sporting power struggle was therefore unconscionable, but there were also issues of branding and association at play.

In the minds of millions of Italians, FIAT, the Agnellis and Juventus were a single entity. Whether the family liked it or not, a dysfunctional Juventus would cause collateral damage to the rest of the family holdings, while a winning team would add still more prestige. That being the case, it made commercial sense to carry on, but the fallout from Monateri's death had taught them that it would require both investment and hands-on involvement. Gianni wasn't interested in the latter, so the issue was whether Umberto wanted a full-time job as president of Juve. He said he did, and so the old guard was invited to resign. Barely out of his teens, Agnelli the younger assumed the presidency of *la vecchia signora*.

The assumption was that he'd start throwing money at the problem straight away, but Umberto – nicknamed *il Dottore* – was initially cautious. Spending money was the easiest thing in the Agnelli world, but he announced that he wouldn't be sanctioning new acquisitions just yet. Juventus weren't in the business of buying other people's mid-season cast-offs, so they'd see out the season and re-evaluate in the summer.

Given that what they had wasn't very much at all, Umberto's first season in charge was hardly auspicious. Nor, in spite of buying nine new players, was his second. Deploying the old *semplicita, serieta, sobrieta* mantra, he chose to work his way out of trouble, rather than lavish money on a handful of marquee signings. It didn't work, and at the end of the 1955–56 season the once-mighty Juventus beat the drop by just four points as Fiorentina claimed the *Scudetto*. That wasn't the worst of it. Umberto engaged Combi, the old rubber man himself, to work alongside Puppo. However he, like his old mate Caligaris, now succumbed to a heart attack. They renamed the training ground in his honour, but Juve had lost another of its heroes. Puppo was sent packing in 1957, and Rizzoli's Milan ran away with the title.

Suddenly the man-child Umberto found himself alone on the long, hard road to Damascus. His brother had won the title with Juventus, and so had their late father.

He had to find a way, and he told himself he *would* find a way, but so far he'd contrived only to turn an ordinary side into a godawful one.

At the San Siro, the Milan clubs routinely attracted over 60,000. It was all well and good that provincial Italy loved Juventus, and all well and good that FIAT reaped the benefit. The problem was Juve's match-day takings were light years behind the *milanesi*'s, and new player regulations which permitted him only one *oriundo* and one foreigner only added to Umberto's woes. He'd promised himself and his brother that he'd run Juventus prudently. He'd tried that, but the *Juventini* wouldn't tolerate a fourth successive season in the Serie A shallows, and he daren't even contemplate the financial consequences. How had it all gone so terribly wrong, and what on earth was he going to do about it?

At Elland Road, with Sam Bolton and a mountain of debt

Leeds United had scored 72 league goals in the 1956–57 season, and Wales' John Charles had accounted for more than half of them. At 25, Charles was in his prime as a footballer. He was a magnificent header of the ball, had a fulminating shot and was calmness personified in front of goal. He was a man mountain of a centre forward but much more besides. His work rate was prodigious, he had two great feet, and he looked after the ball like no other. He was fast and immensely strong, and he loved nothing more than defending his own goal. He could see a pass, he made mugs of really good centre halves, and his team-mates loved him. Charles was a manager's dream, and his goals had propelled Leeds, for a decade a middling Division 2 side, to the upper reaches of Division 1.

The Leeds chairman Sam Bolton had been resisting offers for years, but now his club was in a heap of financial trouble. Elland Road was falling apart, they were £40,000 in the red, and the bank was getting twitchy. They needed cash, but Bolton knew that selling Charles would decapitate the team and wipe thousands off the gate. As likely as not it would condemn them to a relegation scrap, so he was damned if he did and stuffed if he didn't.

Following his sacking at Juve, Jesse Carver had bounced between the English west Midlands and Italy. He'd accepted a job at West Brom, then another at Toro, then Roma and Coventry. Latterly he'd had a season and a half at Lazio, and he'd transformed their fortunes. Rome's 'second' club had finished third in Serie A twice in succession, and Carver's stock had never been higher. He was talking to Moratti about taking over at Inter, and talking to Gigi Peronace, his old translator at Juve, about the mighty John Charles.

Peronace had deployed his English to broker the transfer of one of the more unusual *oriundi*. Eddie Firmani was a South African striker of Italian extraction, but he'd been playing in England with Charlton. With Peronace's help, Sampdoria had broken the British transfer record in paying £35,000 for him, and Peronace had taken a chunk of that for himself. Firmani had been a big success in Genoa, and subsequently at Inter. He'd become an Italian international and, liberated from

English football's derisory maximum wage, made himself a fortune. He was earning ten times his salary at Charlton and, notwithstanding the fact that he was about half the player John Charles was, ten times more than him.

There was big money in Italy, but for a variety of reasons British players had rarely moved there. England was the 'home of football', and the idea that her players might want to live in little Italy seemed presumptuous. Moreover there were significant risks involved. Quite aside from linguistic and cultural barriers, the style of play was completely different and the British were expensive. The Swedes and Danes, on the other hand, cost nothing. They came over as amateurs and in the main assimilated well. By now there were enough of them to constitute a community, and that helped alleviate any homesickness. Furthermore, they had a hell of a lot riding on the move. Their associations forbade them from reclaiming amateur status for five years if they went back, so their work ethic was exemplary.

Meanwhile the fees being asked for the better *oriundi* had become stratospheric. When they came over, it was implicit they'd take Italian citizenship asap, but they too had to adapt. It was by no means a given that they'd succeed, and Juve's recent experiences with the Argentines Juan Vairo and Raùl ('wrong man, wrong time') Conti were testament to that.

The Firmani deal had been a sort of hybrid. He'd been an *oriundo*, obviously, but in facilitating his transfer Peronace had proved that you could do business with the English. He also knew that if anyone could succeed in Italy then Charles could, and that Leeds were in parlous financial straits. He'd been tapping up big John for a while now, and Sam Bolton knew it.

If Charles had to go – and the harsh reality was that he did – then selling him to a big foreign club made perfect sense. It would be more palatable for the Leeds fans than a move to, say, Manchester United, and besides the likes of Real Madrid, Inter and Juventus were in a position to pay much more. They would smash the British transfer record; the bank would be paid off at a stroke, and the fans would have a new stand. Bolton would be seen as magnanimous in sanctioning Charles' dream move, and there'd be a bit left over for some sort of a replacement.

In the spring of 1957 Peronace called Umberto and told him, as breathlessly as he knew how, that there was a brief window of opportunity. Charles would be turning out for Wales at Windsor Park in three days' time, and if Agnelli was genuinely interested he'd do well to be there. Umberto said that interested he most certainly was, and told his skiing buddy turned vice-president Walter Mandelli that they were off to Belfast. The game ended goalless, but it seems Charles played well enough.

Leeds pushed the boat out and asked for £65,000, almost double the Firmani fee but for double the player. That was 110 million lire, and even Inter baulked. Umberto couldn't afford to say no, so he opened negotiations with Padova for the sale of Kurt Hamrin, Juve's Swedish winger.

At the same time, from Argentina, Carletto Levi was in touch. A former Juve shareholder and Agnelli family friend, he'd emigrated and become FIAT's South American distributor. His adopted country had just won the South American championship, and they had a devastating front three. Antonio Angelillo, Humberto Maschio and Omar Sívori were known as the 'trio of death', and their respective clubs were ready to cash in. Umberto made enquiries and learned that Maschio was good and Angelillo better, but that 21-year-old left-footer Sívori was the jewel in the crown. His dribbling was out of this world and, socks rolled down and head up, he was an absolute joy to watch. He was prickly off the pitch and downright combustible on it, and if he had about him the look of a street urchin it was because a street urchin was precisely what he was.

His club, River Plate, didn't particularly want to sell, but like Leeds they were skint and their ground decrepit. They'd begun work on their Stadio Monumental in the late 1930s, but had run out of money before completing the north and south stands. It had finished up looking like a broken horseshoe, and that was just embarrassing.

Milan had paid 52 million lire for Schiaffino, but he'd been 29 when he crossed the Atlantic. River Plate thought of a number, doubled it, factored in the Agnelli family fortune and then, for good measure, rounded it all up to 10 million pesos. That came to 160 million lire (£91,000), and if Juve didn't pay it then someone else almost certainly would.

Umberto and Mandelli went for a long walk in Piazza San Carlo, the baroque square in which Cavour and his pals had conceived the *risorgimento*. They concluded that the Argentinians were barmy, and that no footballer could possibly be worth that amount of money. Then they went and transferred the money anyway. So much for Umberto's probity. So much for balancing the books.

Umberto had opened his piggy-bank, and out had popped a giant Welsh number 9 and a tiny Argentine 10. A tall, balletic 17-year-old winger named Bruno Nicolè, would be the 7. He was the hottest property in the Italian game, and he came with a price tag (70 million lire) to match. Twenty-year-old *torinese* Carlo Mattrel was the best young keeper in Italy, and the old *Juventino* stopper Rino Ferrario, sold two years before, returned to the fold. That was number 6 taken care of, and so all that remained was 8. Boniperti's goals had been carrying the team for two years, but he wasn't getting any younger. The craft remained, however, and he was happy to be redeployed behind Charles and Sívori.

The polyglot Serb Ljubiša Broćić was the new coach. He'd worked in (among others) Albania, Egypt and Lebanon, and most recently been in the employ of PSV Eindhoven. He'd taken it upon himself to write to the club explaining why he was the man for the job, and they'd invited him over for a chat. He was nice enough and enthusiastic enough, and so they took him on. Umberto stated somewhat disingenuously that he wasn't expecting miracles. 'Our objective isn't to win the championship. We've made financial sacrifices in order to offer the Turin public a team which is fun to watch, and if the match-day takings are sufficient we'll reinforce the midfield and defence next season.'

It's not clear whether he was deluding himself or simply baiting the 'Turin public'. The transfer record smashed twice in a week, and 70 million lire for a 17-year-old. Pull the other one, Umberto …

Juve (and Genoa) began the 1957–58 season with nine titles. Umberto, feet firmly under the table now, had persuaded the FIGC that the first to ten would get to add a gold star to their shirt, and it seems to have done the trick. The Charles–Sívori–Boniperti trident spluttered initially, but there was nothing Charles couldn't and wouldn't do for the team. He was three players in one, and Juve won their first five games. The sixth was the Turin derby at the Fila, and it was here that the legend of John Charles *il gigante buono* was created. In Sívori's absence he scored the only goal and managed, uniquely, to unite the two groups of fans in applause. When he and Ivo Brancaleoni clashed heads, the Toro man came off worse. The game carried on, but with blood pouring from Brancaleoni's broken nose, Charles couldn't have cared less. He took Brancaleoni in his arms and tried to offer such comfort as he could.

Over time Charles' greatness as a footballer would manifest itself in myriad ways, but his obvious, innate decency transcended even the most splenetic sporting rivalries. He reacquainted Italians with the idea that chivalry and success weren't mutually exclusive, that decency and respect were of greater value than goals and points.

Almost nobody in Italy had heard of John Charles prior to his arrival, but it was impossible not to admire him both as a player and a human being. By the same token it was impossible – for opposing fans at least – not to despise Sívori. He was a footballing alchemist but also a master of the dark arts. Where Charles cared for and about everyone, Sívori was capable of starting a riot in a phone box. Charles had no ego whatsoever, but Sívori never tired of reminding people just how good he was. Charles was a father and family man, Sívori an inveterate womaniser, smoker and night hawk. Charles was a very good trainer, while Sívori's insolence and tardiness infuriated Broćić and his team-mates in equal measure. Charles was a calming presence in the dressing room with a smile for everyone. Sívori could be surly, recalcitrant and at times just plain ignorant. While Charles was never booked, Sívori missed weeks on end through suspension. The Welshman would jump with his arms down for fear of harming his opponents with his elbows, but the Argentine would punch, gouge and kick them like the most cynical South American defender you ever saw. While his strike partner was the very personification of 'British fair play', Sìvori loved nothing more than to humiliate defenders with his nutmegs and his sublime dribbling.

Big John Charles was a defender's nightmare and so, in an altogether different way, was little Omar Sívori. As the season progressed, so too did the understanding – if not quite the friendship – between the two of them. They were the yin and yang of Juventus, and (here's the thing) Boniperti was the connection between them. By Christmas Juve were almost out of sight, and the *trio magico* tag was being applied by fans and commentators alike. Still today it resonates, because their bond represents the perfect distillation of Juventus as both institution and condition; two diametrically opposed elements maintained in perfect synergy by the black and white.

The Munich air disaster in February 1958 was a chilling echo of Superga, and Charles in particular was deeply moved. Then the *Azzurri* were beaten in Northern Ireland and failed to qualify for the World Cup. But Charles reminded Italians that football was just a game. It could and should be *enjoyable*, and goals, not dour *catenaccio*, were what was best about it. And when Juve played, goals there were. Lots of them. Juve filled the Comunale for the derby, as Toro were demolished 4–1. The following week they almost filled it again, this time against Milan. Charles put them ahead before turning Mario Bergamaschi, his marker, and latching onto a long ball inside the Milan half. Only Bergamaschi went to ground and, as Italian defenders will, started writhing around. Charles was through on goal, but when he realised what he'd done – or what Bergamaschi was claiming he'd done – he just stopped and booted the thing into touch. His team-mates ought to have been incandescent, but how could they be angry with a man like that? How can you upbraid a guy who moves to your country, fills your ground, utterly enchants your fans and scores 28 times in his debut season? How do you berate a gentle giant of a man who wins you Serie A at a canter, and with it Italian football's first gold star?

How was it possible not to love King John Charles?

A new, winning team, then, but also a completely new look. Umberto's Juventus abandoned their old, heavy, round-collared wool shirt. In its stead they wore a lighter, more modern version, made of silk and featuring a fashionable V-neck. The new fabric tended to billow as the players ran, swelling the back of the shirt. Some believe it was this which inspired the *gobbi* – hunchbacks – sobriquet which has attached itself to the club and its supporters. It's unflattering to say the least, and remains the favoured insult of those who wish the Juve ill.

Over the years, different explanations have emerged in regard to the nickname's meaning and origins. In Italian folklore a *gobbo* is a bringer of fortune, and that plays into the idea that Juve is a lucky club. Juve being Juve, everything is scrutinised in minute detail, and interpreted according to which side of the fence you happen to sit. The *gobbi* moniker is a case in point, because it infers that the more the club spends, the more referees go weak at the knees and the 'luckier' it gets. Of course the *gobbi* deny it, but Italian people are hyper-sensitive to institutional corruption and it's a certifiable fact that the club has at times deliberately and demonstrably corrupted football officials. It's also true that the Rosetta case had taught Umberto Agnelli's father the value of gerrymandering very early in his tenure.

No European football culture is more given to conspiracy theories than Italy's, probably because no European society is more given to them. So while many German and English fans believe that Dortmund and Manchester United are favoured by referees, there's no consensus that their boards have set out to subvert the refs' integrity. Their neutrality may be compromised by history, on-field dynamics and whatever subliminal forces are in play at the Westfalenstadion and Old Trafford, but there's little or no verifiable (or even circumstantial) evidence of match fixing, bribery or boardroom malfeasance. In Serie A, where political acumen and sporting success are indivisible, there's mountains of it, and Italians just assume corruption is endemic. They assume it because they know themselves, and because only a damned fool would assume otherwise. The *gobbi* are the most powerful and the most successful, so it follows that they're the most corrupt.

In a tight spot, with Ottorino Barassi

The Italians had been world champions twice in succession pre-war, but in Sweden they weren't even at the starting gate. It was humiliating, and so FIGC delegates set about electing a new president. The outgoing one was Ottorino Barassi, and back in the day he'd been fêted as a national hero. He'd organised the victorious 1934 World Cup, and as president he'd been charged with looking after the trophy, retained by Italy in 1938. Legend has it he'd been tipped off the Nazis were going to pilfer it, so he'd taken it home and hidden it in a shoebox, and told them someone from the Italian National Olympic Committee had whisked it away to Milan. He'd then sent it to his cousin down in rural Puglia. He, in turn, had secreted it in an old olive oil barrel, as you would if you needed to hide the Jules Rimet Trophy.

Barassi's health was failing him now, and on 9 August 1958 he was replaced by the brightest and most moneyed star in the *calcio* administrative firmament. At 23, Umberto Agnelli became the youngest president in the history of the FIGC.

While Juve flaunted their gold star, their stellar team and their limitless wealth at the federation, their neighbours' fortunes reached their nadir. Toro had been haemorrhaging goals, prestige and money for a decade. The board, strapped for cash and as a consequence points, came to an arrangement with a local chocolatier. In exchange for an unspecified sum, the club would change its denomination to Torino Talmone, and the famous *granata* shirt would carry a ginormous T on the breast.

It was sacrilege, obviously, and it would do them not one ounce of good. Poor Toro would be relegated at the end of the 1958–59 season, but every cloud and all that. Talmone declined to renew the contract, and with no takers for a Serie B club which had become a byword for rotten luck, Torino became Torino again. They'd come straight back up anyway, and would spend the next handful of years muddling along in the middle of Serie A.

Notwithstanding Umberto's meteoric rise, Juve's title defence was born under a bad star. Italian football-ing tradition has it that sides begin their pre-season *in ritiro*. The players are taken to the clean, cool air of the mountains, and there they prepare away from the heat and humidity of the city. The idea is that there is liter-ally nothing to do other than work, rest and bond, and for those familiar with the misery of the Po valley in the summer it makes absolute sense. However, non-Italians don't always understand that, and consequently often struggle with the tradition.

For Sívori, capricious and highly strung at the best of times, it was all too much. He was bored witless, he hated training without the ball, and he couldn't have cared less about tactics. Greatness like his couldn't be coached any-way, and he wasn't much interested in the details of how they got him the ball, just so long as they did. His rela-tionship with Bročić was already strained and, amid the tedium of *ritiro*, they fell out irredeemably.

With *catenaccio* in (temporary) remission, in 1958–59 there were a lot more goals. Serie A averaged three per game, and Antonio Angelillo, Sívori's erstwhile partner in the Argentine national side, would score a record-breaking 33 of them for Inter. Conversely, Juve's problem was that, with three strikers and two wingers, they kept leaking them. As Juve's domestic season spluttered into half-life, Milan and Fiorentina embarked on a thrilling joust for the championship.

Meanwhile the European Cup was in its fourth season. By now every major league was represented, and the competition had captured the imagination of fans across the continent. In the three previous editions, the Italian champions had fared extremely well. Milan had made the last four in the first, Fiorentina had reached the final in 1957 and Milan in '58. They'd both been beaten by the great Real Madrid team of Kopa, Gento and Di Stéfano, but there was no shame in that. Their performances had been noteworthy, and that mattered a lot in a sport which was increasingly global. Juventus had aspirations to be the most global of all Italian clubs, so they'd a great deal riding on a successful campaign. They were drawn against the Austrian champions WSC. They were a very useful side, but Juve won the home leg 3–1 and logic suggested they'd prevail in Vienna. Inexplicably, however, they collapsed to the mother of all away defeats, a 7–0 humiliation which cost Broćić his job. The local press crowed about 'the arrogance of the Italian millionaires', and the game also marked a paradigm shift at home.

Italians had more disposable income, and more consumables to spend it on. As a result the sporting press had more advertisers, and more pages to fill. Sports journalism was an increasingly crowded field, and it was moving with the times. Previously the papers had recounted events on the pitch pretty much as a straightforward narrative. With the advent of TV, though, readers were able to see all that for themselves. The papers needed to react accordingly, and that meant more varied content. The result was a new generation of better, more expansive writers who offered opinion and analysis of the background and circumstances which *informed* the football.

As attitudes around the sport evolved, so too did the editorial policies of the sporting dailies. In the past their content had reflected local sporting preferences because people in Turin cared much more about Toro than they did about, for example, Lazio. They'd generally been even-handed though, and they'd concerned themselves with the what as distinct from the why. Now, as they arm-wrestled one another for readers, they became increasingly critical and irreverent, and on occasion downright hysterical. Following the debacle in Austria, *Il Corriere* and *La Gazzetta* in particular rounded on Juventus. They felt the *bianconeri* deserved it, but the tone of the reporting also played to their respective readerships. It simultaneously outraged the *Juventini* among them – and outrage was increasingly the currency of football – and gratified the anti-Agnelli lobby.

With Broćić redeployed as a scout, the legends Cesarini and Parola oversaw a trip to the San Siro. Inter hadn't beaten Juve for four years, but with Toro in terminal decline the meetings between them had increasingly supplanted the Turin derby as *the* must-win fixture. Inter versus Juve was Italian anti-football at its gory worst, and by extension at its dramatic, blood-curdling best. The games were invariably bad-tempered and spiteful, and all the more compelling for it. Some years later the great journalist Gianni Brera would refer to the fixture as the *derby d'Italia*, and the moniker would stick.

For once the *nerazzurri* had the better of it, and at half-time they led 2–0 through Angelillo and Firmani. Then, however, the Milanese fog descended, and with half an hour remaining Boniperti played his card. He escorted referee Orlandini into the Inter penalty area and invited him to see what he could see. They agreed that Mattrel, the Juve keeper, wasn't visible, and Boniperti declared that on that basis the game couldn't possibly continue. A fairly animated conversation between the two sets of players and Orlandini ensued, but Boniperti won the argument because ... well because he was Boniperti. The game was suspended, and that was just as he'd planned it.

Inter argued that matters should be resolved by playing only the remaining half-hour, Juve that the thing needed to be replayed in its entirety. They won that argument as well, so the replay was scheduled for the Thursday before Christmas.

Umberto laid on free travel for a thousand *Juventini*, and Charles opened the scoring with a trademark flying header. The photograph, reproduced countless times over the years, has him towering above three incredulous, shell-shocked Inter defenders. While they look like zombies, he is pure kinesis. Juve went on to win 3–1, as Sívori made enemies of 70,000 *Interisti*. Each time he received the ball he goaded his marker, hapless 19-year-old Bruno Bolchi, matador style. Sívori was ridiculing Bolchi and intentionally inciting the home fans. Thus the antagonism between the clubs grew still further, and an enduring theme of Italian football was established.

They met again at the beginning of the 1959–60 season. Having been mothballed in 1943, the Coppa Italia was at last reinstituted. Inter and Juve reached the final, and they drew lots to host it. Inter won the phoney war, and they reckon 80,000 were shoehorned into the San Siro. Here again, they came away empty-handed as Sívori led them a dance. They lost 4–1, and most neutrals agreed they'd got off lightly.

They reconvened in Turin that December, and this time the gloves came off definitively. The man in black that day was Italy's first refereeing superstar. Concetto Lo Bello came from Sicily, and he'd amass more Serie A games than any other official. Many Italians maintain he was the greatest *arbitro* of all, quite an accolade in a football culture as murky as theirs. He'd officiate at two European Cup finals, and was 50 when he hung up his whistle and became the mayor of Siracusa. His son, Rosario, would enjoy an illustrious reffing career of his own, but he'd never be quite the figure that his father had been. Concetto Lo Bello's *performances* (and I use the word advisedly) were never less than dramatic, but this one was pure panto.

Juve led through Charles, and just before half-time Lo Bello awarded them a corner. The Inter players believed there'd been a prior infringement, however, and the usual handbags ensued. Lo Bello found himself surrounded, and tried to clear a passage for himself with a classic Italian reffing trick. He flung his arms open as theatrically as he knew how, but apparently caught one of the Inter players, Invernizzi, in the mush. He, of course, threw himself to the ground like a three-year-old, and was carted off for 'treatment'.

There was nothing whatsoever wrong with him, and Lo Bello would later claim that if he'd touched him it had been hardly at all. The Inter sponge man, on the other hand, maintained that Invernizzi had been 'concussed by a classic right cross' which had 'almost cut his mouth'.

'Almost cut his mouth'. The great fairy ...

Bolchi was then sent off for 'almost breaking Sívori's ankle', but Juve's anarchist-in-chief evened things out by almost performing an impromptu appendectomy on Amos Cardarelli. The game finished 1–0 to Juve, but Umberto seethed all the same. He'd convinced himself that Lo Bello was a secret Inter fan who had it in for Juventus, and insisted that he be forbidden from reffing either in the future. It was ridiculous, and probably libellous, but also illustrative of the siege mentality which he seemed to be developing.

Nevertheless, Inter had come up short again. The *gobbi* had won ugly, but once more they'd known too much and had too much. In Flavio 'crazy heart' Emoli – so-called because he had tachycardia – and Umberto Colombo, they had a tireless midfield duo. The back line was solid, the wingers Nicolè and Gino Stacchini great dribblers. Charles was a titan, Boniperti the thread which stitched the whole thing together. Most of them were at the pinnacle of their sporting careers and, after two seasons together, there was genuine synergy in their play.

And then there was Omar Sívori. There was nothing imposing about him physically – quite the opposite in fact – but once he crossed the white line he'd the bravery of a lion, the reflexes of a viper and the constitution of an Argonaut. He and Boniperti weren't big buddies off the field, and that was pivotal to their success on it. Sívori envied Boni his relationship with the Agnelli family and also the rapport he'd built with the Juve fans. Boniperti had been at the club ten years, and the fans viewed him as one of their own. Sívori was the better football player, but no matter what he did couldn't usurp Boniperti (or Charles) in their affections. Boniperti knew this and he was smart enough to understood the corollary effect of it. The more he inspired the love of the Juve fans, the more they bestowed it, and the more insecure Sívori became. An irate, pent-up Omar Sívori was the most lethal weapon you could have on a football field, and Boniperti harnessed his ire for the team's good.

For all his human shortcomings, Sívori was sublimely blessed as a footballer. From time to time he'd receive the ball and just stop the game in its tracks. He'd size it up, recalibrate it and reboot it in a completely different cadence. Irrespective of where he received the ball, there was a fair chance it was going to finish in the back of the net. He was devastating in the area and devastating out of it, and he could torpedo any side from any position. Whatever his brain asked, his left foot delivered, and there wasn't a defender in Serie A he couldn't embarrass. He scored every type of goal and made every type of goal, and by the season's end seemed to be operating in a different dimension. What a player.

It had been quite the two years for Umberto Agnelli. He'd assumed control of the FIGC and then married Antonella, heiress to the Piaggio scooter fortune. (Gianni had stolen that particular show, turning up in a Ferrari wearing nought but a pair of canvas shorts and flip-flops.) He'd completed his degree; his football team had won the Coppa Italia, and by April 1960 they were home and dry in Serie A. Fiorentina, runners-up for the fourth time in succession, would trail in eight points adrift. Sívori would outscore his old mate Angelillo to become the *capocannoniere*, and in so doing make a significant down payment on the Ballon d'Or.

At the Cibali, with Sandro Ciotti

The 1960–61 season began without Genoa, demoted following yet another match-rigging scandal. The campaign would develop into a titanic struggle, one of the most dramatic in history. Once more Juventus and Inter would be its lead actors, and once more it would have a quintessentially Italian denouement.

Angelo Moratti had gone through five years, eight coaches and a large fortune failing to win Serie A for his beloved Inter. Whatever they did something always seemed to go wrong, and that something tended to be Juventus. Now, however, he'd prised a brilliant, charismatic coach from Barcelona, and hope sprang eternal. Helenio 'the wizard' Herrera had been successful in Spain, just as he'd been successful in Portugal and France. He'd been successful everywhere he'd been and, for fifteen years, with every club and national side he'd managed.

Hitherto, football coaches had been more or less invisible because they'd been considered functionaries. Obviously they did tactics and fitness stuff, but they weren't in themselves particularly newsworthy. Herrera, a big man in every sense, had turned all that on its head in Spain. Under him the players became the functionaries, the success of the club no less than their *raison d'être*. His teams were organised and super-fit. He had the players weighed each week, and if he considered any of them overweight or undermotivated they didn't play. Their lifestyles were ascetic, with drinking and smoking absolutely forbidden. Timekeeping and respect for authority were paramount and enforced. Herrera's spies monitored the curfews he imposed, and those who didn't respect them didn't play. His players spent three days *in ritiro* before each game, and by the time they took the field their *esprit de corps* was palpable, their bodies incendiary, their minds as sharp as their reflexes.

The wizard demanded total autonomy, absolute discipline from his charges and complete faith in the 5–3–2 system he'd developed. His version of *catenaccio* featured four markers and one *libero*, and three indefatigable box-to-box midfielders. The ball would be 'verticalised' (got forward) as quickly as possible, and the full-backs had to be ready to join in. They needed to be athletic, technically adept and attack-oriented, because they were central to the functioning of the system. Herrera also insisted that the home crowd constituted his twelfth man, and deployed motivational psychology brilliantly. Over time his thinking, like that of Carver before him and Mourinho later, would reshape the football landscape.

Juve began their defence with four straight wins and then, as was by now customary, a horror show in the European Cup. This time they rolled over in Sofia, as CSKA helped themselves to three goals in nine second-half minutes. This presaged a collapse in their Serie A away form, and by the final day of the opening round of fixtures, they were a dismal sixth. They travelled to Bari that day, and were reacquainted with Concetto Lo Bello. Though Charles' late winner stopped the rot, Lo Bello refused to award Juve a penalty when Nicolè went down in the area. Once more Juventus cried foul, and once more Umberto saw fit to lampoon Lo Bello. Meanwhile, over at the San Siro, Inter won one of Italian football's more unusual games ...

Tipped for an immediate return to Serie B, Catania had made mugs of the pundits. Unbeaten at the Cibali, the legendary ground they occupied in the shadow of Mount Etna, they'd reached the midway point of the season in a miraculous third place. In Milan, however, they conceded after 13 minutes, and then Franco Giavara, one of their stoppers, deflected a shot past keeper 'Beppe' Gaspari. Twelve minutes later he diverted a cross past him, so they went in 3–0 down with Giavara on a hat-trick of own goals. In the 69th minute Catania full-back Elio Grani diverted a Firmani shot in before Mario Corti, club captain and club legend, completed the rout with a mishit clearance. Four own goals in one match – takes quite a lot of doing, that.

Herrera wasn't easily pleased, and he wasn't impressed by what he'd seen. While the two points were welcome, he said that Inter had been gifted them by 'a team of office clerks'. The experience seems to have traumatised both sets of players, because each went into free fall after that.

Inter had seemed nailed on, but as their campaign stuttered on the frozen pitches of February, Juve's took off. By the time they travelled to Venice on 9 April they'd won eleven games out of twelve, and Inter had been overhauled.

With Juve 1–0 up in injury time, the referee awarded Venezia a corner. It came in, was headed down, and landed at the feet of the Venezia midfielder Giorgio Puia. He smashed it in, but at that precise instant, the ref blew for full time. The 'goal' was disallowed, and mayhem ensued. Yet more controversy and objectively yet another extremely questionable refereeing decision in favour of the *gobbi*. Why had he let them take the damned thing if he'd intended to blow for time with the ball in the six-yard box?

The following Sunday, Inter visited the Comunale on a pig of an afternoon. When they shut the gates 90 minutes before kick-off, thousands were locked out. The crowd broke down four gates, and with at least 80,000 inside spilled onto the playing surface. These 'peaceful invasions' went on (and off) for half an hour, but then with the score at 0–0 Herrera decided enough was enough. His players made for the tunnel and, as the wind howled and the freezing rain pelted, refused to budge. They'd already had to stop twice; they were completely sodden, and subjecting them to yet another restart in these conditions was inhuman.

On 26 April the league declared that Juventus were 'objectively responsible' for the abandonment, and applied its standard, time-honoured sanction. Inter were awarded a 2–0 victory, and Juve's lead at the top was accordingly reduced to two points. Two days later the president of the FIGC, Umberto Agnelli, chaired a board meeting at Juventus. There it was decided that the club would lodge an appeal with the Federal Appeals Commission (CAF), the supreme court of Italian football.

Club lawyer Vittorio Chiusano produced a 22-page dossier, the thrust of which was that Inter had been *anti-sportivo* in refusing to continue. Regarding the pitch invasions, he claimed – and I'm not making this up – *force majeure*. The storming of the gates had happened *outside* the ground, and as such Juventus had been in no position to do anything about it. Moreover by the Friday, 48 hours before the game, only 40,000 tickets had been sold. The club couldn't have foreseen the demand for tickets on the Sunday, and had halted sales immediately they'd known the ground was full. They'd done everything they possibly could, and the only thing which had prevented the finishing of the fixture was Inter's intransigence.

It was an interesting argument but fanciful in the extreme. It wasn't Inter who had failed to secure the stadium, and it wasn't Inter who had failed to stop the incursions onto the playing surface. While Juve had every right to appeal to CAF, nobody believed for one minute that they had a real case. The three-man CAF committee would meet the first week in May, and pretty much everyone expected them to rubber-stamp the original decision. There was no harm in Juve's trying, but the *force majeure* argument was a load of old nonsense.

Just then Turin in general and the Agnellis in particular were rolling out the red carpet. Italy was celebrating its 100th birthday, and the world's beautiful people had been invited to its first capital. Five million would visit Italia '61, as the city reached the apogee of its industrial and cultural influence. The *centro storico* was revitalised, Parco Valentino replanted, the great boulevard connecting it to Lingotto renamed and reimagined. Corso Unità d'Italia was transformed into a futuristic cityscape, dignitaries like Queen Elizabeth and the Kennedys invited to ride the city's fantastical new overground monorail. Juve, too, played their part, hosting a prestigious football tournament. The Torneo Italia '61 would see Pelé, widely considered the world's greatest player, wow the Comunale for Santos. It goes without saying that Umberto tried to engineer a deal for him, but the Brazilians weren't having it.

Meanwhile CAF shillied and shallied, and reconvened in Rome on Saturday 27 May. There they invited both parties to make a deposition and, having heard them out, decided not to decide anything at all. Rather they announced they'd try all over again the following Saturday, on the eve of the final game of the season.

The aim was to postpone the thing for as long as possible in the hope that results on the pitch would render their decision academic. The problem was that the results hadn't obliged. Juve had lost at Padova, so as things stood they were dead level with Inter at the top. The *bianconeri* would conclude with a tricky game at relegation-threatened Bari, while Inter, firmly back in the groove now, would visit own-goal specialists Catania. The CAF had obfuscated itself into a corner, but now, on the eve of the final day of the season, it could obfuscate no longer.

When the day dawned, only two of the three-man committee sat before the press in Rome. When asked why De Gennaro, the president, was absent, the other two informed the audience that it was really nothing at all. De Gennaro just had a prior arrangement; and so the formalities would go ahead without him. That seemed highly peculiar, but it was no more than an *antipasto* for the weirdness which was to follow. The two remaining members first rambled pointlessly, incomprehensibly and it seemed eternally about the workings of the committee, then, just as the journos were losing the will to live, they came, more or less, to the point.

In that oh-so-Italian, oh-so-verbose way such bodies have, they declared that Juventus had been culpable for the abandonment of the game, but they hadn't *meant* for it to happen. That being the case and all things considered, an overturning of the original findings, a replay of the game and a fine of 4 million lire seemed appropriate. Umberto Agnelli had that sort of money down the back of his sofa.

By the following morning, word was out that an apoplectic De Gennaro had in fact quit the panel. Now obviously there was no suggestion *whatsoever* that his colleagues had been influenced by external factors, but it's fair to state that everyone who wasn't a Juve fan was flabbergasted. Nobody in the press would print it, but whichever way you cooked it this was unprecedented. Nobody in public life dared articulate it, but nobody wasn't thinking it. Umberto Agnelli had absolute power over Italian football, and you know what they say about absolute power …

It was assumed that Inter only needed to turn up in Catania to win. The home side were ravaged by injury; their recent form had been lousy, and on the surface they'd nothing riding on it. If Inter and Juve both won (or both drew) then Herrera's team would need to win the replayed match in Turin to force a championship-deciding play-off with Juve. If, on the other hand, Inter beat Catania and Juve failed to overcome Bari, then victory in Turin would hand Herrera's team the championship outright. The CAF decision had been highly unfortunate, but Inter's fate was still in their hands. If they won two games they *might* be crowned champions, if not they'd just have to win a third. Then they'd have their first title since 1954, the *gobbi* would be left with nothing, and justice – poetic and sporting – would be served.

The difficulty was that Catania weren't much interested in that particular fairy tale, because as they saw it they'd a great wrong of their own to right. They'd embarrassed themselves at the San Siro, and then Herrera had seen fit to disrespect them publicly with his 'team of office clerks' jibe. A win would guarantee them their highest ever Serie A placing, and even better they'd have their pound of flesh. If, in exacting it, they sounded the death knell of Herrera's title pretensions, then so much the better.

In the days preceding the game, the Catania players effectively suspended their own manager and allegedly refused a significant cash offer to throw it. Instead they knuckled down to their work, more determined than ever to give moneybags Inter 90 minutes they wouldn't forget in a hurry.

Every people has its great sporting moments, and obviously they're rooted in some sort of special performance. However for the most part they're not placed in the collective consciousness by those who do the performing. Rather they are audio-visual constructs brought to the masses via the radio or the small screen. Moreover, they are usually remembered not so much for images as for their voiceovers. Very few in England remember the minutiae of the 1966 World Cup final, but everyone can recite Kenneth Wolstenholme's 'Some people are on the pitch ...' voiceover. Jacky Van Der

Gelder's epiphany as Bergkamp eviscerated Argentina in the 1998 World Cup quarter-final is timeless. In Norway (and indeed beyond) nobody will ever forget the late Bjørge Lillelien. Following his country's 2–1 win over England in 1981, he invoked Lords Nelson and Beaverbrook, Churchill, Eden and Attlee, then Henry Cooper, Lady Diana and Maggie Thatcher. Ecstatically and memorably he informed them that their boys 'took one hell of a beating', and the rest is history. It was a scruffy game against a horrible England team, but Lillelien immortalised it with his verdict.

One of Italy's most tumultuous football moments occurred that afternoon at the foot of Mount Etna, and its author was the RAI *radiocronista* Sandro Ciotti. With 20 minutes remaining, the mighty Inter were 1–0 down and all at sea. They'd barely been out of their own half; the Cibali was absolutely stomping, and the home side were all over them like a bruise …

As the ball broke in Inter's final third, Catania crowd favourite Todo Calvanese held off full-back Giacinto Facchetti. He then rounded the keeper and slid home, and legend has it the roar could be heard across the Strait of Messina. RAI switched to Ciotti, their man on the ground, just as Calvanese cavorted in front of Herrera's bench in celebration. Though there's no tape and as such no actual proof Ciotti really said it, all Italians of a certain age recognise the phrase *Clamoroso al Cibali!* It means 'Sensational at the Cibali!' and, whether he actually said it or not, it was all so momentous that millions of people choose to believe he did. Everyone can tell you where they were (or where they imagine they were) for *Clamoroso al Cibali.* It's part of Italian football history because, with the benefit of hindsight, it's come to represent a tipping point in the game.

More of which later, but Juve drew 1–1 with Bari (Umberto Agnelli said it was 'like spectating at Forte Apache'), and the *Scudetto* was theirs. Grubby or otherwise, it was their third in four seasons, but the 1960–61 season wasn't about to go quietly. Though the championship was decided, there was a football match still to be replayed between Juventus of Turin and Internazionale of Milan. On the surface it was a dead rubber, but by now the blood between them was really, *really* bad.

Beforehand, Herrera reeled off a list of the ailments affecting his players. Picchi, Bicicli, Buffon and Firmani were injured, Morbello and Guarneri ill. Balleri was suspended, Fongaro was about to leave the club, and Masiero couldn't play because he'd already booked his holidays. It wasn't fair to detain Lindskog with his family waiting back in Sweden, so he wouldn't play either. The youngsters Bolchi, Corso, Da Pozzo, Facchetti and Mascalaito weren't available because the Inter under–21 side had a really important fixture that day as well. What with one thing and another, they'd just have to send the youth team to Turin. Herrera agreed that it was 'regrettable', but there you go. Sorry.

As a points-scoring exercise it was all a bit futile, but Inter felt cheated. CAF had turned the season into a farce, and Herrera was damned if he was going to legitimise it – and Juve's championship – by sending his first team.

Juve won the non-match 9–1. Sívori scored six of the hollowest, most meaningless goals of his career, but of infinitely more interest was Inter's reply. It was a penalty, and it was converted by the son of an Italian footballing legend. Sandro Mazzola had been six when his father had perished at Superga, but he and brother Ferruccio (named after the Toro president) had chosen Inter over Toro. Now aged 19, Sandro was making his first-team debut, and Inter knew that the symbolism would overshadow Juve's triumph.

Mazzola's was the first game of a truly great career, but for Boniperti it was the last. The following day, Juve's captain and greatest ever player announced his retirement. Giampiero Boniperti was 33; he'd scored 178 goals, and he knew his legs were going. They persuaded him to stay on as a director, but it was mainly window dressing. Boni started a company which specialised in transporting FIAT cars, and another one manufacturing rubber components for FIAT cars. Later he took a call from Umberto and agreed to manage the famous (Agnelliowned) rice fields near Vercelli, his home town. He also looked after another Agnelli agricultural holding down in Umbria because, as-near-as-made-no-difference, he was one of the family.

That was all to come, but for now the era of the *trio magico* was over. For four years they'd cast a spell over Italian football, and Juve supporters had never had it so good. Umberto's timing in signing Charles and Sívori had been perfect, but also fortuitous. By now the mass ownership of television was fundamentally altering Italian daily life, and with it the sporting landscape. Italy's domination of cycling had seen the sport share top billing with football, but aspiring Italians no longer had any interest in old-fashioned pushbikes. Their society was increasingly urbanised, they had good public transport, and they aspired to scooters and cars. Bike ownership fell off a cliff, and interest in the sport of cycling waned exponentially. Moreover there were no TV cameras capable of covering the races, and it was impossible to predict finish times. Bike racing took too long, it was too textured, and there were too many variables. RAI had only one channel, and stadium sports like boxing and football were cheaper to televise and easier to manage.

The 1960s were the golden age of Italian boxing for one reason and one reason only. TV coverage inspired thousands of Italians to try it, and by the law of averages some of them were bound to be good. The more Italians won, the more people were inspired to take up boxing, and so it went. Likewise, football matches were ideal for the great unwashed. They always kicked off on time, there was always a commercial break after 45 minutes, and they always finshed in time for the *Telegiornale* – the news. They were immediate, absolute and partisan, and they took place in the evenings and on Sundays when the factories were shut.

In simple terms, football was televisual and cycling wasn't, and the ball supplanted the bike in the heads of Italian *sportivi*. Soccer became *the* sport on the Italian peninsula just as Juve, already the nation's favourite team, was sweeping all before it. The ubiquity of Charles, Boniperti and Sívori on Italian screens led to their ubiquity on Italian front pages and in Italian discourse, and ultimately to Juve winning still more Italian hearts and minds.

Now, however, Herrera had his feet under the table at Inter, and Milan were assembling a fabulous new side. Anyone could see that things were about to become much more complex for the FIAT factory team, but no one – not Umberto and nor anyone else – could foresee just *how* complex.

Between a rock and a hard place, with Umberto Agnelli

Interviewed by *Tuttosport* in advance of the 1961–62 season, Umberto Agnelli said that he 'always felt a certain hostility' when travelling with Juventus. He didn't elaborate, but he didn't need to. Umberto had convinced himself that that he and his football club were being singled out, but for the life of him he didn't know why. Perhaps if he reflected ...

Aged 25, he was one of Italian sport's most powerful men. He and his brother owned its wealthiest, most successful football club, and he'd been fast-tracked to the head of the national federation at a very young age. Like his father before him he'd been a font of new ideas. At first that had been interesting, but then he'd turned the sport on its axis by signing Charles, Sívori and Nicolè. He'd spent money the club hadn't earned and couldn't earn, and which he himself hadn't worked for. That had distorted everything, and made an uneven playing field still more lopsided.

Aside from the fact that he owned a football team, he had almost nothing in common with the other presidents. They were self-made, middle-aged men who'd survived the war and the post-war, and then prospered by grafting long and hard. They'd made their fortunes and used them to sustain their local clubs, putting something back into their local communities. Umberto, on the other hand, hadn't actually had to *do* anything for his money; it had been handed to him on a silver platter, so he knew the price of everything and the value of nothing. He was able to do entirely as he pleased, so rightly or (more likely) wrongly, the perception among his peers was that his had been a cosseted, privileged upbringing.

Part of the problem lay in his character. There was nothing particularly *wrong* with Umberto, but not a lot to like. For all his idiosyncrasies you couldn't help but like his older brother, and that was mainly because Gianni couldn't help but make you laugh. Umberto had a fraction of Gianni's wit and in truth none of his panache. He was a rather sombre, rather awkward young man, and of late he was forever moaning about something or other.

At the FIGC meetings he'd blither on about the need for football clubs to be tight, coherent, professional organisations. He was acting as he thought an Agnelli should, but the club he presided over was just a rich kid's plaything. It was OK for Juve to be winning the league, and more or less OK for Umberto to buy up all the best players. It was his money and his prerogative, but to imply that it was all a consequence of some modern, enlightened management style was an insult to their intelligence. Did he *really* expect people to thank him for saying it was? Did he not understand that Juve's largesse demeaned guys who earned a fraction of what he'd paid for Sívori? Was he *really* so deluded as to think people didn't suspect foul play at the CAF?

The new Serie A season began, bizarrely, with a glut of British strikers. Peronace had been perspicacious with

Charles and Firmani, and both had been a credit to their profession. England was the cradle of football, and their excellence had convinced Italians that English players were paragons of sporting virtue. What's more there were fortunes to be made 'over there', and so in June 1961 Jimmy Greaves joined the gravy train at Milan. His tenure would be short-lived and not a little turbulent.

Greaves had been a sensational number 9 at Chelsea, but he was a liability in Italy. Having trousered a massive signing-on bonus, he fell out with manager Nereo Rocco and with those team-mates who didn't appreciate his drinking, his tardiness or his general torpor. Greaves couldn't cope with the loneliness, and certainly not with Italian defenders. The less he coped the more they baited him, and he didn't have the gumption to deal with it. He failed to learn the language and made it clear that he wanted nothing more than to get back to London as soon as was humanly possible. There was no suggestion *whatsoever* that his homesickness was related to English football having recently abolished the maximum wage, but by November the whole sorry episode had reached its baleful conclusion. Spurs paid Milan £99,999, which meant Rizzoli had his money back and Greaves wasn't burdened with being the first £100,000 Englishman.

Elsewhere Toro signed two 21-year-old strikers. Denis Law and Joe Baker, from Manchester City and Hibs respectively, are famed in Italy principally for what we'll term their lifestyle choices. Baker in particular made a splash. When he wasn't back in Motherwell 'visiting his mother', there was never a dull moment. He scored the only goal in a thunderous derby at the Comunale (Sívori was sent off for verbally abusing the ref), but his off-field activities were far more noteworthy than anything he did on it. He and Law were manna from heaven for the new *paparazzi*, but Joe didn't much like it that they kept following him around. On the eve of the away game in Venice, he was photographed brawling with one of them in the medieval splendour of Piazza San Marco. The photographer seems to have ended up in the Grand Canal, and obviously it made the front pages. It earned Joe a criminal record, yet another fine and yet another reprimand from the club. However his British-footballer-abroad *pièce de résistance* occurred just after 4 a.m. on Wednesday 7 February.

Baker had just taken delivery of a new car, a lovely Alfa Romeo Giulietta Sprint. He and Law decided to take it for a spin, and to make a night of it in the company of Law's brother Joe. They jumped into the Alfa and toured Turin's night spots, but then Baker had a momentary lapse. He quite forgot that (to paraphrase *The Italian Job*) Italians drove on the wrong side of the road, and as a result he, his Alfa and the Law brothers found themselves upside down at the junction of Corso Cairoli and Corso Vittorio. Oh dear, or words to that effect.

This left Baker in hospital with a smashed septum, and earned the directors of Toro a ticking-off from his mother. She flew in with his girlfriend Sonia, and admonished them for being too soft with him. What he'd needed, she said, had been a thick ear right at the outset. He was a good boy *really*, and it was all their fault because they'd indulged him. And that more or less concluded Joe Baker's Italian adventure. More or less because, while Arsenal agreed to pay £65,000 for his services, Toro insisted he clear his debts before sanctionong the transfer. Baker owed 4 million to the hospital which had fixed his busted nose after the crash, and a further million to the club. They'd paid his fine following the incident in Venice, and the body shop which had repaired the Alfa was demanding payment as well. That was another million, and then there was the hotelier who'd been putting him up these past months.

Law saw it through to the season's end, and on the pitch at least he did reasonably well. Like Baker, though, he struggled with the discipline, with *catenaccio* and with homesickness. There was talk of a move across town, but Law wasn't interested. He literally jumped in a cab to the airport, and scarpered back to England. Manchester United took him, and Toro put it all down to experience.

Over at Inter, Sívori's old mucker Angelillo was perfectly in tune with the spirit of the times. He'd scored copiously in his first two seasons, but then he'd gone and fallen in love with a nightclub entertainer. Attilia Tironi's *nome d'arte* was Ilya Lopez, her musical speciality was the tango, and that seems to have done it for poor Angelillo. He'd come over all nostalgic, and he and Ilya had quickly became the *paparazzi*'s go-to couple. The goals had dried up completely, Herrera hadn't appreciated Angelillo's nocturnal comings and goings, and he'd offloaded him to Roma.

In his stead he bought a swarthy Ballon d'Or winner from Barcelona and the son of a Staffordshire miner from Aston Villa. Luis Suárez and Gerry Hitchens were an unlikely front two, but a very effective one. Hitchens' England career would peter out as a result of the move, but he'd a good work ethic, an eye for goal and no intention whatsoever of skulking off home à la Greavsie.

In the absence of Boniperti, Juve's title defence started catastrophically. He'd been the team's talisman and its brain, and without him the dressing room felt bereaved. His replacement, the Argentine Humberto Rosa, was hopeless, and Nicolè turned up for pre-season a stone overweight. Charles was 30, crocked and eyeing a return to England, while Sívori's newborn son was sickly. The midfield toiler Colombo and the great defender Sergio Cervato had left, and when the team failed to win any of its opening four games the tone was set.

In the meantime, Umberto's term in office at the FIGC was up, his wife was expecting, and there was nothing more to win domestically. He made it plain that he very much wanted to win the European Cup, but he wouldn't commit beyond that. Umberto had been a diligent chairman. While Gianni had always treated Juve as a toy, he'd viewed it as a responsibility and a job of work. He'd tried to forge his own identity, to emerge from the long shadow cast by his big brother. He'd only been partially successful, but it hadn't been for lack of effort. Now, though, he seemed increasingly careworn, and not a little paranoid.

Having incurred Umberto's wrath at Bari, Lo Bello hadn't been invited to officiate at any more Juventus matches. His impartiality had been called into question repeatedly and publicly, and so it simply hadn't been worth the while. Umberto had seen to it that he was *persona non grata*, and he'd done the same with poor Pietro Leita. He'd been the first to send Sívori off, and for Umberto that had been unforgivable. Sívori would receive ten red cards during his Italian career. That's still a record for a Serie A striker and so, in all probability, is Charles receiving precisely zero yellows. In practical terms, Umberto's opprobrium had finished Leita's career, and either Cesare Jonni or Iginio Rigato seemed always to be in charge when Juve played.

However Giuseppe Pasquale, Umberto's replacement at the FIGC, was having none of it. He sat down with Giorgio Bernardi, the boss of the Italian referees' association (CAP), and they agreed the tail would no longer wag the dog. Lo Bello was very deliberately chosen to referee Juve's home game with Inter on 22 October.

Inter won 4–2, but there was not the slightest hint that Lo Bello had favoured them in any way. It goes without saying that the game was violent (Charles was stretchered off following an elbow to the abdomen from Franco Zaglio), but the Sicilian reffed it fairly and squarely. Even Umberto was forced to concede that his decision-making had been impeccable, but he whined on regardless. His players, he claimed, had been subjected to a 'psychological shock' on hearing the announcement of Lo Bello's involvement in advance of the game, and it had undermined their performance. The insinuation – yet again – was that Lo Bello's appointment was all part of a wider plot against Juve.

Umberto's love for the club was intense, but it was impairing his judgement. He seemed to be coming undone, and his departure was a matter of when and not if. Gianni therefore took it upon himself to co-opt one of FIAT's aircraft engineers to the board. Former fighter pilot Vittore Catella was a company man to his boot straps, a *sportivo* and a lifelong Juve fan. He'd distinguished himself on the organising committee of Italia '61, and as regional president of the Italian Olympic Committee had experience in sports admin'. Gianni being Gianni, he neglected to tell Catella, who knew nothing about it until he took a call from the secretary of Juve informing him that he was now a director. When he enquired why he hadn't been told, he was informed that they 'hadn't wanted to worry him'.

For once Juve made a decent fist of it in Europe. In the first round they survived a mass brawl, a pitch invasion and a near-death experience at Partizan Belgrade. As the return flight landed at Caselle it suffered a mechanical failure, and only the pilot's excellence averted calamity. They drew Real Madrid in the quarter-final, and Sívori was awarded the Ballon d'Or before the Turin leg. Real won that 1–0, but in reversing the scoreline at the Bernabéu, Juve became the first foreign side ever to win there. It earned them a replay in neutral Paris on 28 February, and they started very brightly. However they ran out of steam in the second half, and the Spaniards prevailed 3–1.

Then it all went pear-shaped.

The term 'doping' had entered the sporting vernacular in the mid-1950s. In cycling, amphetamine was so widespread as to be almost obligatory, but footballers had escaped testing principally because their governing body was in denial. Everyone knew that the use of *eccitanti* was commonplace, but this was a Pandora's box that the FIGC didn't want opened. Reports had been commissioned and flowery euphemisms uttered, but football seemed always to be talking *around* the problem of doping, as distinct to addressing it. Three weeks before the Paris game, however, the first Serie A anti-doping controls had been carried out. Sixty players had been tested, and the Italian public feverishly awaited the results.

Following the Paris game, an explosive interview appeared in *L'Équipe*. Its subject was a celebrated Parisian masseur named Emil Wanono. He'd worked extensively in cycling, a sport in which the masseur had always been imbued with slightly Machiavellian qualities. The three-time Tour de France winner Louison Bobet had been among his clients, and Wanono had also helped some of European football's best sides. Among them was Herrera's Inter, and no side ran the way they did. Wanono was good, and there were rumours that he'd be accompanying the Italian national side to the World Cup in Chile.

On the eve of the game he'd been on hand to massage Emoli and Castano, two of Juve's walking wounded. Apparently he'd made an offer to 'help them win' and declared that, if they did, he'd expect payment in the form of a FIAT 2300. The players claimed to have laughed it off, but in the interview Wanono pointed to the disparity in Juve's energy levels in the two halves. Their first-half performance had been incredible, but they'd miscalculated with the stimulants. That had caused their second-half 'collapse', and Real had won because their performance levels had been 'normal' over the full 90 minutes. Juve issued a press release stating that it was all lies, and Umberto himself wrote to Wanono informing him he'd be seeing him in court.

Predictably enough, Wanono climbed down at that point. He begged Umberto's forgiveness and claimed, laughably, that his use of the word stimulant had been misinterpreted by the journalist. He'd meant to say that the win in Madrid ought to have *acted* as a stimulant for the replay, and that if Juve had utilised it as such then they wouldn't have been beaten in Paris. *L'Équipe* responded that, while they'd no reason to suspect that Juventus were doping their players, Wanono's reinterpretation of what he'd said was codswallop.

Everyone carried on pretty much as before but on 8 April the tests came back from the lab. Eight Serie A players were positive, among them three from Herrera's Inter. Sandro Mazzola said it was a stitch-up, but then his brother, transferred now to Lazio, gave the lie to his claim by insisting that the use of amphetamine was standard practice at the San Siro.

Nobody from Juve tested positive, but following the defeat in Paris they failed to win another game all season. Inexplicably they picked up a single point from their last ten encounters and contrived to finish only four points above the drop zone. They reached the semi-final of the Coppa Italia, but by then their energy levels and morale seemed to be on the floor. They travelled to Ferrara, but when the minnows of SPAL thumped them 4–1 it effectively concluded this awful campaign.

With gate money down a catastrophic 22 per cent, Umberto had a brainwave. The Brazilian Paulo Amaral, nicknamed 'the iron sergeant', had been fitness coach of the *Seleção* at the 1958 World Cup. Everyone had known that the Brazilians were luxuriously gifted, but under Amaral their physical improvement had been dramatic. They'd astounded the elite of the European game, and so now Amaral accepted Umberto's offer of a job in Turin. In truth, he was a sprat to catch a mackerel. Umberto dispatched Boniperti to the 1962 World Cup in Chile ostensibly as a talent scout, but in reality with a blank cheque. Using Amaral as an intermediary, he was to meet Pelé and convince him to make Turin his home. Boniperti is believed to have offered the player £60,000 in signing-on fees alone, but Santos weren't selling. Pelé was their player, the Brazilian government had designated him a national treasure, and the Santos president, Athiê Jorge Coury, had no need of FIAT's money.

Boniperti came home empty-handed, and so too did *Azzurri*. They were eliminated by the hosts at the Battle of Santiago, still perhaps the most infamous game in World Cup history. In introducing the 'highlights', David Coleman of the BBC famously stated that it was 'the most stupid, appalling, disgusting and disgraceful exhibition of football, possibly in the history of the game', and he wasn't too far wrong.

For the Chilean public, the *oriundi* in general and Sívori in particular were the worst sort of Argentines. They'd whored themselves, their careers and their country for European gold, and the *Azzurri* had been portrayed as smug and superior in advance of the match. The inflammatory reporting of the Italian press contingent heightened tensions still further – describing a country and its people as 'proudly miserable and backward' wasn't perhaps the best, and nor was the modus operandi of the Italian defenders. It wasn't quite the bloodbath it was portrayed, but foreign referees simply wouldn't tolerate the sort of provocation which was grist to the mill in the Italian game. Italy finished the first half with nine men, and the second with their reputation and World Cup aspirations up in smoke. As ever they blamed the ref (in this instance Englishman Ken Aston), but they were their own worst enemies.

Meanwhile poster boy John Charles had his sights set on a return home. The consensus around the place was that he'd given his best anyway, and Amaral was happy for him to move on. Charles began negotiations to rejoin Leeds amid accusations that Juventus had broken (unwritten) financial promises. It was an unbecoming departure for a great player and, as it transpired, the end of an era.

Chapter 5

Black and White and
Red All Over

People who have chosen other colours are to be pitied.
They've chosen to suffer.

Giampiero Boniperti

In Piazza Statuto, with an angry mob

In 1949, when the Marshall Plan money had arrived, one Italian in ninety-six had owned a car. Now it was one in eleven, and over two million of them were FIATs. In Italy, those who couldn't pay upfront bought them through Agnelli-owned finance companies, and insured them through the family's brokers. Nearly 90,000 *operai* were employed at Lingotto and Mirafiori; they were producing 8000 cars a day, and the company boasted a global market share of 6 per cent. FIAT had factories in Turkey and South Africa, in Mexico and Argentina, and even across the frontier in Tito's Yugoslavia.

The FIAT trains ran on time, and Italians travelled on FIAT-managed and -built *autostrade*. FIAT tractors tilled the land, FIAT trucks moved Italy's freight, and FIAT cement built her tenements. The wealthy flew in FIAT helicopters and aeroplanes, and the military relied on FIAT tanks and fighter planes. Productivity was up, profits were staggering, and living standards were higher for everyone. The Agnellis' wealth was as infinite as the political muscle it bestowed.

However, the perceived disparity between the living standards of the bosses and those of the workers – the people actually *producing* the wealth – was increasingly stark, and on Wednesday 13 June 1962 three Italian metalworkers' unions went on strike. Inflation was outstripping wage growth, and they were unhappy with the terms offered by Confindustria, the Italian employers' federation. At Lancia's Turin factory some 60 per cent downed tools, at the white goods manufacturer Westinghouse 63 per cent. At Viberti, where they made trams, buses and suchlike, seven out of ten stayed at home.

As usual, things were different at FIAT. Of the 85,000 due in, only 303 failed to show up. The 'FIAT way of life' was a factor, but so too was the composition of the workforce. Many had come from the agrarian south and had a feudal mindset. Some hadn't joined a union because they'd no idea what they were for, most because they feared their (northern) bosses' reaction if they did. Membership was discouraged more or less overtly, the line being that as FIAT workers they had no need of it anyway. The company was their home-away-from-home, their family and their protector, so joining the *sindacati* was by definition an act of rebellion. While strictly speaking it couldn't be said that FIAT refused to employ trade unionists, it refused to recognise the legitimacy of many of them.

Now, however, a new breed of *operaio* was emerging. They were better educated and more politicised, and they refused to toe the line. Another strike was called for the following Tuesday, and this time FIAT was targeted. Flying pickets showed up, there were skirmishes outside the factory gates and complaints of intimidation. The absentees still numbered under 5 per cent, but in admonishing the strikers publicly through a badly worded press release in *La Stampa*, the management inflamed matters.

On 23 June the situation escalated, as an estimated 60,000 joined the strike. They effectively paralyzed Lingotto and Mirafiori, and Valletta reacted by shutting the gates entirely for the following two days. As miscalculations go it was a whopper, because it alienated both strikers and loyalists. The atmosphere grew still more febrile, as the delicate relationship between the company and its staff began to fray.

A meeting was called for Wednesday 4 July, but Confindustria's new terms didn't find favour with the workers. A further walkout was called the following day; they stayed out on Friday, and on Saturday a big crowd gathered in Piazza Statuto. It felt like a tipping point, and by mid-afternoon the riot police had been mobilised. The first tear gas was fired shortly after 2 p.m., and trouble continued on through Sunday and into Monday. It would be Tuesday morning before the police regained control of the square, and by then the sackings had already begun at FIAT.

The company was extremely imaginative with its pretexts for dismissals, but paradoxically that served only to weaken its hand, as FIAT's employees began to view their bosses in a different light. Many more felt emboldened to join the unions, and thousands felt they'd no choice. The company had displayed a ruthless streak, so they would need the protection of union membership. Most agreed that FIAT had changed Italy for the better, but over the next decade Italy would change FIAT – and by extension its football team – in ways nobody could have foretold.

Away from the chaos in Piazza Statuto, Umberto was beset by personal tragedy. He and Antonella lost their newborn twins, Enrico and Umberto, and on 19 July 1962 Juve's chairman announced that he was stepping down and taking a 'normal' job as the head of the family insurance business. The going had got tough at Juventus and at home, and the Agnellis were taking another sabbatical.

Vittore Catella, the personification of *semplicita, serieta e sobrieta*, was elected president, but his appointment was never going to be universally popular. Technically speaking, Juventus was part of the FIAT 'family', but neither Gianni nor Umberto had been working for the business when they'd taken charge. They'd run the club because they could, because it was theirs and because, fundamentally, they were *tifosi*. Catella, on the other hand, was a FIAT white collar parachuted in by Gianni. His arrival dispelled any pretence that Juventus wasn't simply an extension of the brand.

The family were at liberty to do that, but there were tens of thousands of Toro fans on the FIAT payroll who had been able to convince themselves (or delude themselves) that Juve was nothing to do with them. It belonged to the people they worked for, but it wasn't FIAT per se. In redeploying Catella to the football club the company had removed the facade of independence. That might seem a minor issue, but to many Toro fans it mattered a lot. At a time when the workforce was beginning to question the degree of control the family exerted over them, it felt at best insensitive and at worst like a slap in the face.

None of which altered the fact that, with Charles and Boniperti gone, Juve had need of a new standard bearer. He'd need to reflect the values of the company the way Parola had, and galvanise the team à la Monti. The old lady needed a talisman to line up behind, and in the event a couple emerged. When, in 2010, the fans elected the 50 inductees into the new Juventus 'Walk of Fame' outside the ground, only two made it from the post-*trio magico* era. One was a defender who'd grown up a stone's throw from the San Siro, the other a midfield general from northern Spain.

During the previous season's Real Madrid trilogy, their midfield dynamo Luis del Sol had told the press that his family had originated from (of all places) Vercelli and intimated he'd be interested in a move to Italy. The guy was a brilliant, irrepressible player, precisely the sort of dynamo Amaral needed in his new-fangled 4–2–4. Toro were keen on him as well, but Juve had the money they'd received for Charles and the defender Bruno Garzena, and del Sol boarded a flight to Malpensa.

Bruno Nicolè had enjoyed a meteoric rise. At 21 years and 61 days old he'd been Italy's youngest-ever captain, but now, just eighteen months on, his career seemed moribund. He'd hardly played the previous season, but worse still he hadn't seemed bothered. His career would be finished before his 28th birthday but, in Bruno Mora, Juventus had unearthed a ready-made replacement. He'd been just about the only bright spot in a dismal season, but now the club provoked outrage by trading him for a centre-half from Milan.

Sandro 'Billy' Salvadore (so-called because Billy Wright was his idol) had been born in Milan and was a natural sweeper. The problem was that so was Cesare Maldini, and Milan coach Nereo Rocco preferred him in the role. Salvadore, deployed as a man-marker, had bided his time, but as he took the field for a post-World Cup friendly in Argentina, he was told he'd been sold to Juventus, and that Mora was coming the other way. Salvadore would become a Juve mainstay, captain and legend. He'd play over 330 games in twelve years, and would even captain the national side.

At the start of the 1962–63 season the new Juventus punched above their weight. They were level with Inter until late February, but fell away following successive defeats against Sampdoria and Toro. They won only three of their last twelve games, while Herrera's extraordinary young Inter side held their nerve to finally deliver the championship to long suffering, big-spending Angelo Moratti. In Tarcisio Burgnich, Aristide Guarneri and buccaneering full-back Facchetti, Inter had three outstanding young defenders, and in 21-year-old Mazzola an immensely talented inside forward. They returned to the summit of Italian football after nine long years, and two days later their neighbours beat Benfica at Wembley to become European champions. Milanese football was in the ascendancy once more, and Inter were well on their way to becoming the best team not only in northern Italy, but in all the world.

Over at Juve, the early months of Amaral's reign had been characterised by optimism, but then he'd become grouchy and uncooperative. All considered, second was no mean feat, but the 1963–64 pre-season would be a joyless experience. Like it or not, *catenaccio* was the order of the day in Italian football, and evidently it worked. Amaral, though, was totally intransigent, insisting on his Brazilian 4–2–4. That was all well and good in theory, but he had no Pelé, no Zagallo and no Garrincha. Those he did have were unaccustomed to the system, and his refusal to adapt strained his relationship with Catella.

Sívori had been appointed captain, but he was too self-centred to lead a team, and his performances were increasingly mercurial. Some felt his form had suffered because he'd started an insurance business, others that he simply didn't care enough. The hope was that the captaincy would ginger him up, but the plain fact was that he and Amaral didn't get along. In fact Sívori didn't seem to get on with Brazilians full stop, and the 21-year-old striker Nené was a case in point. He was the club's first black player, and he was a talented, humble kid. He'd been signed from Santos on Boniperti's recommendation, but for some reason Sívori didn't rate him and he went the same way as his countrymen Bruno Siciliano and Miranda the previous season. Miranda in particular had looked a player. He'd scored 12 goals in 17 games, but still Sívori had taken against. His power base at Juve was considerable, and he wasn't prepared to share top billing with anyone who wasn't Charles or Boniperti. Miranda and his mate had been moved on at the season's end, and now the same fate befell poor Nené.

In advance of the trip to Modena at the start of the 1963–64 season, Amaral threw a tantrum. He insisted that the players travel by bus and not, as was customary, by train. The club let him have his way, but then he demanded they take the train home. It was absurd, and ten days later he effectively sacked himself. On the eve of the Inter-Cities Fairs Cup (precursor of the UEFA Cup) game against OFK Beograd, he announced that he'd be resting Sívori and four other first-team players. Sívori's absence was guaranteed to reduce attendance, and this at a time when Catella was attempting to balance the books. Worse still it was an international match, and Juventus sold itself as a big, important, international football club. That only 2062 spectators turned up was simply humiliating.

Catella had no choice but to let Amaral go, and the club installed the 1934 World Cup winner Eraldo Monzeglio in his place. It did the trick initially – as it tends to – but the dressing room was riven with petty disputes and rivalries. Juve lost the Coppa Italia semi-final against Toro, and staggered home sixteen points off the pace in the league. They were clueless, but that's not to say this wasn't a dramatic season in Serie A.

Inter were everybody's favourites, but an unlikely challenger emerged in Bologna. They hadn't won the league for 22 years, but new coach Fulvio Bernardini had guided them to successive fourth-place finishes. Now they blazed a trail through the winter months. When they beat Toro 4–1 at the Fila to record their ninth straight victory on 2 January, there seemed to be no holding them. When, however, the doping test results came back from the match, no less than five *bolognesi* were positive. Following years of denial and obfuscation, Italian football's doping culture was exposed. The five miscreants were absolved from blame on the grounds they'd ingested the drugs unwittingly, but Bernardini and club doctor Poggiali were each suspended for eighteen months.

The samples had been tested in three different labs – in Florence, Milan and Rome – and were consistent, but Bologna maintained they'd been framed. The players had eaten their normal pre-match meal (steak and risotto) in their normal restaurant. The owners, cooks and waiters there were all *rossoblu* fans, so it was inconceivable someone had interfered with their food. Afterwards they'd each drunk a coffee and an *amaro* in their normal café, then set off for Turin. It therefore followed, given that Bologna didn't dope their players, that somebody must have got at their samples.

Three Bologna magistrates joined forces to contest the results. They visited the lab in Florence, and noted that the samples had been stored close to a fridge containing … amphetamine! That didn't seem right, and nor did the fact that, while five *bolognesi* had been positive, none of the Toro players had. A neutral might have suggested that may have been because one side was doped and the other not, but they weren't having that. Bologna had also been tested following their game against Milan, and none of those tests had come back positive. The main thrust of their argument was the sheer *quantity* of amphetamine present. They stated, quite correctly, that the samples contained enough to power a racehorse.

The inevitable question was ... *Chi l'ha fatta?* Whodunit?

Oddly, they pointed the finger at Milan. Their players were suspected of illegal betting practices, so according to Bolognese logic they must have been involved in some sort of dirty tricks campaign. The suggestion seemed to be that they'd somehow got their hands on the non-positive samples from the Milan game, added some amphetamine and swapped them with the samples from the Toro game. (If at this point you're thinking you couldn't make this stuff up, don't worry. It's probably because you haven't lived in Italy.)

The *Caso Bologna* enveloped all of Italian society and – you've guessed it – began to assume a political dimension. Bologna is a medium-sized central Italian city far from the economic, political and sporting powerhouses of Milan and Turin. The *bolognese* narrative, eagerly picked up by the Roman press and by those in the south, was that rich, corrupt, northerners were gerrymandering Italian sport in precisely the same way they'd always gerrymandered Italian wealth and power. They'd stop at nothing to protect their cartel, and this was yet another example of their ruthlessness. Italian football, they claimed, had become a dictatorship. Same old, same old ...

Next Enrico Niccolini, head of the anti-doping commission, was beaten senseless at his home in Florence. That was grist to the mill, and so too the fact that Bologna had two players sent off against Sampdoria. Best of all though – pure Fellini in fact – was their away game at Roma. Having travelled incognito to the game, Bernardini put on sunglasses and fedora and took a seat in the stand with the hoi polloi. His attempts to look inconspicuous failed, however, on account of him being a dead ringer for Fulvio Bernardini and this being a football match involving Bologna. There was another unusual thing as well – the people sitting around him couldn't fail to notice that he kept leaning into his over-coat and talking. He was a man alone at a football match, and he kept talking to the inside of his coat.

One of the Roma directors informed the ref that the man was the suspended Bernardini and that he was com-municating, via walkie-talkie, with his assistant on the Bologna bench. The ref therefore stopped the game and confiscated the assistant's apparatus. Then Bernardini got into a slanging match with the Roma fans around him, and then that calmed down. Then 32,000 people watched 22 young men in short shorts run around a huge lawn kicking a bag of wind this way and that.

The final verdict came with three games remaining. Bernardini and Bologna were absolved of all wrong-doing, and their points restored. They failed to deter-mine the who, what and why of any of it, and the upshot was that Bologna finished the season level on points with Inter.

A Felliniesque someone suggested they resolve mat-ters by awarding not one title but two. The 1927 *Caso Allemandi* championship had never been conferred, so why not simply give that one to Bologna and this one to Inter? That would have evened things up after a fashion, but the idea was canned on account of it being extrava-gantly stupid. Instead a neutral-venue play-off would have to decide matters, so Rome's Olympic Stadium was booked for Sunday 7 June.

On the afternoon of Wednesday 3 June 1964, the chairman of Bologna FC climbed into his car in the company of his wife and personal physician. Genial old Renato Dall'Ara, now 72, had been at the helm in Bologna for over thirty years. He'd been advised not to go to any more matches because of a heart issue, but he had to attend an important meeting in Milan with his counterpart from Inter. Dall'Ara and Angelo Moratti, Inter's *presidentissimo*, had been invited to break bread together by the league. Tensions were running high, what with the doping and everything, and it was felt that a cordial handshake between the two of them might help to ameliorate the situation.

When they arrived in Milan, Dall'Ara's wife duly made her excuses. She left him in the care of his personal physician, with Moratti and with host Giorgio Perlasca. Dall'Ara began by congratulating Moratti on Inter having won the European Cup Final the previous week, sat down and then ... (How best to put this?) then he just dropped dead. Fellini would have loved that.

Doped or otherwise, Bologna sent Dall'Ara on his way with a *Scudetto*. For their part, Milan had a wealthy new president in Felice Riva and a dazzling young playmaker in Gianni Rivera. Notwithstanding the defeat against Bologna, conventional wisdom had it that Herrera's Inter were the best team in Europe. They'd outrun, -passed and -classed the mighty Real Madrid to win the European Cup in Vienna in May, and the football they'd played had been scintillating. Defensively they were rock solid; their work ethic was great, and in Mazzola they had a genuinely outstanding player up top. They had flair, method, discipline and purpose, a mirror of the man who had made them. Herrera had very good players, but that was only half of it. He'd institutionalised a clearly defined set of behaviours, delivered continuity and a winning culture, and the club was reaping the rewards.

At Juve there was none of that; the club's fall from grace had been spectacular. The Monzeglio experiment had failed, and by the season's end the eleven who took the field were a team in name only. Their playing style, insofar as one could be inferred, seemed almost decadent. The post-Umberto Juve had become a byword for stasis, and the club desperately needed a new broom.

Herrera had been in post for four seasons at Inter, while the manager's job at Juventus had become a revolving door. The players understood that they were supposed to win football matches, but nobody was telling them clearly and consistently how to do it. That had been fine with Charles, Boni and Sívori, but they'd been virtuosos.

Like everyone else competing with Inter, Juve needed to unearth a facsimile Herrera. A tall order, but, lo and behold and out of nothing, they found one. He was holed up in a provincial town down on Spain's Mediterranean coast, and in time he'd drag the club kicking and screaming out of the dark ages …

At loggerheads with Heriberto Herrera and Omar Sívori

In 1962 Español had been steered back into the top flight by a tall, angular Paraguayan named Heriberto Herrera.

He'd subsequently moved to tiny Elche and, despite a stadium capacity of only 12,000, guided them to a miraculous fifth in La Liga. Like his namesake at Inter he brooked no nonsense, and the brand of high-octane football he'd instilled had compensated in large measure for the technical shortcomings of the players.

Gianni had been hearing good things about Herrera from FIAT's Spanish distributor, so Catella drove down to the Côte d'Azur to meet him. He informed the brothers that this was precisely the man the club needed; he was hired, and the Italian press immediately dubbed him HH2. Herrera started out by stating that he didn't subscribe to notions of 'talent', because in isolation it was neither use nor ornament. Neither did it matter whether the players liked him, his methods or his ideas, because they'd a job of work to do just as he had. If they did precisely as he instructed they'd likely be successful, and if they didn't they wouldn't. Herrera by name ...

Pre-season was essentially a boot camp, and Sívori for one wasn't having it. Five days before the first competitive match, a Coppa Italia game at Alessandria, he cried off with a calf strain. He declared himself fit on the morning of the game, expecting to play, but HH2 stopped him in his tracks. Having missed almost a week of training there was no way he'd be able to contribute adequately, so best he stayed at home, rested some more and redoubled his efforts to be ready for the opening league game.

Sívori had always been untouchable at Juventus, and in leaving him out Herrera was planting his flag. Juve had engaged him because they felt they needed a disciplinarian, and this amounted to a direct challenge. Either they threw their weight behind him, or they continued to indulge Sívori, but the consequences of the latter would likely be more of the same – inertia, poor results and absent fans.

Pressed by a journalist to explain his philosophy, HH2 famously stated that he made no distinction between players according to reputation: 'Coramini and Sívori are the same.' The message was clear. Alberto Coramini was a 19-year-old defender with little ability to speak of, but he was first onto the training pitch of a morning and he desperately wanted to play. Sívori, on the other hand, was a capricious superstar. Former Ballon d'Or or otherwise, he'd no longer be permitted to contaminate the dressing room. HH2's Juventus had started to resemble a totalitarian mini-state, but that was what the directors had signed up for.

His playing style, *movimiento*, was unlike anything Juve fans had ever witnessed either. Some have suggested it was a precursor to Dutch 'total football', but it wasn't nearly as expansive. It required huge physical commitment, because the players needed to cover more ground and, critically, press much higher than with *catenaccio*. They'd work in their respective zones, but they also needed to accustom themselves to the idea that they were no longer *specialisti*. There were no stars or drudges, and everyone needed to learn to do everything. HH2 valued physicality, desire and discipline over artistry, and defence over attack. Those who didn't subscribe knew where the door was, and if the players didn't particularly warm to him then so be it. He needed them to play for *one another*, and if their mutual loathing of his training methods was the catalyst then all well and good.

Off the pitch the players were forbidden from talking to the press, and even to their own fans. He demanded that they were in bed by ten, and tea and coffee were strictly off-limits. HH2 seldom smiled, and he never, *ever* spoke about his private life. That was probably because, aside from studying diet, sports science and medicine, he didn't have one. There was no wine, no women and (Paraguayan folk music aside) resoundingly no song. *La Gazzetta dello Sport* described him as a Trappist, and not without reason.

His team started poorly and on 8 November 1964 travelled to Florence minus Sívori and right-winger Giampaolo Menichelli. They parked the bus, but conceded on the hour and never looked like equalising. HH2's verdict was that Fiorentina had converted their one and only chance, but Juve had created nothing whatsoever. He was at loggerheads with Sívori and Gianfranco Zigoni, a talented but wayward young striker, and his side had scored the sum total of five goals in the season's eight league games. The fans were convinced he was a charlatan, and there were rumours he was talking to a Spanish club about going home.

When *La Stampa* revealed that HH2 was to meet Catella, it seemed Juve would be looking for another new *mister*. When Herrera emerged, though, he simply reiterated that Rome wasn't built in a day, that Zigoni was to be loaned out to Genoa, and that he'd be fulfilling his contract unless informed otherwise. The following Sunday Juve beat a useful Sampdoria side 2–0, and then thumped a very good Toro one 3–0. By now Turin's 'second club' had moved out of the Fila and in with their neighbours, but they were being outmuscled both on and off the pitch.

Herrera's squad was in no way ready to sustain a title challenge; he therefore pinned his managerial future on the Coppa Italia and the Fairs Cup, because he knew that if he could deliver one or the other there'd be a contract extension. That would see off Sívori, the enemy within, and guarantee him gainful employment for years to come. In public he took pains to sound conciliatory, but in private this was a battle of wills.

By May the Milan clubs were out of sight, but Herrera was on course. Sívori had been injured and then marginalised, and Salvadore, del Sol and captain Ernesto Castano had reclaimed the dressing room. Juve were alive and kicking, and in the Coppa Italia they travelled to Bologna for the quarter-final. Without Sívori they defended resolutely for 120 minutes, then won a penalty shoot-out as Bologna's Marino Perani took all five and missed three. Dramatic denouement or otherwise, the game itself wasn't up to much as a spectacle. It did, however, showcase the rigour and pragmatism HH2 had instilled. Juve had travelled to Bologna to win a game of football, but in order for that to happen they'd needed to avoid losing it. For two hours they'd been absolutely resolute, and ultimately they'd prevailed. They'd done so without their most talented player, and his non-selection had engendered precisely the *esprit de corps* Herrera's namesake had patented at Inter.

The Fairs Cup semi-final with Atlético Madrid went to a replay, and Juve won the coin-toss to host it. With Sívori once more indisposed, they came from behind to win 3–1, and the following week Menichelli scored the only goal as they beat Toro to reach the Coppa Italia final. A very slick Ferencvaros side beat them 1–0 in the

Fairs Cup final, but the game crystalised the progress they were making. The Hungarians were more talented, but Juve were brave, committed and extremely fit. The players were unremarkable, but the blueprint was right.

Gianni had been at the game, and rumours began to circulate that he was minded to return to the club. That, however, was wishful thinking. Valletta was 83 now, and he was tired. Approaching the 100th anniversary of his grandfather's birth, it was time for Gianni to take the reins at FIAT.

Gianni was 45, and the feckless playboy of yore had grown up. Though still prone to indiscretions, he was in the office bright and early of a morning, Saturdays included, and in the main he relished the work. He still lacked patience and rigour, but he'd developed the diplomatic or intellectual bandwidth to compensate. He still didn't entirely trust Umberto, and the undercurrent of rivalry between them had never truly dissipated. There were all sorts of reasons for that, but chief among them were the age gap and the unique circumstances in which they'd grown up. Gianni cared about Umberto, but he didn't want him under his feet as he grappled with his life's great calling. Little brother was dispatched across the Alps to run the French subsidiary.

For now at least, there would be no blank cheques for Juventus, so if Catella wanted new blood he'd need to sell. The club's most saleable assets were Salvadore and Sívori, and Milan were keen to take the former back in exchange for the Brazilian striker Altafini. It was clear that Juve urgently needed a goalscorer, but Salvadore was a mainstay of the team. In the main he'd been deployed as a full-back. It wasn't his natural position, but he'd got on with it because he understood that he was part of a collective. The back line was the rock upon which Herrera was building the new Juve, and they'd conceded just 24 league goals in 34 matches. Salvadore had been central to that, and to the mentality which informed it. He was one of Herrera's men, and Catella knew that if they sold him from under his nose there'd be hell to pay.

During a post-match interview Gianni stated that the club didn't need to sell Sívori, but that if he wished to stay he'd do well to 'accept the discipline of the team and demonstrate more wisdom'. He saw no reason why he and HH2 couldn't co-exist, but Sívori needed to 'avoid making the mistakes of this season'. Herrera read this and understood that it represented the vote of confidence he needed to move against Sívori. In the normal course of events he was a master of emollience, but now he told a group of journalists that he struggled with 'certain individuals who created disorder'. The subtext was clear for all to see, and the following morning Turin's sporting hacks beat a path to Sívori's door.

They shoved their papers under his nose; the red mist duly descended, and all manner of anti-Herrera invective spewed scandalously forth. Sívori concluded by stating that he'd be speaking to Catella about this, and if no assurances were forthcoming he'd be on his way. He reckoned he had three more good years in him, and it wasn't as if Juve would be short of offers. The time had come. Either Herrera went or he did.

Big mistake. Juve fined him and declared themselves open to offers of around 130 million. Newly promoted Napoli offered 90 million, but their owner also agreed to buy FIAT engines for his flotilla of yachts. Gianni never could resist that sort of deal, and besides even Sívori's team-mates were fed up with him by now. In essence they chose Herrera over him, and Juve cut one of their greatest ever players adrift.

On 29 August 1965, Juventus travelled to Rome for the final of the Coppa Italia against mighty Inter. Before 70,000 spectators, HH2's spoilers hustled and bustled, and Inter never once got round the back of them. Burgnich and del Sol were sent off for a punch-up; as a spectacle it was rank, and Giampaolo Menichelli's winning goal was just about as scruffy as they come. HH2 said he liked it. He liked it a lot.

It was perfect. Sívori was out, and Heriberto Herrera settled in for the long haul.

At the Comunale, with a bunch of blue-collar workers

The club replaced Sívori, but only after a fashion. The Piedmontese Silvino Bercellino had come through the youth system, and had been dispatched to Serie B Potenza for a season. He'd done well down there, but it's fair to say he was no John Charles. Sívori partisans joked that it didn't really matter, because a good striker would be wasted on this Juve side anyway. Someone referred to them as the *Juve Operaia*, the 'factory worker Juve', presumably because they played with the elan of the blue collars at Mirafiori. The sobriquet stuck because, quite simply, the cap fitted.

So curmudgeonly were their tactics that they accumulated just 38 goals in 34 league outings. They conceded only 23, and the games seemed always to be mired in a tactical gluepot. They were boring and, in the absence of the sort of plot twists mavericks like Sívori and Zigoni were able to provide, at times unwatchable. Under HH2 the objective seemed to be 0–0 away and 1–0 at home, and the more proficient they were the more mind-numbing matches became. Not for one minute did anybody doubt his tactical acumen, and nor for that matter the players' endeavour. They meant well, but life was too short to watch football this bad, and as ever the fans voted with their feet. The previous season, Juve's average league gate had been a paltry 25,666. That was less than Bologna, Milan, Inter and Roma, and only fractionally more than Toro's 24,000. Now the attendances plummeted once more, as Napoli (average 68,000), Fiorentina and even Brescia proved bigger draws.

For all their appeal out in the provinces, Juve had never attracted particularly large crowds. The Turin public's apparent indifference had been a bugbear for Umberto, who'd portrayed the signings of Charles, Sívori and Nicolè as 'gifts' to the fans. That he did so spoke of his own sense of entitlement, but also of the relationship between the family and the city. Many maintain that the endless fascination the *torinesi* have with/for the Agnellis is the inevitable legacy of centuries spent prostrating themselves before the Catholic Church and the Savoys. Though doubtless there's some truth in that, when it comes to crowd size, it's also a fact that the Milanese and Roman conurbations have always been much bigger, that there are no large satellite towns close to Turin, and that the majority of the Piedmontese still regarded Toro as their club.

HH2's *operai* managed eleven 0–0 draws; Liverpool beat them in the first round of the Cup Winners' Cup, Serie B Catanzaro in the Coppa Italia. Was that *really* all the mighty Juventus aspired to? Maybe not, but Catella was convinced they were on the right road. It had taken the other Herrera three years to deliver a trophy at Inter, and so, while the football was rancid, in the circumstances there wasn't much to be gained by sacking him. Yet.

Italy travelled to the 1966 World Cup full of optimism, and came home (yet again) in disgrace. The defeat in Santiago had been grotesque, but losing to North Korea in Middlesbrough was unconscionably awful. As usual, Italian football blamed the failings of its national team on foreign players. The FIGC placed a ludicrous five-year embargo on them, forcing Inter to abandon deals for Franz Beckenbauer and, allegedly, the great Eusébio.

Juve hadn't the cash for that sort of thing. Sensationally, Gianni had signed the deal of the century with the Soviets. The FIAT 124 was to be produced under licence at Stavropol, a city on the Volga renamed Togliattigrad in honour of the late president of the Italian communist party. Gianni's dreams of bridging the east–west ideological divide were well intentioned, but totally quixotic. The factory would be four years and millions of dollars in the building, and so for now he wouldn't be funnelling money into Juve. Necessity being the mother of invention, Catella set his sights close to home. At the eleventh hour he scraped the money together to renew with Salvadore and keeper Roberto Anzolin, both of whom had been threatening strike action in advance of the new season. Gianni thought that hilarious. At times it seemed the whole country was either striking or threatening to.

For all his idiosyncrasies, Gianfranco 'crazy horse' Zigoni was a *Juventino*. He'd grown up in the youth teams, and before HH2's intervention looked set to be a big star. He fancied himself as the white Pelé, albeit with long hair, a Porsche and an ego completely disproportionate to his abilities. Beseeched by one of the directors to pacify HH2 by cutting his hair, he'd agreed on condition that the director 'cut off his cock'. He was by no means a natural fit for the *Juve Operaia*, because defensively he was rubbish. That said he wasn't disruptive for the sake of it and unlike Sívori got on well with his team-mates. He'd been playing in Serie B these past two years, but Herrera knew the team needed an injection of creativity. He couldn't afford to go out and buy it, and Zigo promised to keep his head down and respect the all-for-one credo. He was joined up front by Gigi De Paoli, a tough-as-teak striker from Brescia, and by the scuttling right-winger (and prototype HH2 player) Erminio Favalli.

Inter began the 1966–67 season as runaway favourites and led from the outset. They won their first seven games but – hold the back page – Juve weren't awful. Everyone knew they'd be good without the ball, because that was HH2's thing. The football they produced was very far from pretty, but it was admirable and just a tiny bit watchable. The whole was much greater than the sum of the parts, and as Milan and Bologna fell away, they alone clung to Inter's coat-tails.

With five games remaining, Juve travelled to Milan trailing by three points. AC Milan were enduring a miserable season, but Rivera produced a sublime performance and they won 3–1. Inter were held at Cagliari, but afterwards Catella all but acknowledged that it was over. Juve were four points adrift with four games left. They'd have to beat Inter in Turin, win their final three games and hope Inter tripped up against Napoli, Fiorentina and/or Mantova. On the Wednesday after the Juve game, Inter beat CSKA to book their place in the European Cup final. Two days later, Helenio Herrera flew to Glasgow to watch Inter's opponents Celtic in the Old Firm derby, while his namesake took his players off to Villar Perosa for *ritiro*.

HH2 told his players in no uncertain terms that Catella had been talking nonsense. If they could win on Sunday the gap would be down to two points, and then it would all be up for grabs. Inter still had to play fifth-placed Fiorentina, and they were a very decent side. What's more, they were drawing games they'd have won before Christmas, and anyone could see they were starting to look jaded. Moreover, between the Fiorentina game and the trip to Mantova, they'd have to play Celtic in Lisbon. They'd come back exhausted emotionally and physically, and Mantova were good at home. That game was a *Clamoroso al Cibali* waiting to happen, so there'd be no defeatist talk and absolutely no thought of finishing second. If, he assured them, they won all their remaining games, the title would be theirs.

Gino Stacchini had been an unsung *Juventino* hero. He'd served the club faithfully for twelve years, and he was the last man standing from the *trio magico* era.

Now, though, his knee was knackered, and HH2 called up bit-part Favalli for the Inter game. He hadn't featured for three months because, to coin an Italian phrase, his second touch was invariably a header, but also because he and HH2 couldn't stand one another. Favalli had told Herrera to 'go to hell', but with nobody else available it fell upon him to try to contain the marauding Facchetti.

Juve started well but then got entangled in Inter's *catenaccio*. Their efforts became progressively more frenetic and exponentially less precise, but with 20 minutes left a hopeful cross was slung into the visitors' box. It seemed much ado about nothing, but an Inter defender made a hash of his clearing header under challenge. Keeper Giuliano 'ice man' Sarti could only parry it onto the post, and when it ricocheted back into the six-yard box even Favalli couldn't miss. There was the usual argy-bargy, but Concetto Lo Bello rightly decreed that the goal was good.

With two games left and two points in it, Inter entertained Fiorentina. They scrambled a 1–1 draw with a late penalty, but they were out on their feet. Mazzola was half-fit and Luis Suárez a dead man walking, while Brazilian winger Jair would miss their remaining games. Juve closed to a point with a scratchy 1–0 win in Vicenza, and now the umpteenth row erupted between the two clubs ...

Inter requested – and were granted – a four-day deferment of the final-day fixtures. The league took account of 'extenuating circumstances', and in so doing ensured that Suárez would be fit to face Mantova. Catella said he saw no reason not to acquiesce, but then Catella was a nice man who hadn't been a professional footballer. HH2, who wasn't and had, was absolutely furious.

Inter were overrun by Celtic's 'Lisbon Lions' in the final, but they arrived in Mantova having rested for seven days. Juve were hosting Lazio for their final game, and at half-time both matches were scoreless. Juve took the lead shortly afterwards, and now thousands of crackling transistor radios tuned into Mantova. There the ball broke on the right-hand corner of the Inter area, and Beniamino 'Gegè' Di Giacomo, a former Inter striker, rushed towards it together with Armando Picchi.

Di Giacomo and Picchi had known one another all their professional lives. Both were 31, both had enjoyed distinguished careers, and for two roller-coaster seasons they'd played together under Herrera at Inter. Picchi had been a fixture in the side, while Di Giacomo had been in and out. He'd been prolific when he'd played, and had felt he'd done enough to be selected for the 1964 European Cup final against Real Madrid. In the event, Herrera had left him out and, because he was Herrera, hadn't thought to explain why. At the season's end Di Giacomo had been unceremoniously shunted on to Mantova. Not good.

On this occasion, he and Picchi reached the ball almost simultaneously, but the striker stuck out a leg and got something on it. He managed to waft it in the general direction of the six-yard box, and it turned into a cross of sorts. Whatever. It was too close to Sarti and, as it looped towards the keeper's arms, too far from any of his teammates. Then it happened. The ice man, consummate all season, allowed it to melt through his fingers and to drip apologetically over the goal line. It remains the most

Juve-Nazionale: Combi and Rosetta lead out the Italian team at the 1934 *Mondiale*, with Allemandi, Bertolini, Borel *et al* in attendance. The sign behind reads 'Buy Italian Products'.

The calm before the storm: Parola and Campatelli, his Inter counterpart, exchange gifts. In the fifties and sixties, matches between the two clubs were invariably violent, and utterly compelling.

Boom town: Gianni, front and centre at the 1955 Turin motor show. He's showing Luigi Einaudi, the Italian president, the chassis of the low-cost FIAT 600. Mirafiori would produce 2.7 million of them.

Absolute power: Umberto Agnelli, president of the Italian football association at the ripe old age of 23, sits proudly beneath a portrait of his late father.

The power of three: The *Trio Magico* of Boniperti, Charles and Sìvori lit up the Italian game between 1957 and 1962.

Attention seeker: Gianni with Jackie Kennedy's sister and other socialites. Note the non-accidental carpet slipper on his right foot. He was forever making fashion 'statements' like that.

Winning ugly: Heriberto 'HH2' Herrera (top step, grey suit) and his blue-collar *Juve operaia* team. Their football was painful to watch, and yet somehow they won Serie A.

The new football:
The success of the
Sicilian Anastasi,
pictured here
alongside Fabio
Capello, predicated
a shift in northern
Italian attitudes
towards their
southern cousins.

1979 and all that:
L-R the late, great
Gaetano Scirea, the
'heart-stealer' Cabrini,
the *Sardi* Cuccureddu
and Virdis. Then the
redoubtable Brio, the
icon Zoff and the arch
Juventino Bettega.

The great and the
merely very good:
Trapattoni schools the
poster-boy Rossi, the
stopper extraordinaire
Claudio Gentile and
the flying Pole Boniek.
Platini doesn't need
any schooling.

A singular talent:
Prior to Diego
Maradona's arrival
at Napoli, Michel
Platini was irrefutably
the most complete
footballer in Serie A.

The worst of times: Police horses rush across the pitch as violence erupts in a 'mixed' section of the Brussels' Heysel Stadium.

New order: By the early nineties, Silvio Berlusconi had amassed a vast fortune. His Milan would outspend and outplay Gianni's Juve, but not outlast them.

Ill-gotten gains? Gianluca Vialli lifts the 1996 Champions League trophy. It was never rescinded, but the era is synonymous with the alleged use of performance enhancing drugs.

Useless beauty: It's 1998, and as ever the Delle Alpi is half-empty. Here, before a league game against Sampdoria, the champions seem nonplussed by all the empty seats.

The smartest guy in the (trophy) room: Inexplicably, a section of the Juve *tifoseria* still venerates Luciano Moggi. The mother of the idiot is always pregnant, as the Italian saying goes.

All for one: Nobody embodied the spirit of the FIAT factory team like the great Pavel Nedvěd. Here he takes on another midfield tyro, the Inter legend Javier Zanetti.

The perfect 10: Alessandro Del Piero scored over 200 goals in black and white. Here he converts a Champions League penalty against Chelsea.

famous goalkeeping howler in the history of Italian football, and the most expensive one.

For five years Herrera's thoroughbreds had run and run and run, but now they had nothing left to give. When Zigoni headed in a second goal over in Turin, their time was up. Sarti's tears broke Milanese hearts, and the era of the *Grande Inter* was over.

Six years earlier, the *trio magico* had won Serie A with 80 goals in 34 games. Now HH2's *operai*, barely a striker to their name, had done it with 44. Gianni said he'd turned 'aristocrats into social democrats', and he was right.

The Juve Operaia had won Serie A. Good Lord.

On Corso Re Umberto, with poor, heartbroken Tilo Romero

Images of terrible barbarity were emerging from Vietnam. Unspeakable atrocities were being perpetrated in the name of capitalism, and Western democracies were increasingly politicised and polarised. The opening stage of the Giro d'Italia had to be cancelled due to protests in Milan, and large demonstrations took place in Bologna, Rome and Turin.

The latter was the cradle of Italian capitalism, FIAT its beating heart. Its post-war revival had been financed by US money, and Gianni in particular had never disguised his admiration for American culture and values. Now, though, America was engaged in an imperialist war in south-east Asia, and the Stars and Stripes were set ablaze in Piazza San Carlo. To the progressives, the liberal intelligentsia and communists, the Agnellis were guilty by association. The left saw them as capitalist-colonialist pariahs, American proxies in Europe.

Like his grandfather, Gianni believed in markets, but he'd made it his business – publicly at least – to steer clear of ideology. Now, though, ideology was refusing to steer clear of *him*, and people – including the ones who kept the Agnellis in the style to which they had become accustomed – were losing faith in capitalism. Some were losing their patience and some were losing their temper.

The student riots in Paris, events in Vietnam and the Prague Spring had focused European minds on issues of power, individual liberty, female emancipation and worker's rights. In Italy the so-called Hot Autumn, ushered in by a sit-in at Turin University, saw students, trade unionists and social commentators coalesce around revolutionary philosophies and behaviours. Absenteeism at FIAT increased dramatically as the unions demanded higher wages and better representation. Productivity declined exponentially, as northern workers and students accused the ruling class of profiteering and railed against the perceived exploitation of and discrimination against their southern brethren.

The post-war *boom economico* had attracted droves of southerners to Turin. The mid-60s had seen a slowdown in inward migration, but now, as FIAT expanded once more, agents were dispatched to entice still more young men from the south. In the 16 years since 1951, the city's population had increased by 400,000. There were over 1.1 million residents now, and the social discord was palpable. Schools, hospitals and social services weren't able to cope, and large sections of the *seconda cintura*, the new developments on the outskirts, were inhabited almost exclusively by migrant families. Ten years previously, places like Grugliasco, Venaria and Collegno had been quiet, rural villages. Now they'd been swallowed whole by the third city of the *Mezzogiorno*. Turin's southern population was eclipsed only by those of Naples and Palermo. In the Apennines, entire villages had upped and left. Much more of this, they said, and the Abruzzo would be a wasteland.

FIAT's domestic market share was declining, but it was enjoying unprecedented growth elsewhere. There were approaching 3 million 500's in circulation, the 124 had won European Car of the Year, and the company was attempting to buy Citroën. Exports had increased fourfold in five years, and Mirafiori needed more workers. Moreover, a new plant, south-west of the city at Rivalta, was almost ready to begin production. It would need an initial 15,000 *operai*, and all being well an additional 25,000 within a couple of years. Every morning the 'train of hope' pulled in at Porta Nuova, disgorging more and more families and more and more chaos. The infrastructure couldn't keep pace and, worse still, there just weren't the beds. People would fight, quite literally, for a bench in the waiting room at Porta Nuova, and thousands slept in trucks. Inflation was running at 3 per cent, but rents in Turin, for those lucky enough to find a flat, were rising at 10 per cent annually. The mayor called a meeting with FIAT senior management and argued, probably uniquely, for an economic freeze. But if, the city fathers argued, the company was hell-bent on increasing its workforce, it needed to assume responsibility for housing the newcomers. FIAT couldn't carry on like this, because the city belonged to everyone and it just wasn't fair. Aside from a vague assurance that they'd try to recruit only single men this time, the company paid no heed. Turin would be on its knees without FIAT, and so they would carry on regardless.

Herrera winning the title with the players he had was a miraculous achievement. Gianni's gag about a team of social democrats had been good, but also apposite. The *Juve Operaia* had been bang in tune with the zeitgeist, but fitness, organisation and endeavour would only get you so far. By inclination and design, Juventus was a bourgeois club with global aspirations, and the European Cup remained the Holy Grail both for the Agnelli brothers and for the fans. Both Milan clubs had won it, and for Juve it was becoming something of an obsession. However nobody – not even HH2 – truly believed you could win it without the sort of creative impulse Italian football sorts refer to as *fantasia*.

Surprise, surprise, Toro were up the creek again. Once more there were rumours of a merger and, interviewed by *Tuttosport*, club president Orfeo Pianelli admitted there had been preliminary discussions. The atmosphere, however, was so febrile that Gianni didn't dare countenance it. Any such venture would have been perceived as a Toro surrender, and in the prevailing climate that would represent an existential risk to the Agnelli family holdings. The idea was dropped, and instead Catella began negotiations to buy Toro's brilliant, maverick winger Gigi Meroni. The fee, reputedly between 800 and 900 million lire, was astronomical, but Meroni was a stellar footballer and Toro were in urgent need of cash.

Besides, Juve needed to evolve. They hadn't made a marquee signing for two years, and both Napoli and Inter were sniffing about.

Not only was Meroni a mesmeric dribbler but also, in the vernacular, a *personaggio*. On the field he put one in mind of George Best, but off it he was a very atypical sportsman. He was shacked up with a beautiful blonde divorcee he'd met at a fairground; he had artistic pretensions, and he dressed not unlike a fifth Beatle. In the final analysis football was show business, and Catella reckoned Meroni would put thousands on the gate. Juve had taken over 100 million lire that day against Inter, and almost as much in winning the title against Lazio. A winning team featuring Meroni ought to be able to repeat that against Toro and Milan, and to fill the ground for the European games.

The problem was that Meroni was a Torino hero, and Toro were the team of old Piedmont. They were also the team of the left, and Gianni Agnelli was acutely aware of the fact that the left needed, more than ever, to be kept onside. Pianelli had overextended himself in trying to recreate the glory days, but Torino had other saleable assets in keeper Lido Vieri and midfielder Giorgio Ferrini. The prevailing mood among Toro fans was anyone but Meroni and anywhere but Juve, but on 27 June Pianelli admitted that the deal was all but done. He blustered that it was better that Meroni represented 'the city' by wearing the black and white of Toro's 'neighbours', but that was never going to wash.

They came out in their multitudes and, because this was Turin, failed to see the irony in gridlocking the city with their FIAT 500s. The anger was genuine though, and so was the idea that Juventus were robbing the poor to feed the rich. They stopped short of violence but made it known that this was a bridge too far. If Pianelli and Agnelli decided to complete the deal then so be it, but it would probably end badly for each of them.

Gianni had always been at pains not to tread on Catella's toes, but he was nothing if not perspicacious. There was much more at stake here than football, and he recognised that no good could come of going through with the deal. He called Catella and told him it was off, and it's impossible to overstate the wider significance of that phone call. Politics and sport had never been indivisible, but for the first time a Juve transfer had been directly affected.

Gianni rang Pianelli after having spoken to Catella. He apologised for messing him about and told him that what Juventus really needed was a new midfielder. He said he quite liked Luigi 'Gigi' Simoni, a sort of poor man's del Sol, and Pianelli's opening gambit was 250 million. That was about 50 million too much, but Gianni told him 500 million would be fine. When Pianelli explained that he must have misheard, Gianni repeated that it was fine, and he'd have Catella transfer the 500 million straight away. Juve would pay 500 million for Simoni, and under no circumstances whatsoever would Meroni be sold. Pianelli understood then. He turned down a big offer from Inter for Meroni, and he stayed right where he was.

Disaster averted, Meroni ran Sampdoria ragged on 15 October at the Comunale. Toro won 4–2, and he and team-mate Fabrizio Poletti went out to celebrate. Sprinting across Corso Re Umberto, they were hit by a FIAT 124 driven by Attilio 'Tilo' Romero, a 19-year-old

Toro fan (and neighbour of Meroni) who'd been at the game that afternoon. Poletti suffered only superficial injuries, but Meroni was flung into the air. He landed under an oncoming car, which dragged him 50 metres. They got what was left of him to hospital, but there was almost nothing which wasn't broken. Gigi Meroni was pronounced dead at 10.40 p.m.

Toro hammered Juve 4–0 the following Sunday. Some have questioned its validity as a sporting contest, but it precipitated a dramatic collapse in form for Herrera's team. By the new year, Milan led the championship, with the rest, Inter and Juve included, out of their depth.

On 4 February 1968, the *bianconeri* visited little Varese. Newly promoted and bankrolled by a rich, lugubrious domestic-appliance manufacturer, they were tearing it up in Serie A. Owner Giovanni Borghi was the self-styled '*comandante*'. He was broad-beamed, rough-hewn and not a little uncouth, but he was a sporting vision-ary all the same. He very well understood that, for all that there were more women in the workplace, Italy was still a regressive country. For the most part it was hus-bands who made the buying decisions, particularly with 'technical' products like his fridges. Italian womanhood couldn't be expected to understand their intricacies, and with that in mind Borghi's IGNIS brand had spon-sored Italy's best boxers, athletes and cyclists. In IGNIS Varese he'd transformed a nondescript provincial basket-ball team into a championship-winning one, and then, because he could, he'd bought the football club.

Doing well in Italian football was mostly about money, but Varese's success was due in large measure to serendipity. In 1966 they'd travelled to Catania for a

Serie B game at the Cibali. It had finished goalless, but then a chance meeting in a bar had changed the face of Italian football and, it could be argued, the face of Italian society. As Varese boarded their flight home, the airline had announced that it was overbooked. A young woman expecting a baby needed to get back to Milan urgently, so they were looking for someone to give up their seat. One of the Varese directors, a guy named Alfredo Casati, had stood up and said he'd be fine to fly home the following morning. He'd then walked out of the airport, into a bar, and into Italian sporting legend.

When the *barista* asked him what had brought him to Catania, he'd explained his job and the situation with the flight. The *barista* had said that being the case he'd do well to get back to the Cibali sharpish, because there was a local derby between Massiminiana and Paternò. It was a Serie D game, but it mattered a great deal in these parts and the ground would be heaving. Massiminiana were top of the league because they'd unearthed their very own 'white Pelé'. The kid, Pietro Anastasi, wasn't yet 18, but it was only a matter of time before one of the big boys discovered him.

Casati had heard it all before, and Sicily had produced a grand total of zero top-class footballers. Of the eleven who'd stunned Inter that famous afternoon in '61, not one had hailed from south of Rome, let alone Catania. Football was a northern sport, and that was because the north had infrastructure, commerce and history. It was *played* in the *Mezzogiorno*, but Neapolitan Antonio 'Totonno' Juliano aside, the south still hadn't produced a single outstanding player. Moreover even Napoli, easily the most successful of the southern teams, had spent protracted periods in Serie B. However, it wasn't as if Casati had anything better to do, so he jumped in a cab, went back to the Cibali and discovered what all the fuss was about.

After the match he walked straight down to the Massiminiana dressing room and asked to speak to the kid. He asked Anastasi, nicknamed 'the Turk' on account of his Moorish appearance, whether he was interested in moving to the north. Anastasi told him that where he came from *everyone* wanted to move to the north, and Casati said that was settled then. At the end of the season he'd be moving to Varese, and as as-near-as-made-no-difference that was Milan. He wouldn't be working on some dead-end production line either, rather he was going to become a professional footballer. Anastasi thanked him very much and said Varese wouldn't regret it.

Regret it they hadn't, and by the time an understrength Juve came to town, his goals had propelled Varese to fourth place in Serie A. He was still only 19, but he so embarrassed young Coramini that HH2 redeployed Salvadore to mark him. Only he too was made to look foolish, as Anastasi helped himself to a hat-trick and Varese ran out 5–0 winners. The champions had been dismantled by a 19-year-old from Catania, and Gianni Agnelli had taken note.

With the Italian championship out of reach, Juve overcame Braunchsweig to reach the European Cup semi-finals. They were powerless, though, in the face of the one and only Eusébio. Benfica's finest put them to the sword in Lisbon and again in Turin.

By the time Italy hosted the 1968 European Championships, Anastasi was to all intents and purposes a Juventus player. He'd been due to sign for Inter, but with Moratti gone there was nobody on hand to sign the cheque. With a power vacuum at the top of Inter and with Borghi anxious to get it done, Gianni had stepped in. He'd agreed to match Inter's fee (650 million lire) but also to throw in a load of cut-price compressors. Borghi liked that sort of thing, and so 'Pietruzzu' Anastasi agreed to sign for the club he'd supported, like so many Sicilians, as a boy.

Italy drew 1–1 with Yugoslavia in the final, but Anastasi scored a fulminating volley as they won the replay 2–0. He wore number 9, but there was infinitely more to his game than grubbing around in the penalty area. He had speed, talent and an eye for goal, but he also worked prodigiously for the team. There was a selflessness to his play which the fans couldn't help but appreciate and so, aged just 20, he became one Italy's best-paid players.

Anastasi became a successful sportsman, but fundamentally he was no different from the millions of young southern Italian males trying to make a go of it in the north. Like them he was a migrant in search of a better life, and they adopted him as their inspiration and exemplar. He was warm, open and generous, and his goals transcended the north–south divide. This was a godsend for the city because it started, in a very real sense, to sweep away age-old prejudices. You couldn't help but be moved by his character and his fairy tale, and so, consciously or otherwise, he seemed to embody the new Italy. The Juve side he joined was still HH2's, still fundamentally negative. However, his presence added 7000 to the gate, and many of the newcomers were from the south.

The Meroni affair had convinced Gianni that Juve needed to be more attuned to social issues, the Anastasi transfer that the team had to better reflect Italy's new demography. Juventus had always purported to be Italy's team, but the playing staff had been drawn almost entirely from the Po basin. The *Mezzogiorno* hadn't been represented at all, but with the Anastasi signing the penny had finally dropped and Gianni had understood that the geographical composition of the dressing room needed to change drastically. Change it would, because more than ever the company needed to be seen to be listening.

Anastasi had revolutionised the way Juventus thought and acted, but he couldn't change HH2's approach. The club invested in German schemer Helmut Haller and midfield general Romeo Benetti, but the tactics were the same and so were the consequences. The *Juve Operaia* had been fine while they were winning, because Herrera had turned ordinary players into good ones. Now, however, a sort of reverse alchemy was at play. They finished fifth in Serie A, and failed yet again in Europe. Eliminated in the second round of the Fairs Cup by Eintracht Frankfurt, the club had to change tack. Herrera had to go, and in June 1969 go he did. To Inter Milan.

At the *Stadio*, with the new *Juventini*

Having acquired the failing Lancia and Ferrari automotive companies for a song, *l'Avvocato* had been in *extremely* good spirits. Then, however, he'd watched Juve lose the derby 2–1, and it had quite ruined his Sunday evening. Juve had serious problems, and he knew just the man to solve them. It was October 1969, and Gianni called that old scallywag Boniperti.

Catella had appointed Argentine coach Luis Carniglia and bought in half a dozen new players. Among them was Sampdoria's blonde man-marker Francesco 'Morgan' Morini. The nickname, a reference to the mythical Welsh pirate, was applied on account of his unerring ability to relieve forwards of the ball. With Salvadore assuming the captaincy and the sweeper role, Morini was detailed to replace the stalwart Castano, with 20-year-old Giampietro Marchetti at left-back.

All of the above had seemed like a very good idea, but the consequences had been unutterably bad. Juve had won only one of their opening six games, and Toro's last-gasp winner had been the final straw. The team was hovering just above the drop zone, the new defence was at sixes and sevens, and Carniglia seemed to be making it up as he went along.

Catella was 60 now, and his mandate would expire in 18 months. Gianni therefore told Boniperti they needed to start again from scratch and that he was the man to do the starting. Because Agnelli knew Boni extremely well, he framed it as a deal. He'd be installed as CEO and shadow Catella for a while. The club's working capital would be doubled, and when Catella retired he'd have absolute autonomy in rebuilding the squad. The playing staff would need to reflect the new Italy, but beyond that his one and only remit would be silverware. Boniperti said that would all do nicely and – typical him – put Carniglia out of his misery on day one.

On day two (or as near as made no difference) he spent 390 million lire on a young left-sided midfielder from Sardinia. Antonello Cuccureddu would play 300 games in black and white over a decade or so, the majority in the company of midfield wrecker Giuseppe 'Beppe' Furino. Born in Sicily, Furino had moved to Turin as an adolescent. He'd graduated through the Juve youth teams, spent a couple of seasons out on loan, and now he'd become the first *torinese* son of migrant parents to represent the club. Like his idol Sívori, Furino played without shin pads, and like Sívori he was a snarler. As a southern kid in Turin he'd had no choice but to learn to scrap, and for 15 years and over 500 games he'd do precisely that. They called him 'the fury', and never was a nickname so apt. He was slight and only moderately talented, but no *Juventino* was ever so emblematic and so pig-headed.

What Anastasi had started at Juve – the legitimisation of southern accents, southern people and southern cultures – Cuccureddu and Furino continued. They made it OK to be a *meridionale* at the Comunale, so while politicians had been harrumphing on about social harmonisation for years, Juventus simply put it into practice.

Boniperti's new coach would be the *torinese* Ercole Rabitti. He appropriated Herrera's old 'iron sergeant' persona, and by and by the team hauled itself back into contention for the title. A disastrous run of results in March saw them lose ground, however, and the players didn't appreciate Rabitti's preening, bare-chested vanity. Nor did they care for the fact that he continually criticised them publicly, and though a third-place finish was a decent return, Rabitti was shown the door. It's a truism that footballers sack their managers, and they couldn't wait to see the back of him.

As a youngster, Boniperti had trained alongside a reserve-team player from just north of Turin. Pietro Giuliano had combined his football career with studying and had only ever made one first-team appearance. He'd always said that was enough for him, a boyhood dream come true. He was too brainy to be a footballer anyway, so he'd finished his economics degree and drifted away from the game.

Giuliano was the Piedmontese archetype. He was diligent, undemonstrative and resourceful, and his CV was testament to that. Now he and Boniperti bumped into one another at Sunday mass, and Boni offered him a job. Boniperti claims he never told him *which* job, but Giuliano agreed anyway, and for the next two decades he'd be Juve's *éminence grise*. Nothing of significance would happen without him, and he'd take care of all the humdrum stuff Boni wasn't cut out for.

While Giuliano busied himself off camera, general manager Italo Allodi set to on the hard-nosed practicalities of procuring success in Italian football. He'd worked with Herrera during Inter's hegemony, and was widely regarded as the Italian game's greatest administrator, transfer specialist and fixer. Stories of the refs he had corrupted were already legion, and it's scarcely credible that Inter not conceding a single penalty in 100 games was coincidental. Though he always denied it, Milan's jewellers and fine-art dealers are thought to have appreciated his patronage a very great deal. It speaks volumes about the Italian game that he continued in gainful employment for 30 years, and that the governing body of the sport saw fit to induct him into its hall of fame in 2017.

It also says a lot about Boniperti's ambitions for Juve that he employed Allodi, not least because he didn't particularly like him. It suggests that old *semplicita, serieta e sobrieta* ideal had been sacrificed on the altar of pragmatism. Boniperti knew full well what Allodi was about, and what he was about was winning at all costs. If Luciano Moggi is widely held to have been Italian football's shadiest operator, it's because Allodi, whom the World-Cup-winning trainer Enzo Bearzot called Brutus, taught him everything he knew. Allodi it was who gave Moggi his first meaningful job in football, as a talent scout for Juventus. Prior to that Moggi had worked on the railways, like Allodi's dad. His travel heavily subsidised, Moggi had spent his spare time roaming around central Italy looking for talented kids to recommend to big football clubs. Boniperti had Moggi down as a wrong'un, and legend has it he was banned even from entering his office. That said, Moggi discovered the legends Paolo Rossi and Claudio Gentile, the sharp-elbowed Italian stopper par excellence who would play over 400 games in black and white.

In the here and now, the club appointed Armando Picchi as coach. Under Herrera he had emerged as Inter's captain and undisputed leader on and off the pitch. At 35 he was the youngest coach in Serie A, but was universally respected by his peers. The winning blueprint had been drawn up at Inter, and Boniperti knew that if it were to be replicated in Turin, Picchi and Allodi were the men best qualified to do it.

The weakness of the squad they inherited was demonstrated by Mexico '70. With Anastasi unable to travel due to a testicular problem, the club had only one representative at the World Cup, the reserve Furino. Italy performed splendidly in reaching the final, but the composition of the national squad was highly unusual. Eight years earlier a law had been enacted for the economic redevelopment and 'Italianisation' of Sardinia, the country's poorest and most desolate outpost. In building the largest oil refinery in the Mediterranean, Inter's president Moratti had kick-started the industrialisation of the island. New money had flooded in, and now Cagliari boasted six *Azzurri* and, for the first and only time, a Serie-A-winning team. There were also two players from Napoli (Juliano and reserve goalkeeper Dino Zoff) and two from a resurgent Toro.

For eight years, Luis 'the postman' del Sol had been Juventus' midfield redoubt, a great player manfully shoring up some pretty ordinary sides. Now, though, he was 35, and so Allodi did a deal with Roma. The details are still somewhat opaque, but in practical terms Juve replaced one old pro with three new ones. Luciano Spinosi was a promising 20-year-old defender, Fabio Capello a resourceful and authoritative midfielder, Fausto Landini a gangly teenage striker. Landini would disappear without trace, but Spinosi and Capello would become pillars of the new Juve. So would Franco Causio, a winger from Lecce down in Puglia. The fans nicknamed him 'the baron' partly for his moustachioed, aristocratic appearance, but also because his play was intelligent, mannered and precise. He'd delight them for eleven years before signing off with a World Cup winner's medal in 1982.

On 27 September 1970, Juve began the season down in Anastasi's Catania. They had eight starters under the age of 25, and debutant Roberto Bettega scored a highly portentous winning goal. Bettega was a class act, and this new team would be inspired by the strike partnership he and Anastasi created. Rational and austere like the city of his birth, Roberto 'Bobby gol' Bettega was the son of a FIAT *operaio*. Although he'd always eschew the traditional number 9 shirt in favour of the 11, no Italian striker was ever better in the air. Few possessed a right foot as adroit either, so while Anastasi was a very fine player for the club, it's fair to say that Bettega would become a genuinely great one. In an era of low-scoring football he'd accumulate 130 league goals, and for a decade he'd assume Boniperti's old mantle as Juve's champion, factotum and kingpin.

Off the pitch, he and Anastasi were as different as sober Turin and tumultuous Catania. Anastasi was warm-hearted, generous of spirit and pig-ugly, Bettega detached and Marlboro-man handsome. They were black and white, and that was entirely the point. Their partnership had no right to work, but on every imaginable level it just did.

Progress was being made, but by November Picchi was complaining of back pain. By January he was no longer able to work, and by February he'd been diagnosed with a tumour in his spinal column. In his stead the club appointed one of their own. Having survived Dachau, the Czech Čestmír Vycpálek had joined Juve in 1946. He'd only spent a season there, but had carved out a successful career with Parma and Palermo. He'd stayed on in Sicily, but Boniperti liked him a great deal. It was impossible not to, and Cesto had been invited to coach the youth section the previous season. Now Boniperti asked him to replace Picchi, and he accepted. The players liked him, and in rallying round him they sustained Picchi insofar as they were able.

While Inter and Milan had two European Cups apiece, Juve's record in European competition had been abysmal. The club had reached the Fairs Cup final in the formative years of the competition, but then so had Birmingham City. The results had been as dispiriting as the Turin public's indifference, but this was a new team and a new start. They defeated Barcelona over two legs in the second round, and were comfortable against the Hungarian side Pésci in the third. In the last eight they scraped by Dutch outfit Twente Enschede with two extra-time goals from Anastasi, and reached the final by seeing off Cologne at a packed Comunale.

For Armando Picchi, each win for Juventus had been a palliative of sorts, but on 26 May 1971 he passed away. That evening the team he'd helped to build entertained Leeds at the Comunale, but with the pitch waterlogged the referee called it off after 56 goalless minutes. On the day of his funeral they reconvened, but the Englishmen twice came from behind to force a draw and began the second leg as overwhelming favourites.

Anastasi levelled Allan Clarke's opener, but the ref denied Juve a penalty when Billy Bremner appeared to catch Haller. Leeds hung on to win on the new away-goals rule and Juve, who hadn't lost a single match in the competition, failed to scratch a 20-year itch. They drew nine of their last ten league games – bit weird, that – but fourth in Serie A wasn't too shabby for such a young side. A decent 1970–71, then, but '71–72 would be one of the best in Serie A history. One of the best and, because they're two sides of the same coin, one of the very worst ...

Cagliari were financed by Milanese petrochemical money; Toro had an exciting new team, and in Gianni Rivera Milan had arguably Europe's most talented player. Juve had the same roster as the previous season, but from February no Bettega. He was struck down with pleurisy, and for a while it seemed he might not play again. Cesto plugged the gap by redeploying Haller up front, and the net result was that Capello, his erstwhile partner in midfield, exerted more influence on the games.

So much for Serie A's glittering cast. As ever their talent was all eclipsed – or at least besmirched – by the perennial *Sturm und Drang* about refereeing decisions, refereeing standards and refereeing propriety. It would come to a head one unhinged afternoon in March, defile the sport as never before, and Juve would emerge as the big winners.

With ten games remaining, the *classifica* was as follows.

Juventus	29 points
Torino	27 points
Milan	27 points
Cagliari	26 points

Juve were at Bologna, and trailed 1–0 with 20 minutes remaining. The *bolognesi* were aggrieved that Morini hadn't been sent off, Juve that they'd been denied two penalties.

All 22 players agreed that the pitch was unfit for purpose, and *Tuttosport* had it right in describing it as a 'rugby match'. Juve's equaliser made the point perfectly. They were awarded a free kick on the left, but as Causio crossed, Furino appeared first to elbow Perini in the kidneys and then to wrestle Adani, Anastasi's marker, to the ground. Pietruzzu headed home unmarked, and a minute later Marchetti completed the comeback to secure the points.

Over at Sampdoria, Toro were initially denied an equaliser following a header which finished a good foot over the line. The players urged the ref to consult the linesman, and having done so he awarded it. The Samp' players promptly besieged the lino', and the ref, Enzo Barbaresco, changed his mind again. He re-disallowed the goal he'd just undisallowed, and completed his *opera d'arte* by sending off the Toro captain Giorgio Ferrini for protesting.

Under a deluge in Cagliari, the hosts and Milan were level at 1–1 with three minutes remaining. There was a gentle coming-together on the edge of the Milan box, and the referee alone saw an infringement. Milan's Riccardo Sogliano, hopping mad, was sent off for dissent, and Cagliari scored the pen'. Gianni Rivera was apoplectic. Emerging from the tunnel he claimed that the ref had 'awarded 80 fouls against us and laughed in our faces when we tried to protest'. He then accused the referees' association of corruption, asserting that this was the third championship they'd stolen from Milan. He said that while Giulio Campanati was in charge it 'couldn't be otherwise' and that he was past caring whether or not they sanctioned him. 'Milan,' he concluded, 'would need a nine-point start to win the title, because seven wouldn't be enough. I've heard they're paying the refs before the games these days.' Sogliano added that the referee would be 'sorry for having awarded a penalty like that', and that sort of talk had quite sinister overtones back then.

The association opened an inquiry, *Caso Rivera* became front-page news, and at times it seemed was the *only* news. But, as usual nothing of substance happened, and the net result was that Rivera, the messenger, was shot summarily, publicly and uselessly. He was banned for the final five weeks of the season; Milan's title challenge ran aground once more, and the *calcio* merry-go-round whirred on regardless.

On Friday 5 May 1972, Cesto Vycpálek's son, 28-year-old Čestmír Junior, boarded a flight at Rome Fiumicino. Like many of the 108 passengers he was travelling home to vote in Sunday's general election, but he never made it. Three miles from Palermo, Alitalia AZ112 crashed into Monte Lunga, and there were no survivors. On the eve of the funeral, his father's team hosted second-placed Cagliari at a sold-out Comunale. Sixteen minutes from time, with the score at 1–1, *siciliano* Anastasi received a pass from *sardo* Cuccureddu on the left-hand edge of the Cagliari box. He skipped by Niccolai and, as Cera closed in, got a match-winning left-footed shot away into the corner of the net. After the match he spoke tearfully of the pact the players had made among themselves before kick-off. The win, he said, was for Cesto and because of Cesto. Three weeks later, Haller and Spinosi scored within the space of five first-half minutes against Vicenza – that old Allodi magic – this most dramatic of championships was theirs.

Winners or otherwise, the team had been short of a top-class keeper for a few years now, so when Boniperti sat down with the brothers Agnelli to discuss the club's title defence strategy, it amounted to convincing Napoli to sell them theirs at whatever cost. Allodi called Corrado Ferlaino, the Napoli president, and arranged a meeting.

As a 15-year-old, Dino Zoff had undergone a trial at a Juventus boys' club in his native Friuli, but they'd decided he hadn't been big enough to keep goal. So had Inter, and a very Italian legend has it that his grandmother had intervened at that point. *Nonna* had prescribed a diet of eggs, eggs and more eggs, and the results had been miraculous. He'd shot up, earned a contract at Udinese and kept right on all the way to Serie A Mantova. Then to Napoli and Italia '68, a silver medal at Mexico '70 and finally, having usurped Cagliari's Albertosi, a regular starting berth for the *Azzurri*.

Napoli had been on fringes of the title race here and there, but they'd never broken the northern stranglehold. The city was beautiful but underdeveloped, and many in the north argued that, while technically and geographically it was Italian, it remained a different country. Literacy levels still lagged behind, life expectancy was short, living standards pitiable. So while Cagliari seduced players with promises of clean air, sandy beaches and obscene riches, Ferlaino's side tended to attract promising youngsters and guys, like Sívori, whose best years were behind them. In common with other football-mad port cities like Liverpool and Marseilles, Naples' 'island' reputation defined it. For a century it had been synonymous with violence, vulgarity and squalor, and that kind of thing takes generations to wash through. It wasn't the football club's fault, but to most Italians it was a good place to escape from.

Anyway, Napoli had won only six league games the previous season, and this had had a disastrous effect on attendances. Ferlaino therefore saw no option but to deconstruct the team and build a new, fresh-faced one in the hope that it would entice the Neapolitan public back.

Boniperti would have expected to pay upwards of 800 million lire for Zoff, a world-class 30-year-old goalkeeper in the prime of his career. In the event he got him for 330 million and Juve's current incumbent Pietro Carmignani, whom he was looking to offload anyway. Ferlaino threw in veteran striker José Altafini as well. He'd won a World Cup winners' medal with Brazil in 1958, but he was still contributing even at the age of 34. Giving him away would probably have made sense if his legs had gone and Juve were paying a realistic price for Zoff, but they hadn't and they weren't. Ostensibly it was an awful deal for Napoli, so what was Ferlaino playing at?

Although Italo Allodi's ethics were debatable, nobody was in any doubt that he was an outstanding wheeler-dealer. He'd been central to Herrera's success at Inter, and he'd just repeated the trick in Turin. Nothing moved in Italian football without him knowing about it first, and his genius for the *calciomercato* had acquired shaman-istic qualities. Everything he touched seemed to turn to gold.

Corrado Ferlaino had only recently bought Napoli, and he was extremely ambitious. He therefore did a deal which worked for Juve in the short term and which would later transform the city of Naples and the whole of Italian football. Allodi shook hands on the basis that, when the time was right, he'd do for Ferlaino's Napoli what he'd done for Moratti's Inter and now Agnelli's Juve. He'd keep his promise and would build the supporting cast when Diego Maradona touched down in Naples 12 years later. Nobody knew it at the time, but Ferlaino's apparent folly in flogging off the family silver represented a down payment on Napoli's first *Scudetto*.

Dino Zoff wasn't much of a talker. He was, however, intelligent enough not to overthink his job, and he'd no interest in showing off. He was the strong, silent type, and there was always a sense of economy about the way he kept goal. He was a serious athlete, and it's incontestable that he would become the most iconic goalkeeper in Europe. While it's safe to say that Juve was evolving under Boniperti and Allodi, if ever a player epitomised the old *semplicita, serieta e sobrieta*, it was Zoff.

Some argue that Gigi Buffon was a better keeper for Juve, but it's undeniable that Zoff's acquisition was among the best business Allodi ever did. He wouldn't miss a league match in 11 seasons, and he'd break goalkeeping records like no one else. He hardly ever dropped a clanger, seldom made bad decisions, and his equanimity reassured those in front of him. He was famously careful with money and very well understood his value to Juve. It was inestimable, and goodness knows what he'd be worth in today's marketplace.

At the jeweller's, with four beautiful young women

As a young man, I was friendly with a top linesman. He was forever flying off for big European games, and at a certain point he told me he'd been selected to officiate in a massive match in Turin. When he got home he explained in bemused detail what had happened to him. Because it was nearly 30 years ago I can only really remember the bones of it, and there are libel laws I don't want to fall foul of. So apologies in advance for the rather sketchy nature of what follows, but it's all true and hopefully you'll get the gist.

Essentially a guy in the employ of the hosts collected my pal and his colleagues, and drove them into town. They were met by four beautiful young women; they ate copiously and lavishly, and then, because they had time to kill, the guy said he'd show them the sights. It turned out that by 'the sights' he didn't mean the jaw-dropping beauty of Palazzo Carignano or the peerless baroque majesty of the Church of the Consolata. What he meant was the designer boutiques on Via Roma and the jewellers in Via Cavour. One of the girls told my lino mate that everything was 'at their disposal', and the tailor, the jeweller and the watchmaker were instructed to take their measurements. They were obliged to try stuff on, the whole thing started to become ludicrous. Their host was massively overdoing it with the 'hospitality', but they didn't know what to do and they'd no choice but to play along. They were in a foreign city, and they found themselves in a situation they couldn't get out of.

During the match one of the visitors went down under a challenge just inside the box. It was a penalty, and the ref, perfectly placed, duly awarded it. It was converted, and the visitors left with a positive result. I can't remember what my friend said happened after the match, but the essence was that their host was nowhere to be seen.

Presumably he was busy elsewhere, because they never saw him again.

Where were we?

On 11 April 1973, Brian Clough's Derby came to Turin for the European Cup semi-final first leg. At the conclusion of an ill-tempered first half it was 1–1. Entering the tunnel, the ref, Gerhard Schulenburg, was in light-hearted conversation with Haller, Juve's German substitute. Clough's assistant Peter Taylor didn't much like that, and he and Haller started pushing one another. The two of them had to be pulled apart, and the ill-feeling continued in the second half. The game was littered with (Derby) fouls, and Juve ran out 3–1 winners.

Someone counted and said that Schulenburg had awarded 42 free kicks to Juve and 19 to Derby. Clough was incensed and initially stated that he'd speak to the media for 'no more than five minutes'. Then, however, he and Taylor launched into a tirade against Juventus and the referee. He told the visiting John Charles to advise the press that he wouldn't be speaking to 'any cheating Italian bastards', which was not a little awkward for big John. When he declined to translate, Clough famously prevailed upon the Italian-based journalist Brian Glanville.

Taylor claimed that Derby had 'played against 12 men'. He suggested that Schulenburg's having booked Gemmill and McFarland, both as a result now suspended for the second leg, had been no accident: 'Maybe he had a list of the players who were on a booking.' When Clough said sarcastically, 'The Juventus coach probably motivated his players well at half-time,' Taylor interjected once more, 'There's a Portuguese ref for the second leg. Maybe someone from Juventus will go to Lisbon and try to buy a player there.' One would like to assume no one did but, without the stars Gemmill and McFarland, Derby never laid a glove on them at the Baseball Ground. The better-off Juve *tifosi* made for the travel agents and booked their flights to Belgrade for the final.

Four days before the final league games of the season, Rivera's Milan travelled to Thessaloníki for the Cup Winners' Cup final. Their opponents were another of those poor, gullible, bovine English sides. The perception at home was that Don Revie's Leeds were a pretty hard-nosed bunch, but here they were made to appear positively Corinthian. They conceded from a questionable free kick after five minutes and spent the next eighty-five camped in the Milan half. Aided and abetted by a sublimely bad Greek referee named Christos Michas, the *rossoneri* hung on for one of the greatest miscarriages of footballing justice in history.

Michas was so crooked that even the locals turned on him at the final whistle. Rocco, the Milan coach, admitted that he'd been 'the best player on the pitch', and so too, in a roundabout way, did the (Italian) president of UEFA. Artemio Franchi was a champion glad-hander, and he felt that Michas was to be 'commended'. Later, with the trophy safely domiciled at the San Siro, Michas was investigated and banned for life. In that sense a form of justice was seen to be done (though not if you were a Leeds fan), but the wider issue was the nature of the Italian game. Notwithstanding Rivera's outburst at Cagliari and subsequent ban, corrupting officials was intrinsic to it. Nothing and nobody was off-limits.

Milan had secured a win in Greece, but the big prize lay in wait for them at Verona's Bentigodi stadium. They'd led Serie A by five points in April, but were haemorrhaging goals and points in the run-in. They still led by a single point though, and needed only to beat Verona to wrap up the double. Juve and surprise package Lazio were a point behind, and each would conclude with visits to mid-table sides. Juve travelled down to misfiring Roma, Lazio to Napoli.

Milan needed just one more big shove, but their nerve failed them completely. They conceded three times in the first half, while Juve went in 1–0 down at a packed Stadio Olimpico. With Lazio goalless in Naples, Serie A was a virtual dead heat between them and Milan, with Juve a virtual point behind.

(Here's where it starts to get quite murky, but see if you can follow it anyway.)

At half-time the Roma president, Gaetano Anzaloni, made his way down to his side's changing room. According to club captain Franco Cordova, he complimented the players on having taken the lead but then urged them to lose it as soon as possible. They'd nothing to play for; he needed to keep Juve onside in view of the upcoming *calciomercato*, and if that hurt Lazio's *Scudetto* chances then so much the better.

Meanwhile, down in Naples, a delegation from Lazio were in conversation with their Neapolitan counterparts. So the story goes, when the Lazio contingent enquired as to whether Napoli were amenable to a deal, they were rebuffed. They'd already done one elsewhere, and they were men of their word.

Three-way parity was restored on the hour. Substitutes had been introduced to the Italian game in 1966. Initially they'd been used exclusively to replace injured players, but Altafini's arrival at Juventus had changed all that. While he struggled to do the full 90 minutes, he was still clever and dynamite over ten metres. He had replaced Haller at the break, and headed in his 200th career goal. With three minutes remaining Juve were awarded a corner, and you can guess the rest. The ball broke to Cuccureddu on the edge of the box, and he belted it in. Next Lazio – bidding to be hanged for a sheep rather than a lamb – got done on the break in Naples, and Milan finished 5–3 losers.

Juve had their *Scudetto*, while Lazio's legendary season is remembered as a manful struggle against two much bigger, much more affluent football clubs. Their failure had been heroic, but not so Milan's. They'd just bottled it. Again.

That last day is etched into the collective memory of Italian football, and with good reason. While Roma skipper Cordova denies going easy in the second half, he doesn't deny having been *instructed* to by his chairman. Besides he was one of eleven, and he can't possibly be sure that all his team-mates were similarly committed. It may very well be that some of the Roma players followed their chairman's instructions, and there's ample evidence suggesting they did. Shortly before his death in 2011, former Roma defender Giovanni Bertini is alleged to have said that on this occasion five of his team-mates took bribes. That may or may not be true, and that's kind of the point. Nobody really knows what to believe, though everyone believes there was some sort of deal. It may also be that someone extraneous to Napoli (or Verona) paid their players to turn up. You'd like to think that as professional athletes they wouldn't have needed any extra incentive, but that would be to misunderstand Italy and the Italians.

Juve being Juve, the European Cup final in Belgrade turned out to be a damp squib. There was no shame in being beaten by the great Ajax side of Cruyff, Johnny Rep and Neeskens, just proof that there were some referees that money couldn't buy. It couldn't quite buy the Coppa Italia either, as Milan won the final on penalties. It was a pyrrhic victory in light of their epic Serie A failure, but two cup competitions in one season was a decent return on whatever they'd invested in Michas and his colleagues. So much for Rivera's assertions that they were handicapped by corrupt match officials.

With Rivera's best days behind him, Milan's star would wane the following season. In 1974 Juve finished second, as Lazio, a Serie B side only two years earlier, led thrillingly from post to wire. The day after the season finished a classic Serie A *giallo* revealed itself. Antonio Fesce, the president of relegated Foggia, found himself in a bit of a tight spot. His team had needed to beat Milan on the final day to stay up, but had drawn 0–0 at home. After the match Foggia's fans had attempted to burn down their own stadium, and that hadn't been ideal. Fesce wasn't about to take relegation lying down though, because as he saw it his club had been the victims of a monumental miscarriage of justice. Not only had the ref failed to award them a stonewall penalty, but he had information that his counterpart at Verona had bought their game against Napoli to beat the drop. And so began the famous *Scandolo della Telefonata*. Here we go again ...

The Verona president, Saverio Garonzi, was a tremendously able Italian football administrator. One of his former players, Brazilian Sergio Clerici, was on the books at Napoli. He was also at the fag end of his career, so Garonzi had called him up before the game and, according to Fesce's sources, offered him a leg-up. Clerici was minded to return home to Brazil when he retired, and Garonzi had told him that he could set him up with a FIAT dealership if Napoli allowed themselves to be beaten. They had been beaten, 1–0, and as a consequence Verona had stayed up at Foggia's expense.

Fesce demanded an inquiry, and it turned out Garonzi was bang to rights. Clerici came clean; Verona were stripped of the points, and Foggia leapfrogged them in the table to survive.

It had seemed like a smart move on Fesce's part but then, in the interests of fairness, the inquiry spoke to the referee from Foggia's final game against Milan. He remembered that before the game he'd found himself in conversation with Fesce's secretary, who had offered him and his linesmen a nice watch apiece. The upshot was that Fesce's Foggia joined Garonzi's Verona in Serie B, and Sampdoria, who'd begun the season with a three-point penalty for 'fiscal irregularities' and had finished second-bottom, stayed up.

There's a bloke from Foggia who lives just across the way from me. He tells me Fesce's '*un grande*', and that they recently named a street after him.

Italy failed at the 1974 World Cup in West Germany. A side containing six *Juventini* was eliminated in the group stage by Poland, and Allodi accepted a job at the federation to sort it all out. Boniperti put Cesto out to pasture and prevailed upon another old mucker. The great Carletto Parola signed up for a third stint as manager; crowd favourite Anastasi got the captain's armband, and the retiring Salvadore was replaced by an elegant young sweeper. Gaetano Scirea had been uncovered by Moggi, and he wouldn't have looked out of place in the revelatory Dutch side beaten in Munich by the hosts.

In December, Juve travelled to high-flying Naples for the legendary 'tennis match', a 6–2 win regarded as one of their greatest. It was watched by over 90,000 – still a Serie A record – and by all accounts Juve played something approaching total football. When they put five past Vicenza in May 1975, the Agnellis had their third *Scudetto* in four years.

This Juve team was very good, but for Gianni and Umberto there was trouble – lots and lots and lots of it – ahead.

Chapter 6

The Years of Lead

To be an enemy of America can be dangerous, but to be a friend is fatal.

Henry Kissinger

In purgatory, with Gianni and Umberto

The team's European misadventures aside, Juventus was a sanctuary for the Agnelli brothers. Umberto's marriage to Antonella Bechi Piaggio was broken (he'd remarry the following year), and Gianni's management skills were being tested as never before. Unlike Valletta he tended towards spontaneity in his decision-making, but this was a time for prudence. The 1973 oil crisis had seen a four-fold increase in petrol prices, and that, allied to a series of strategic mistakes, had seen the company post a loss for the first time. FIAT was Europe's biggest car maker, but far from its best.

Gianni's ambition had always been to rival the US giants Ford and General Motors, but he'd failed to get the Citroën deal over the line and the business had become shockingly inefficient. He'd assumed he could handle

the unions by being nice to them, but he was a bourgeois Agnelli and they weren't. Their negotiators didn't
own villas on the Côte d'Azur, didn't flounce around
on boats with Jackie Kennedy, and didn't own oils by
Renoir, Matisse and Canaletto. Gianni's diplomatic skills
stood him in good stead when dealing with expansive
American capitalists, but he was out of his depth with
union officials. In attempting to ingratiate himself with
them he made a huge miscalculation, and the more
money he threw at them the more they demanded. The
balance of power swung from the company to the workforce, and labour costs soared. By 1974 productivity was
down 25 per cent, and the *operai* were joking that they
were 'spending all day' at FIAT as distinct to working
there.

Italians like to joke that the FIAT acronym stands for
'Fix it again, Toni,' and that's a testament to a downward
spiral in perceived quality. FIAT had always been good
at producing cheap cars, but now it had need of new and
better models. It needed to invest in technology, research
and development, and it needed build quality and mes-
saging to compete with the Germans, the Swedes and
the French. Instead Gianni, who much preferred quixotic ideas to dreary detail, focused on the things he liked
to do. He decided he wanted to diversify away from
the core car business, but with 300,000 unsold vehicles
in stock and sales in free fall, the wisdom of that was
questionable.

At times he couldn't do right for doing wrong. That
hadn't really mattered in the past, because he'd been a
playboy and a joker. Now people looked to him for
solutions, and every mistake he made had serious and

palpable consequences. FIAT had 112 separate cost centres, and nobody quite knew which of them made money. That said, it was abundantly clear that the major one – automotive – was losing it hand over fist.

It was a mess, and Gianni, who'd never had to fight for anything in his life, was openly discussing chucking it all in and moving to America. Eventually he resolved to knuckle down and assumed the presidency of the Italian employers' federation Confundustria. There he'd do an inflation-linked pay deal with the unions which would almost prostrate the Italian economy. It increased the cost of imports by forcing the devaluation of the lire, but the consequence was that FIATs became more affordable abroad.

Umberto, on the other hand, jumped ship. He'd always fancied politics, and with the company in trouble he decided the time was right to extricate himself from his role as CEO. He'd started a relationship with Allegra Caracciolo, a member of an old Neapolitan noble family, and Rome represented an escape from the Turin goldfish bowl and from a failing business. The company appointed one of his old classmates in his stead. Carlo De Benedetti's recovery plan was relatively straightforward. The company was overstaffed and undercapitalised and had layer upon disastrous layer of useless middle management. He told the board that there would have to be mass redundancies, perhaps as many as 65,000 globally. The unions wouldn't like that, and the lawyers would be kept busy as a consequence. However, the unions were destroying the business from the inside anyway, and if they didn't act there'd be nothing left to save. There'd be a cash injection by way of a share issue, and that would enable them to get new models onto the books. There'd be no dividends until the business returned to profit, but for that to happen management would have to be re-centralised and tightly controlled. This all made absolute sense, but De Benedetti hadn't factored in the *realpolitik* around the Agnellis.

Gianni and Umberto had run FIAT for themselves and their coterie. They'd always been profligate with money, and that profligacy had permeated the running of the business. For much of the extended family and their hangers-on, it was essentially a provider of free money. Gianni knew this but was disinclined to do anything about it. Nor did he have it in him to play second fiddle to De Benedetti. Intellectually he understood that the business needed to be rethought and restructured, and deep down he must have known he couldn't do it himself. There was too much history though, and he was too concerned with his own place in it all. For all sorts of reasons, he couldn't cope with the reality of ceding control to an outsider.

Moreover, there was more at stake now than the balance sheet. The 1962 demonstrations in Piazza Statuto had been just the start of it. They'd mutated into widespread – and ongoing – strikes in a country and a continent undergoing tectonic change. Vietnam and the Prague Spring had generated a maelstrom, and Italian politics in particular had been radicalised. Right-wing terrorists had planted a bomb which killed 17 in Milan in November 1969, and several left-wing paramilitary groups, most notably the Red Brigades, had come into existence.

FIAT was a leviathan of Italian capitalism, so an obvious target. Communist activists had made it their business to infiltrate the shop floors at Mirafiori, Lingotto
and Rivalta, while the militant Lotta Continua group,
so powerful that it published its own daily newspaper,
represented the greatest threat of all. Aided by the CIA,
FIAT senior management had developed a secret operation designed to root out the more malign elements, but
it had been uncovered. The company, it transpired, had
files containing 350,000 documents detailing the political orientation and activities of its staff. It's important
to note that Umberto and Gianni were never directly
implicated, and it's quite possible that they knew nothing about it. Possible, but perhaps not probable.

The Turin branch of Lotta Continua was centred on
Falchera Nuova, an estate of prefabricated dwellings
on the northern edge of the city. There lived Tonino
Miccichè from Sicily. A 24-year-old FIAT *operaio* and
Lotta Continua activist, he'd been incarcerated for chucking Molotov cocktails in 1973. While inside he'd gone on
hunger strike, and he and his co-defendants had eventually been released.

Having lost his job at FIAT, Miccichè had devoted
himself to securing social justice for the residents of
Falchera Nuova. It had earned him the nickname 'the
mayor of Falchera', and he'd clashed with members of a
right-wing vigilante group. In April 1975 he fell out with
one of them, a 41-year-old *pugliese* named Paolo Fiocco,
over a garage the latter was occupying illegally. Fiocco
was told that Lotta Continua was commandeering it for
one of the residents, and the whole thing escalated into

a turf war. On 17 April, Fiocco shot Miccichè dead in the street.

In isolation, Miccichè's assassination doesn't seem particularly important. He was a nobody in a nothing part of town, but the point is that it didn't happen in isolation. It happened because everything was now politicised and because extreme violence was the new normal. The *anni di piombo* – Italy's 'years of lead' – had begun, and nothing would ever be the same again.

On 11 September Gianni Agnelli's daughter, 20-year-old Margherita, married the writer Alain Elkann. His mother, Carla Ovazza, was 53. She worked as a tour guide and lived in a small apartment with her second husband and their 15-year-old son. She'd joked, 'Now we're related to the Agnellis, let's hope we don't become too important!' Two months later she'd become more important than she – or anybody else – could possibly have imagined. Arriving home from work on the evening of Wednesday 26 November, she parked her car beneath her flat as normal, and simply vanished.

Carla had been kidnapped because she was an Agnelli now, and Gianni knew it. From here on in, every decision he'd make would need be informed by the violence, and by the threat of violence. People like him would live in genuine fear for their lives, so much so that he's believed to have carried a cyanide capsule in case of kidnap. He knew that De Benedetti was right about restructuring the business, but he worried that if he laid off thousands of *operai*, the terrorists would come for his family, his friends and his staff. He signed an agreement with the unions granting them partial responsibility for the running of the business. It cost him a fortune, but he hoped that the bone he was throwing them would buy off the terrorists. Maybe they'd think twice before trying to assassinate him and Umberto or kidnap their kids. Maybe, but maybe not.

His political career stillborn, Umberto made it known that he was minded to return to the fold. De Benedetti was paid off handsomely and left quietly, and the brothers were in it together once more. Turin was, though, a place of intolerance, darkness and fear, a city of violence and of strangers. The beneficiaries of the economic boom, the architects of modern Italy, lived cosseted lives behind wrought-iron gates on tree-lined avenues. While Gianni Agnelli took a helicopter to the roof of Lingotto of a morning, the blue collars seemed hell bent on tearing one another apart. Humble accountants, engineers and secretaries had to utilise armed escorts in order simply to get to work. How had it come to this?

As Turin lawyers, police officers and journalists were murdered in cold blood, as FIAT security officers, directors, managers and workers were slaughtered for simply going about their daily business, the struggle for Italy's soul continued.

La Lotta continuava ...

At the Comunale, with the goal twins

On 6 December 1975, Umberto became a father again. Allegra gave birth to a boy named Andrea, and the city's football teams met at the Comunale the next day. A derby win would have been a great way to celebrate, but Juve fluffed their lines.

Toro finally had a team to be proud of again. In Gigi Radice they had a dynamic new manager, and he'd brought a new swagger to the way they played. Claudio Sala was a strong, skilful, two-footed attacking mid-fielder, a thoroughbred capable of bullying virtually any side out of the game. In front of him the 'goal twins' Paolino Pulici and Francesco 'Ciccio' Graziani were fantastic together.

With Bettega and the old lion Altafini injured, Juve's erstwhile captain Pietro Anastasi had returned to their starting eleven. Parola had upset the fans by sidelining him, but there'd been no obvious adverse effects. On the contrary; Juve were scoring goals and winning games, and fully justified their position as runaway favourites for a 17th *Scudetto*. The football was less spectacular than that of the previous season, but they were still Italy's most complete team. Here though, Toro got about them in a frenzied first half. But for two outstanding Zoff interventions they'd have led at the break, and Parola reacted by hauling Anastasi off once more. Something had to change, so he decided to give Toro something new – substitute Oscar Damiani – to think about. Anastasi left the ground immediately, and his supporters rounded on Parola. In the event Damiani's introduction was irrelevant anyway. Toro carried on where they'd left off, and a Graziani header and Pulici's penalty earned them the points. It was a cracking game, and everyone's second-favourite team had rolled back the years with a stunning victory.

Parola was unrepentant. Anastasi, he said, had been virtually invisible, so his withdrawal hadn't materially changed anything. Derby or otherwise, it was only two points, and the team would dust itself down and carry on regardless. He was right; when they drew with Milan in March, Juve were unbeaten in 13 games. Anastasi had been reduced to the odd cameo, but the old lady led Serie A by five points. To the casual observer all seemed well, but history informs us otherwise ...

Bettega and new captain Furino had coalesced around Parola, while Anastasi had found an ally in Fabio Capello. Following the Milan game, the two of them are thought to have asked for a meeting with Boniperti. Whatever was said, Anastasi didn't even make the bench the following Sunday at Cesena, as Juve lost away for the first time. *La Stampa* called the team's non-performance 'strange', and on the Monday Anastasi felt the need to speak to the press. The situation with Parola had become intolerable, so while he loved Juventus, as things stood he couldn't *stay* at Juventus.

Amid the turmoil there was another derby to be played, this time with Juve as hosts. By half-time they were 2–0 down, and for the first time the fans turned on Boniperti. He'd allowed Allodi to leave, and replaced Cesto with his old mucker Parola. Damiano and even Sergio Gori were always selected over Anastasi, and that was just plain wrong. Amid the tempest a flare, thrown from the stand, hit and temporarily blinded the Toro keeper Castellini. He wasn't able to continue, but Toro won anyway. Fortress Juve had been breached.

The following Sunday Juve lost again, this time at Inter. They'd contrived to turn a five-point lead into a deficit, so, heading into the final weekend, Toro needed only to beat Cesena at the Comunale to realise the impossible dream. Juve, the pantomime villains, travelled to verdant Umbria for a meeting with Perugia. Radice's young side was visibly overawed by the magnitude of it all and could only manage a draw, but they needn't have worried. Juve blew it once again, as Perugia's goalscorer Renato Curi became a hero to the millions of Italians praying for them to trip up. It's quite a schlep to Superga from the city centre, ten uphill kilometres. It's a good two-hour walk if you're fit and strong but, 27 years on from the disaster, they reckon about 250,000 made the pilgrimage.

If there was one thing Giampiero Boniperti hated more than losing, it was losing to Toro. As a young man he'd dreamed of locking horns with Mazzola, Loik and the rest, but he'd never been on the winning side pre-Superga. Subsequent to the tragedy, Juve hadn't lost a *Stracittadina* for seven years, but then Toro's psychological stranglehold had reasserted itself. Even Bettega, seen by many as the arrogant Juve archetype, admitted the club had an 'inferiority complex'. Worst of all for Boniperti was the sense that his team had handed it to the old enemy on a silver platter. Though he denied it publicly, the plain fact was that the business with Anastasi *had* destabilised the dressing room, and the three defeats that had followed *had* been its direct consequence. Although it was undeniable that Toro had a very good side, very few of them would have made a combined Juve–Toro eleven. Juve's had been a breakdown not so much of discipline as humility, and that was intolerable. Poor Carlino Parola was shown the door once more.

Back to square one, with Giovanni Trapattoni

As a child of the bombed-out, scraped-out Milanese hinterlands, Giovanni Trapattoni had known genuine hunger. Unusually for a *milanese*, he'd grown up a Juve fan, his idols Hansen, Præst and Boniperti. That said he'd earned a trial at Milan with his friend Sandro Salvadore. He'd gone on to serve the club with distinction, predominantly as a scurrying midfielder or a clingy man-marker. Wherever he'd played he'd combined energy, enthusiasm and savvy. 'Trap' hadn't been the most expansive footballer, but he'd been a pretty good one.

He'd made his international debut in Boniperti's last game for the *Azzurri*, a friendly against Austria in 1960. He'd gone on to represent his country 17 times, but his finest achievement had probably been the taming of Eusébio in the 1963 European Cup final. For half an hour, the Portuguese had been rampant. He'd opened the scoring and generally made a mug of Victor Benitez, Milan's Peruvian defender. Coach Nereo Rocco had invited Trap to have a go; Eusebio's influence had been curtailed, and Rivera's amplified exponentially. He'd garnered the plaudits and Altafini the winning goals, but Trapattoni's intervention had been pivotal.

When Trap finished playing, his natural authority and diplomacy earned him the assistant manager's job. In Rivera, Milan had been blessed with a major talent, but also a demanding and at times irascible personality. Trapattoni had to mediate between him and Gustavo, Giagnoni, the disciplinarian coach famous for his Cossack hats. He and Rivera struggled to co-exist, and when Rivera failed to show for training for the third time, Giagnoni overplayed his hand by dropping him. He was fired shortly afterwards. *In extremis*, the club installed Trap, and in tandem with Rocco he guided them to third. Despite this, Milan decided not to renew his contract, and he'd agreed to coach Atalanta.

Trapattoni wasn't hugely experienced, but he was a man after Boniperti's heart. He was all about enthusiasm, conviction and zeal, and Boniperti could find nothing in him that he didn't like. They arranged to meet at a hotel on the Milan–Turin motorway, but Trap told him he'd given his word to the Atalanta president Achille Bortolotto. Boniperti told him he'd square it with Bortolotto, and Giovanni Trapattoni became the new coach of Juventus.

Amid an epidemic of dissent, the crowd-pleaser Anastasi was exchanged with a raging but ageing bull of a centre forward. Inter's Roberto Boninsegna had twice been *capocannoniere*. For four years he'd averaged almost a goal a game, and he'd been a big star at Mexico '70. However in the previous two seasons he'd scored only 19 times in 55 starts, and he hadn't played for Italy in two years. He was four years Anastasi's senior, and as an Inter standard bearer he was loathed by Juve fans. Only a churl would deny that Boninsegna had been a good player, but objectively his race looked run. So unpopular was his signing that Juve fans daubed graffiti denouncing it on the walls of Boniperti's house.

Capello was also shunted out – to Milan in exchange for a Juve old boy. As a blond, square-jawed young man, Romeo Benetti had played for a season under HH2.

The club hadn't been convinced, and he'd been sold to Sampdoria. He'd gone on to Milan, and there he'd evolved into a midfield destroyer. Off the pitch, Benetti was a shy guy with a house full of canaries, but on it he was a psycho. Like Boninsegna he was the wrong side of 30, and like Boninsegna he was generally reviled by the opposition's supporters. That, of course, was the very best accolade for a player like him, proof positive that he was doing something right.

He was (in)famous in Italy for the mother of all late 'tackles'. During a 1971 game at the San Siro he'd wrecked the knee of Franco Liguori, a talented young midfielder from Bologna. To all intents and purposes it had finished Liguori's career and had provoked outrage even in the testosterone-fuelled world of football. Benetti had been reported to the police *and* the Ministry for Health, and there'd been a serious debate about his mental stability. He'd escaped serious censure and he was precisely the sort of player Trap wanted in his corner. So too was the workaholic Tuscan Marco Tardelli. He'd be immortalised by *that* goal in the World Cup final of 1982, but already was probably the closest thing to the complete midfielder in Italy. He could do almost everything, and it's no coincidence that his decade in Juve's engine room would be among the club's most fruitful.

Juve began their 1976–77 campaign with a UEFA Cup first leg at Manchester City's Maine Road. They lost 1–0, but Boninsegna's first goal for the club in the second leg saw them through. Having accounted for the blue half of Manchester, he then did for the red. Juve lost 1–0 at Old Trafford, but a brace from him and a belter from Benetti served notice: the two of them weren't going anywhere, and the fans had best get used to the idea.

By now colour TV had come to Italy, but the nightly news made for grim viewing. Ideologically-inspired violence had mutated into a crime wave, with extortion and kidnappings an everyday occurrence. The *Torino bene* in particular were picked off. The teenage son of a TV escapologist disappeared from a village in the hills, while the family of a 51-year-old building entrepreneur paid his ransom to no avail; it would be four years before the cadaver of Adriano Ruscalla was found. In November a bank security guard was murdered in broad daylight, and five armed terrorists from the left-wing Prima Linea demanded FIAT staff hand over shareholder details at gun point. Two directors were kneecapped, the local police chief assassinated …

Between 1973 and 1982, hundreds of Italians would be murdered or maimed, and Turin was the city most afflicted. In 1979 alone, some 32 Italians would be assassinated, the majority by Prima Linea and the Red Brigades. Of those, seven would be *torinesi*, among them FIAT's director of strategic operations Carlo Ghiglieno. He was a good man, but that didn't stop Prima Linea killing him on the steps of his apartment as he went for breakfast with his wife.

With output declining and the violence escalating, the census confirmed a small contraction in Turin's population. It was only a trickle, but over the next 15 years, as the company moved production to cheaper, safer, more mechanised facilities, the southern diaspora was substantially reversed. This, combined with a decreasing birth rate, saw the population tumble by 250,000.

At times it seemed that Gianni's dream of Turin as a great European metropolis was mutating into a hideous dystopia.

It may seem trite, but pride in their two football teams gave people something around which they could coalesce. Juve won the opening seven games of the 1976–77 season, among them a stunning 3–2 success at Milan having been two down. When Italy beat England in a World Cup qualifier in Rome, seven of the starters were *Juventini*, but this Toro side was nothing if not obdurate. On 8 November, Giorgio 'the dam' Ferrini, still today their most emblematic post-Superga player, died aged 37. Ferrini had played 568 times for the club and been central to the creation of this new team. He and Radice had constructed it in his image, and it honoured his memory in the derby. Toro neutered Causio, outplayed Juve once more and won 2–0. The game, though, is remembered for another reason.

In the second half, Benetti stamped on the leg of Castellini, and the Toro keeper stayed down. It was a grotesque 'challenge', whose intent had clearly been to do physical harm to Castellini. As the players gesticulated and the stadium erupted, Zoff ran the length of the pitch. He first upbraided the warring factions and then attempted, à la John Charles, to comfort his stricken counterpart as they stretchered him off. Zoff had done a small thing but, given the general situation, a symbolic one. Turin was a city in crisis, and a city in need of a shared identity. Above all it was a city in need of kindness, and Zoff's act resonated with everyone. Luciano Castellini was his friend and his neighbour, and that mattered a lot.

By late April, when Juve thumped AEK Athens to qualify for the UEFA Cup final, the two Turin sides were locked together 12 points ahead of third-placed Inter. Trap's side had the harder schedule, but Toro blinked with a draw at Lazio. With three games and a two-legged final remaining, Juventus led by a point. Serie A was theirs to lose, and the Holy Grail of a European trophy theirs finally to win. Juve's eleven Italians spluttered through the home leg against Atlético Bilbao's All-Basque team. Tardelli scored the only goal as Boninsegna limped off, but hanging on in Bilbao would be tough; Atlético were a highly accomplished side, San Mamés a notoriously difficult place to play.

In the meantime, Trapattoni's team overcame two major stumbling blocks to the Serie A title: they won superbly at Inter and then nervously at home against Roma. Heading to Bilbao they knew a draw would suffice, and a final-day win at relegation-haunted Sampdoria would immortalise them.

It was a filthy night in the Basque country, but the San Mamés was heaving three hours before kick-off all the same. The players emerged to a wall of sound, but seven minutes in Bettega punctured it with a sensational header. Atlético replied after twelve minutes but needed three now, and three against a side containing Furino, Gentile, Scirea and Zoff was a Herculean task. Juve spent the next 80-odd minutes doing what Italian football teams do better than almost anyone else – defending their 18-yard box resolutely, dutifully and capably. Atlético got a second twelve minutes from time but, try as they might, they couldn't get a third. It had taken 19 years, but the Agnellis finally had an international trophy worthy of their brand. Trapattoni's starting eleven, drawn from eight of the country's twenty regions, remains the only all-Italian *squadra* to win one of the continent's great footballing prizes.

By the time the team bus left San Mamés, visibility was next to nothing. With the airport still closed the following morning, Gianni chartered a private jet out of Biarritz and got them home. On the eve of the final day, *La Stampa* gave away 25,000 Toro flags and 25,000 Juve. The paper sold out by ten o'clock and, uniquely, was reprinted at midday. In Turin, Toro galloped to a three-goal lead against Genoa inside 15 minutes. Juve spluttered through the first half, but on the hour Bettega produced a stunning back-heeled finish. The ref helped them on their way by sending two Samp players off, and Boninsegna finished the job six minutes from time.

The usual debates raged about whether Juve had paid off the officials, the opposition or both, but the broad and the short of it was that Italy's sweetheart was once more her most successful club. Trap and Boniperti had synthesised a very good side, and the beginnings of a great one. Meanwhile Toro were devastated. In 30 Serie A games, they had scored 51 goals and conceded only 14. They'd lost only once and accumulated 15 points more than third-placed Fiorentina. They'd actually won five more games than the previous season, and yet they'd come away with nothing.

That summer, Boniperti did a deal with Mariano Delogu. He was president of Cagliari, and they'd unearthed a live-wire teenage striker named Pietro Paolo Virdis. He and Paolo Rossi, a lithe 21-year-old Tuscan playing for Vicenza, had lit up Serie B with their goals.

Rossi had started his career at Juve, but knee problems had hampered his progress. The club had retained a 50 per cent stake in him, but thought Virdis the better bet to replace Boninsegna.

Sardi are famously insular and famously – at times hilariously – obstinate. They refer to Italy as 'the continent', implying it has nothing whatsoever to do with them, their sheep or their implacable stony landscape. Young Virdis, dyed in Sardinia's famous wool, was highly intelligent, but also as stubborn as a *sardo* mule. He told Delogu he wasn't going because he'd heard that Turin was noisy, dangerous and strange. Sardinia was his home and the *sardi* his people, and he wasn't interested in being somewhere else. Boniperti loved that, and the more the kid dug his heels in the more he relished the challenge of snaring him. Boni being Boni, he got him on a flight eventually, but Virdis being Virdis he hated Turin and couldn't settle. The mononucleosis he contracted didn't help, and Juve would wind up loaning him back to Cagliari after three fairly miserable seasons.

No such problems for a precocious teenage left-back named Antonio Cabrini. He came from Cremona, along the Po valley, and Juve had optioned his signature two years earlier. Cabrini was a converted winger, and he'd something approaching Causio's technical ability. Conventional wisdom has it that Paolo Maldini was Italy's best ever full-back, but Cabrini was its most innovative. He was a watertight defender with a whippy tackle, but he'd discover attacking possibilities hitherto unimagined for a *terzino*. Moreover, at a time when soccer was overwhelmingly a male preserve, *Il Bell'Antonio*

enchanted millions of Italian women. When he got off
the team bus they'd throw their knickers at him.

Juve won the 1977–78 Serie A title and reached the
European Cup semi-final (they folded in Bruges as
Gentile got himself sent off for handball), but the season
was touched by tragedy on and off the pitch. In October
they had travelled to Perugia, site eighteen months earlier
of the final-day defeat which had cost them the championship. Popular midfielder Renato Curi had scored the
winner that day, but now he collapsed to the turf having
suffered a heart attack. He was stretchered from the field,
but died shortly afterwards aged just 24.

Acts of barbarity were so commonplace as to be barely
newsworthy in Turin. However, the kidnapping of four-
year-old Giorgio Garbero, grandson of the Toro president Pianelli, provoked revulsion. He was a *child*, for
Christ's sake, and what kind of ideology condones an act
like that? They paid the ransom and got him back after
a month, but this was a country in the grip of a nervous
breakdown.

On the morning of 16 March 1978, The Red Brigades
assassinated five of Aldo Moro's bodyguards and kidnapped Italy's former prime minister and foremost political figure. Juve clinched the championship on 7 May, but
by then Moro had been captive for 53 days and The Red
Brigades had issued their ultimatum. They'd demanded
that 16 of their members be released in exchange for the
prisoner, but the state had refused to negotiate. To capitulate to extremists would signal the end of democracy,
and Italy 'would not yield'. Two days later, Moro's corpse

was bundled into the back of a Renault 4 and abandoned on a Roman side street.

Italy's '55 days of fire' had run their terrible course, but not so the years of lead. The Red Brigades had generally been tolerated by the extreme left. Some believed the armed struggle was entirely legitimate, others that it was a necessary evil. The killing of Moro, however, was a watershed. It alienated ordinary Italians and trashed any hope the communist party had of achieving power.

As a young man, Guido Rossa had worked at FIAT. Then he'd moved to Genoa, found a job at the Italsider metalworks and, as a card-carrying communist, joined the union. In his spare time he was a mountaineer, and by all accounts he was a popular member of the workforce. He was 33 and his daughter, Sabina, was 15.

At Italsider as at thousands of Italian factories, workers gathered around the espresso machine at break times. Flyers promoting this and that would be left there, but increasingly the workers noticed illegal Red Brigades propaganda which glorified the violence. Rossa and some of his colleagues suspected a guy named Francesco Berardi, and when they opened his safety deposit box it was full of Red Brigades literature. Berardi was arrested and tried, but when he committed suicide in prison The Red Brigades went after Rossa. Ostensibly he and they shared an ideology if not a methodology, and yet they murdered him as he set out for work one morning.

Some 250,000 attended the funeral, but it seemed like all of Italy had come out. Among the mourners was Sandro Pertini, the popular president of the republic. As a socialist and a partisan during the war, he'd fought for democracy and against extremism. Now the impassioned speech he gave, denouncing The Red Brigades unequivocally, resonated throughout the land.

The human cost of all of this was incalculable, but the tide was beginning, very slowly, to turn.

At the fish and chip shop, with Gigi Peronace

While Virdis had netted just one league goal, Paolo Rossi had fired Vicenza into Serie A. He'd then plundered 24 goals in 28 starts in 1977–78 as Vicenza – that's right *Vicenza* – finished second in Serie A. Vicenza and Juve each owned 50 per cent of his registration, so now the federation invited each to make a sealed bid to determine outright ownership. Juve valued Rossi at 3.5 billion lire, just over £2 million, so they bid 1.75 billion for Vicenza's stake. That was a dizzying amount of money for half a football player, but Rossi was the generational talent they felt they needed to win the European Cup. Vicenza's chairman was Giussy Farina. He liked to boast that he knew everything and everyone, and one of his acquaintances had tipped him off that Juve would be offering 2.5 billion. Farina factored in the revenues from an extended UEFA Cup run Rossi's goals would bring, offered 2.6 billion for Juve's half, and won.

Rossi was a top player – Farina called him the 'Mona Lisa' of the Italian game – but 2.6 billion lire for half of him was crazy. Ordinary Italians were so outraged by the numbers that the head of the FIGC, Franco Carraro, would fall on his sword. Even Gianni Agnelli, a man not given to parsimony, struggled to comprehend it all. In Paris on business, he felt compelled to call Boniperti back to confirm that he hadn't made a cock-up with the numbers. Boni was so stupefied by what Farina had done that he rang Felice Colombo, his counterpart at Milan. The two of them agreed that there was no way Vicenza could ever generate that sort of cash, and they'd be boy-cotting the transfer market in protest.

A very good Italian side comprising nine *Juventini*, Rossi and Toro's Zaccarelli lost out to the Dutch at the 1978 World Cup in Argentina, and their employers paid a heavy price. Following an inadequate pre-season, Juve crashed out in the first round of the European Cup against Glasgow Rangers and, having won only two of the opening eight league games of the season, never really got going. A Coppa Italia win was recompense of sorts, but the football was by and large leaden and utilitarian.

Boniperti's troubles were as nothing compared to Farina's over at Vicenza. He had thought he could finance the Rossi folly by selling two-year season tickets, but that barely made a dent in it. He therefore flogged off Roberto Filippi and 'Beppe' Lelj, the right side of his team. In their absence the supply line to the boy won-der choked, and the UEFA Cup windfall never materi-alised. They were knocked out in the second round by Aris Thessaloniki, and when Rossi got injured the goals dried up completely. The buccaneers of the previous two seasons failed to win any of their final ten matches, and found themselves relegated back to whence they came. That might have been awful for the fans, but it was ruinous for Farina. He still owed Juve over a billion lire for Paolo Rossi; he didn't have it, and he knew that if he didn't cough up Juve would bankrupt him.

Farina needed to sell Rossi, but with Juve and Milan determined to make an example of him and Inter out of the frame, he was left with a choice of Napoli and Lazio. The problem there was that Rossi was a small-town kid from lovely Prato. He made it quite clear he didn't want to live in Rome and refused point blank even to contemplate Naples. He said, 'What am I supposed to do in Naples, save the place?' You can imagine how well *that* went down. But he was Italy's best striker, and he couldn't very well play in Serie B. Farina knew this, but he also knew that Rossi was a young player with a dodgy knee.

Perugia (of all people) had finished second behind Milan. They'd gone the entire season without losing a Serie A game, though bizarrely they'd contrived to draw 19 of them. Like everyone else they wanted Rossi, and the city's climate, the quality of life, the proximity to home and European football appealed to him. As a small, provincial club they didn't have the money to buy him, but in Franco D'Attoma they had a smart, resourceful chairman. He called Farina and told him he had a very good idea.

Neither Farina nor Rossi were averse to the idea of a season-long loan, and Vicenza eventually settled on 500 million, two loan players, and 50 per cent ownership of one of them in return. That was fair enough, but it didn't alter the fact that D'Attoma didn't have a spare 500 million to spend. What he did have, however, was a local PR company keen to do business. CPA agreed to pay him 300 million lire, and for that they'd get gate money from some friendlies, revenues from advertising hoardings at the ground and a share of the profits from a local TV station wanting to buy the rights. This was genuinely ground-breaking stuff, but D'Attoma wasn't done yet.

Teofilo Sanson was the owner of both an ice cream brand and of Serie B Udinese. The previous season he'd borrowed an idea from cycling, his great sporting passion. This was a sport whose very reason for being was the creation of brand awareness, and yet football's commercial model made no provision for it. Sanson therefore tested the waters by having his brand name stitched onto his players' shorts, at least until the federation ordered him to take it off. They'd wittered on about the sanctity of the sporting ideal (In Italy. In football. As if.) but had conceded that the addition of 'technical sponsor' logotypes on the team's shirts would henceforth be permissible. A small victory perhaps, but the ramifications would be far-reaching. Juve's shirt would feature the logo of Robe di Kappa ('K's Stuff'), a local sportswear maker; Inter had Puma and so on.

Meanwhile, over in Perugia, D'Attoma, something of a lateral thinker, had a conversation with the Mignini brothers. They were the owners of the Ponte pasta company, and Perugia was their team. They were as keen as anyone to see Rossi join, so they opened an ancillary business as suppliers of technical sportswear. They didn't actually manufacture it, but then the wording of the new rules stipulated only that they needed to supply it. Notwithstanding the fact that they had only one customer and that the logotype was identical to that of the pasta, there was a paper trail confirming they'd done precisely that. It became a cause célèbre, and obviously they garnered a huge amount of publicity as a consequence. They got a billion lire's worth of brand awareness for 200 million lire; D'Attoma got the money he needed to do the deal with Farina, and little Perugia got Italy's most prolific striker. They'd gamed the system, and opened the door to a completely new type of football. It was *Italianismo* at its brilliant, creative, intelligent best, but what happened next was the other side of the same extraordinary coin.

On 4 March 1980, Lazio's Maurizio Montesi was interviewed by the Roman newspaper *La Repubblica*. Unusually for a footballer, Montesi was a thinker, a socialist and a pacifist. The previous autumn a Lazio fan had been killed during the Rome derby, and Montesi had spoken out against the culture of violence which increasingly pervaded the sport. He'd publicly denounced the clubs' support – tacit and financial – of violent ultra groups, but nobody had taken much notice. When he claimed that football was lousy with illicit betting practices, he was ignored. Montesi was a mediocre squad player seeking attention, and he'd do well to keep his stupid mouth shut.

Three weeks later Italians settled down to watch *90° Minuto*, the Sunday afternoon football round-up show. Essentially the format hadn't changed in ten years. As the final whistle blew at each match, the studio would cut to the ground. With the players leaving the pitch, the RAI reporter present would offer a brief synthesis, with the promise of a more detailed analysis to follow. It was the most immediate way to get the results, and was watched by millions. This Sunday everything seemed perfectly *tranquillo* until the director cut to the game between Pescara and Lazio. There was a police car parked outside the players' tunnel. It wasn't immediately obvious why, but it *was* obvious that something odd was going on.

What was happening was the breaking of an extremely long and profoundly Italianate story, beginning with the arrest of four Lazio players. Elsewhere three from draw specialists Perugia found themselves in handcuffs, and the scene repeated itself in stadiums up and down the land. Two Milan players were carted off, and one each from Palermo, Lecce, Avellino and Genoa. Others were invited to present themselves before magistrates, and among them, unthinkably, was the superstar Rossi. Bologna's precocious winger 'Beppe' Dossena was summonsed, as were Italian internationals Oscar Damiani and 'Beppe' Savoldi. Directors and administrators were implicated, among them both Boniperti and Trapattoni. And so began the betting and match-rigging scandal which would bring down the board of the FIGC, and once more call into question what sport was all about.

The story of *Totonero* (the word is a portmanteau of *Totocalcio*, the Italian pools, and *nero*, Italian for 'black') is long and not a little complicated, but fundamentally a Roman fruit and veg merchant had been in receipt, via a restaurateur he supplied, of tip-offs from the Lazio team. The results of matches were said to be ordained in advance, but somewhere along the way it had all gone wrong for the fruit and veg guy. He'd bet the house, lost the lot and made for the police station.

As usual in Italy, the wheels of justice turned slowly, but it was abundantly clear that the football industry was systemically corrupt. Milan and Lazio were each demoted to Serie B and the Milan president, Felice Colombo, banned for life. *Azzurri* Giordano, Wilson, Zecchini, Albertosi, Savoldi and Manfredonia received bans, and so too, most shockingly of all, did the pin-up boy Rossi.

At Juventus, federal agents (nicknamed '007s' in the press) interviewed Bettega and Causio, Boniperti and Trapattoni. They wanted answers about one game in particular, the 1–1 draw at Bologna. In the event Bologna were sanctioned for having fixed another match against Avellino, and Juve alone were acquitted. The rest cried foul, and the Bologna players, almost to a man, still maintain that Bettega called Savoldi in advance of the game to fix it. Carlo Petrini, banned for 3½ years, stated that with the exception of two players the entire Bologna team had bet on the result. Causio has always denied it outright, and Bettega's memory has deserted him entirely. Neither they nor Savoldi were censured.

That said, nobody with an intimate understanding of Italian football is deluded enough to think match fixing didn't go on. One April in the early 90s I saw a Serie A match between two sides for each of whom a point would suffice for UEFA Cup qualification. On the eve of the game there was a TV debate about what might happen, and a former player stated with absolute conviction that it would be a draw. The presenter waffled on about the wealth of attacking talent on both sides, but when he'd finished the ex-player simply said, 'Believe you me – this football match will be a draw.'

And a draw it was, because for 90 interminable minutes nobody attempted to score a goal. They just went from side to side to side in the middle third. It's quite probable that no money changed hands, and it could be argued that it was all entirely reasonable. Over a long, hard season the two clubs had earned the right to play that way, and a non-aggression pact might well have been agreed without a word being spoken. It's like that at the business end of the season, because if Italians are anything they're *furbo* – clever. The people sitting around me understood precisely what was going on, and spent 90 carefree minutes chatting and awarding subconscious marks for artistic impression. It wasn't sport, but it was a pleasant enough afternoon all the same.

We've all witnessed end-of-season games in which precisely nothing happens for 70 minutes, and then a goal apiece is scored in a riveting final 20. The paying public is thus duped into believing it's witnessed a sporting contest, where in fact it's been the polar opposite. In the pre-VAR universe, I watched a defender carefully position himself fully a metre behind the goal line, from where he hacked a very tame shot to 'safety'. Obviously the goal was given; obviously he remonstrated with the ref like a good'un, and obviously the ensuing 1–1 draw suited both sides perfectly well. I've watched that incident a few times since, and I still struggle to believe that I was so guileless as to be taken in by it.

Juve escaped sanction then, but for them 1979–80 was a season of two halves. The first had them grovelling around on the edge of the drop zone, the second racing up the table and flirting with Cup Winners' Cup glory. Ultimately they couldn't quite catch up in Serie A, and in the latter were derailed by an uncommon midfield talent. Following a 1–1 draw at Highbury, Liam Brady dominated the second leg of the semi-final in Turin. Paul

Vaessen's 88th-minute header saw Arsenal through, as England's fourth-best team overcame Italy's finest.

Juve had come close, but the pattern of recent years had once again repeated itself. The top Serie A clubs were wealthy but, Juve's victory against Bilbao aside, they'd won nothing in Europe for a decade. The embargo on foreign players had been in place for 14 years and had proved wholly counterproductive. When, therefore, it was lifted that summer, the net was flung far and wide. Inter had had an agreement in principle with Nancy's brilliant Michel Platini. His family had emigrated to France from Agrate Conturbia, a ten-minute drive from Boniperti's home town Barengo, and he'd been open to a move. He'd subsequently broken his leg though, and when Inter's interest cooled he'd joined Saint-Etienne instead.

Inter secured the Austrian playmaker Herbert Prohaska, while Napoli signed Ruud Krol, the Dutch star of Argentina '78. Roma, 40 years without a *Scudetto*, took a punt on the graceful Brazilian midfielder Falcão, while Boniperti and Giuliano flew to Buenos Aires for a rendezvous with Sívori. They made Argentinos Juniors a money-no-object offer for a 19-year-old footballing prodigy named Diego Maradona, on loan if necessary. No dice; he wouldn't be going to Europe before the 1982 World Cup, and Barcelona had first call on him then.

Arsenal's Liam 'Chippy' Brady (so-called because he was forever at the fish and chip shop) was no Maradona, but he'd been the best player on the pitch in both legs of Juve's Cup Winners' Cup semi-final, so Gigi Peronace started frequenting the chippies of north London. The club needed a midfield strategist, and the fans a reason to turn up. At Juve, more than at any other Italian club, the disparity between prestige and actual income was stark. Whether for fear of terrorism or because of the rather pedestrian team, people had stopped coming. Juventus had less than 11,000 season-ticket holders and an average gate of 31,000. That irked Boniperti no end, because for all that the club was 'Italy's sweetheart' on the TV, at the turnstiles it ranked alongside old trollop Cagliari. Italy's seventh-best-supported team needed Brady to be box office. He signed on 30 July, and the sports journalists at *La Stampa* settled in for a late night at the office.

On the march of the 40,000, with Luigi Arisio

Ten minutes to the north of *La Stampa*'s offices in Corso Marconi, the owners of FIAT gathered together their senior managers. The business was losing sales, its reputation and above all its capital. The unions were on top; anarchy reigned in its factories, and there were rumours that the state would have to intervene to save it. FIAT had been the architect and symbol of the *boom economico* and the standard bearer of Italy PLC. Now it was a national disgrace and in imminent danger of bankruptcy.

Millions of Italians depended on its health, but if its losses weren't sutured soon it would bleed to death. With that in mind Umberto, rather than Gianni, stood up to make an address. The following morning, *La Stampa* announced that Brady was in, Umberto out.

The business needed to lay off at least 20,000 workers, and probably twice as many again. Umberto had decided that his presence would be prejudicial to that process, as well as dangerous both for himself and his colleagues. Thus, as the factories prepared to shut down for *Ferragosto*, the annual holiday, the unions girded their loins for the fight of their lives. They knew Umberto's replacement, and he was a different kettle of fish.

Cesare Romiti was a belligerent, no-nonsense Roman. He'd shadowed Umberto since De Benedetti quit, and he knew exactly what needed to happen. FIAT was at war with large sections of its workforce, and Romiti, unlike Umberto, was perfectly comfortable with seeing the fight through to the bitter end. He understood that this was essentially a numbers game and, crucially, that the state wouldn't and couldn't allow FIAT to fail. As he saw it he had all the cards, and besides he wasn't about to surrender to a bunch of Marxist crackpots.

The very next morning, as Italians awoke to the gravity of the situation, their republic was prostrated by yet another horrific act of violence. A right-wing terror group detonated 23 kilograms of explosive at Bologna Centrale railway station on 2 August 1980, killing 85 and wounding hundreds.

With the country in mourning, Romiti began the fightback immediately. He sent redundancy notices to 13,000 workers, fast-tracking the dispute directly to parliament and informing Italian lawmakers that they – and their country – were at a crossroads. If they capitulated to the unions, the company would go under, and the violence would likely escalate further still. The state declared itself ready to broker a compromise, and Romiti cleverly declared himself open to mediation. He was gambling on the unions becoming still more intransigent, and he was right. They downed tools and refused to listen, but instead occupied the factory floors and intimidated staff attempting to cross the picket lines. This battle of wills lasted 35 seminal days, and the longer it went on, the more ordinary Italians came down on the side of the company. By now all of Italy was familiar with the 'FIAT situation', and everyone knew what was at stake. Turin aside, communities in Sicily, Campania, Molise, Lombardy and Reggio Emilia relied on the company, and with each passing day the stakes were raised.

Then an unlikely hero, the most common of common men, emerged to save the day. He saved the company, the city and, it could be argued, the republic itself.

Luigi Arisio was a 55-year-old middle manager at FIAT, just one white collar among hundreds. He was an ordinary guy with an ordinary job, an ordinary family and ordinary bills to pay. He wasn't much for politics, but like his colleagues he was thoroughly sick of it all. He was sick of the threats and the violence, sick of the uncertainty and the lost income, sick of watching his company and his city self-immolate for no good reason. Arisio had never demonstrated in his life – he wasn't the sort – but he wanted, just for once, for his voice to be heard. He talked to some like-minded colleagues at work, and told them that on Tuesday 14 October there would be a march to Piazza San Carlo. It wasn't ideological, but rather the opposite. It was a chance for normal, moderate FIAT employees, the silent majority who cared about the company and wanted it to succeed, to have their say. Arisio reckoned on maybe a few hundred coming along, but it turned out he was way off.

The 'March of the 40,000' redefined Italy. Not only did it end the unions' hegemony at FIAT, but it dealt the radical left a fatal blow. Within a week the unions would be sitting down with Romiti discussing redundancy payments for 23,000 staff, and Italian employment law would be recast and rebalanced. It would be an exaggeration to state that Arisio had single-handedly ended the *anni di piombo*. However, the march and Romiti's fortitude had seen the company regain control, and had altered the socio-political landscape. There would be further sporadic killings in Rome, in Milan and elsewhere, but not in Turin. These had been the very worst of times, but FIATville had survived itself.

On the field it was the same, but different. The same because there were referees, controversies, scandals and, at the heart of it all, arch-*Juventino* Roberto Bettega. Following a 2–1 defeat in the derby, Bettega claimed that referee Luigi Agnolin had threatened to thump him for protesting too vigorously. (As a result Agnolin, the best in Italy and twice voted the second best in the world, received a four-month suspension.) Different because for once the title race involved all of Italy: Juve from the north, Roma from the centre and Napoli from the south. While Juve played the entire 1980–81 season without a natural number 9, Falcão's arrival transformed Roma into authentic title contenders, and Krol made a goodish Napoli side much better.

Napoli faded in the spring, but on 22 March Roma and Juve were dead level. The former travelled to deepest, darkest Calabria for a meeting with Catanzaro, while Juve entertained their bête noires Perugia. They parked the bus and, with eight minutes remaining, grabbed an unlikely goal on the counter. With his side trailing 0–1 and only four minutes on the clock, Juve left winger Domenico Marocchino picked up the ball on the left. He took on his full-back, but the ball appeared to cross the byline before he delivered his cross. The ref, Roberto Terpin, thought otherwise, and it broke to Furino on the opposite side of the box. Daniele Tacconi tackled and, though Furino went down, won the ball cleanly. Furino didn't appeal (unusual given that he was a serial remonstrator), but Terpin pointed to the spot anyway. Brady converted it, and in the last minute Marocchino bundled home the winner.

After the match Molinari, the Perugia manager, was spitting with indignation: 'Last season there was a sort of summary justice, aimed at convincing the public that it's all fine. Then this happens today.' His chairman, D'Attoma, was slightly more cryptic, though no less angry: 'I'd always thought that Jesus was on the side of the poor, but I need to think again.' On leaving the dressing room, midfielder Cesare Butti deployed good old-fashioned sarcasm: 'If I tell you what I know they'll disqualify me for years. The referee was their best player today.' Finally Paolo Del Fiume, picking up D'Attoma's biblical theme, detonated the bomb: 'They spent the entire game imploring him, "Give us this day our daily penalty." Bettega? He was like the Wailing Wall! He spent the entire game asking Celeste Pin to let him score.' And so, yet again, to an inquiry ...

When Perugia conceded five at Roma, Gianni joked that Bettega's imprecations must have taken a while to sink in and said the Perugia players 'must have an elephant's memory'. That was lovely and fruity, but heading into the home fixture with Roma, Juve led by a point. Tardelli was injured, and everyone associated with *calcio* awaited the outcome of the Bettega inquiry. In time-honoured fashion it arrived, with maximum dramatic effect, on the eve of the biggest game of the season. The league hit him with a three-match suspension, so Juve went into the de facto championship decider minus two of their better, battle-hardened players and lacking a specialist centre forward.

Rome is 700 kilometres from Turin, and the world was a much bigger place in 1981. Public transport was relatively expensive, and Italians didn't generally travel to watch their teams the way that, say, the English and Germans did. In the normal course of events Roma would have expected maximum 1000 *tifosi* to make the trip north, but this time they transformed the ground into a seething mass of red and yellow. By conservative estimate there were upwards of 15,000 of them – a Roman colony.

The game itself is infamous. As a spectacle it was abysmal, Italian football at its cynical worst. The 'play' was spoiled by fouling, play-acting and name-calling, with only the *stranieri* Falcão and Brady exempted from the media condemnation. With half an hour remaining, Furino was dismissed for a sadistic, career-threatening assault on Roma's Domenico Maggiora, but the real story of the game – and in truth of all subsequent games between Juve and Roma – came with 15 minutes remaining.

With Juve's ten men playing for the draw, Roma *libero* Maurizio 'Ramon' Turone was making increasingly frequent incursions into their box in the hope that something would drop for him. When Bruno Conti crossed and Roberto Pruzzo headed down, something did, all lovely and easy and gift-wrapped and soft. He headed past Zoff from six yards and then wheeled away in celebration. The ref initially awarded the goal, but then noticed his linesman's flag was up. The action replay isn't perhaps entirely conclusive, but that's only because the camera wasn't in line. Suffice to say nobody in their right mind believes he was off.

If ever one incident encapsulated a sporting career this was it, and that's why Turone can never escape it. When asked recently he said, 'It was criminal, what happened, but it doesn't matter what I say or what I think. Everyone remembers that moment, but not the other 400 or so games I played.' And he's right. They remember it because it's never gone away, and while football is played in Italy it never will. It's Italian football's most famous disallowed goal, and it's come to symbolise both Roma's endless malaise and, rightly or wrongly, the spell Juve has over officialdom.

Two weeks later, Cabrini volleyed the only goal in the game against Fiorentina, and the Comunale was *in festa*. Gianni Agnelli, recovering from a triple fracture of his left leg sustained while skiing in February, celebrated his clubs' 19th *Scudetto*. He wasn't deluding himself, however: 'We'll do our best in the European Cup, but our clubs are a long way behind. We ought to be able to have as many foreigners as we like, but to be competitive we need at least one more.'

L'Avocatto had spoken.

Down in Catanzaro, with Liam Brady

Heading into the final 45 minutes of the 1981–82 season, Juventus and Fiorentina were dead level. Each had 44 points, each was level at 0–0 (away to Catanzaro and Cagliari respectively), and everything was to play for. The two of them had pulled clear of the rest in January, and in the circumstances that had been a notable achievement. Fiorentina had played half the season without their best player. The brilliant midfielder Giancarlo Antognoni had fractured his skull in November, around the same time Bettega had suffered the knee injury which would rule him out of the World Cup the following summer.

Sponsored now by the Ariston white goods company, Juve had been compelled to make do and mend with a front two of Virdis (Remember him?) and teenager Giuseppe Galderisi. As stopgaps go they'd done pretty well, but now the club had been reacquainted with Paolo Rossi. His suspension had finished at the end of April, and Boniperti had taken him off Vicenza's hands in lieu of a debt rumoured to be 3 billion lire including compound interest. Ten years on from signing for the club as a callow teenager, the prodigal son had scored on his league debut in a 5–1 thumping of Udinese.

Liam Brady had been the club's stand-out player for two seasons. With Causio departed and Bettega well into his thirties, he'd been the creative fulcrum of the team. He had a terrific left foot, and like all truly gifted players seemed to have more time on the ball than everyone else. Brady was high class but probably not quite *world* class, and that had informed Gianni's lobbying of the FIGC to allow clubs two foreigners apiece. They'd acquiesced, and he'd decided to indulge himself once more. Initially the transfer window was to close at the end of May, but the FIGC saw fit to move it forward a month. Boniperti and Giuliano flew to Paris and Warsaw respectively, and within 72 dramatic, nerve-racking hours two European footballing aristocrats were secured.

The signings of Michel Platini and Zibì Boniek left Brady surplus to requirements, though nobody at the club thought – or had the decency – to tell him. Brady was anything but stupid though, and he was more than capable of reading *Tuttosport*. He'd been to see Trap, who told him he knew nothing about it. Brady's manager had lied to him, and Brady knew he'd lied to him. Trap had known Brady had known he'd lied to him, but he'd also known Brady was a good pro. He had a duty to his team-mates; there was a *Scudetto* to win and nothing to gain from sulking. When the announcement was made he'd shrugged his shoulders, made the right noises and vowed to leave Turin with a second championship on his CV.

Catanzaro was a kiln that afternoon, and the home side was particularly stubborn. In theory they'd nothing to play for, but that theory tends to go out of the window when Juve are in town. The *calabresi* were resolute; the tension was growing with every passing minute, and there was no obvious indication that Juve had enough to break them down. Seven minutes into the second half, Trap, who didn't really do patience, replaced the ineffectual Virdis with speed merchant Pietro Fanna.

Meanwhile, at Cagliari, Fiorentina were laying siege to the home side's goal. Antognoni delivered an outswinging cross from the right, and the Cagliari keeper missed his punch completely. He contrived only to clatter into Fiorentina's Argentine midfielder Daniel Bertoni, and the old Toro favourite Graziani volleyed in from four yards. Bertoni had been more impeded than impeder, but the referee chalked it off anyway. There was nothing unusual in that (goalies were untouchable back then), but the Fiorentina *tifosi* were added to the list of those convinced that Juve were in league with the authorities. They coined the saying *Meglio secondi che ladri* – 'Better to be second than to be thieves' – and it's fair to state the enmity has never gone away.

With fifteen minutes left, Juve finally got round the back of Catanzaro. Marocchino skinned the left-back; Rossi headed his cross against the post, and the ball ricocheted to an unmarked Fanna. His shot was goalbound, but then a Catanzaro defender on the line stuck out an arm to save it.

Brady had been the club's penalty taker for two seasons. His technique was almost flawless, and he didn't suffer from nerves. He'd missed one in the Turin derby, but otherwise his record was impeccable. He was on his way out, however, and the club had treated him shamefully. Interviewed some years later, he admitted that the decision had been made to transfer penalty-taking responsibilities to Virdis. That Trapattoni had been worried the Irishman might miss on purpose probably tells us more about the club's morality than Brady's, but Virdis was in the dugout. Brady therefore put it on the spot, waited for the protests to run their course and won Juventus a second gold star.

That summer the famous *blocco Juve* won their country the World Cup in Spain. Head coach Bearzot started six of them in every game, with 40-year-old Zoff cast as the gatekeeper of Italian conscience, Italian history and Italian virtue. Cabrini, Gentile and Scirea comprised the defensive citadel, Tardelli the gallant infantryman, Rossi the rapier. His hat-trick against Brazil is comic-book stuff, Tardelli's goal against Germany in the final an indelible component of modern Italy's collective DNA.

Most sports wax and wane in popularity, but it's almost impossible to articulate just how present football is in Italy. Juve have been absolutely central to its development as a cultural phenomenon, and three moments in particular are pivotal. The 1934 team of Combi, Monti, Orsi and Rosetta was appropriated by Mussolini, its World Cup win hawked as fascism's great sporting triumph. The Charles–Sívori–Boniperti *trio magico* is redolent of a different football and a different time, but it's linked to the birth of TV and to a uniquely optimistic moment. If Tardelli's winning goal completes the triptych – and it categorically does – the question is why?

Professional sport matters not for what it is, but for what it does to its audience. Madrid still resonates not so much with the geometric beauty of the move that led to the goal, but for the wider significance it's come to assume. Looking back at the footage, it's little wonder Tardelli is overcome by the magnitude of what he's achieved. On the surface he's won a very important football match, but there's much more to it than sporting hearts and flowers. There's much more to the 1982 World Cup than (for example) the 2006 edition, and much more than mere football.

For over a decade Italy had been enfeebled by ideological extremism and by its direct consequence – quotidian brutality. Lingotto, the nerve centre of Italian industry during the boom years, had become synonymous with tension, with failure and with angst. Following the March of the 40,000, Romiti had spent two years redeploying FIAT's workers to Rivalta and Mirafiori, or not redeploying them at all. The place had become a stain on Italy's collective conscience so, when the final Lancias rolled off the line that spring, most had viewed its passing with a mixture of relief and nostalgia. The closure, unthinkable even five years earlier, was symbolic as well as actual.

Two weeks before the tournament began, Italy had passed Criminal Law no. 304. It prescribed reduced penalties for those who confessed to having been involved in terrorist-paramilitary activity, on condition that they collaborated in bringing their comrades to justice. The so-called Law of the Repentant had provided a way out for those trapped in the cycle of criminality, and it had an immediate effect. They'd started to surrender, and that had decapitated the terrorist organisations.

If, therefore, Spain '82 looked and felt like an epiphany, it's because that's precisely what it was. What Romiti and the March of the 40,000 had started – the repudiation of the terrible *anni di piombo* – Marco Tardelli unwittingly finished. He couldn't have known it at the time, but the goal he scored was the final act. It brought Italy's tortured, fragmented tribes back together, and herded them towards the light. That's why it's such an extraordinary thing, and why it remains a 'Where were you?' moment in Italy's recent journey. The *blocco Juve* was the catalyst for Italy's victory, and so, subconsciously or otherwise, still more Italians assimilated the idea that the club, the company and the *tricolore* were all one and the same.

Chapter 7

Il Nuovo Calcio

I always win. I'm condemned to win.

Silvio Berlusconi

In Athens, with Felix bloody Magath

The Rossi–Boniek–Platini combination took a while to gel, but by the new year Rossi had delivered the club's first Ballon d'Or. Moreover Boniek finished third, Zoff eighth and Platini ninth, while both Scirea and Tardelli featured in the top twenty. FIAT was recovering; Juve had six World Cup winners and allegedly six of the top twenty players on the continent. What they didn't have – yet – was absolute primacy in Turin, as four minutes of derby-day madness amply demonstrated ...

Some maintain that Roberto Bettega was the last of the true *Juventini*. He'd been born in the city and known no other club. Over the years the old *stile Juventino* construct had become a double-edged sword, and Bettega more than anyone evinced it. On the pitch and off it he was much smarter than the average footballer, and there was something substantial about his personality. It went without saying that he was a brilliant athlete, but he was also straight-backed, handsome and confident. With his prematurely grey hair and Savoy elegance there was something of the courtier about him, but also something of the knave.

Non-*gobbi* liked to deride 'Juventus style' as synonymous with chicanery, with Bettega cast as its living, breathing, swindling epitome. Their assertion was that he'd stop at virtually nothing to win football matches, and he had been the subject of rumour and suspicion for some time. The Juve hardcore adored him because he was talented and cunning, but also because he was one of their own. Conversely and inevitably he was abhorred on the other side of Turin's great divide, because for Toro fans he was an Agnelli stooge. He represented the arrogance and hubris of the ruling class, and the moral bankruptcy of those who believe themselves above the law.

Bettega was 32 now, and his time was almost up. He'd played nearly 500 games, and Boniek, Platini and Rossi were the medium-term future of Juventus. Bettega was still a very resourceful player, but with Trapattoni alternating Marocchino's young legs with his old ones, he agreed to a lucrative move to Toronto Blizzard.

As a young *Torinese*, Bettega in particular had been hamstrung by Juve's inferiority complex vis-à-vis Torino. So, as a young player, had Boniperti, but as the club's president and special envoy respectively the two of them had made it their business to eliminate it. They'd been hugely successful, and under Trap, they'd had much the better of the *derby della Mole*. Of the fifteen most recent encounters they'd won six to Toro's two, with seven drawn. It went without saying that Bettega's last derby was a huge occasion. There were six games of the season remaining, so six games both of his Juventus career and that of Zoff. Juve trailed Roma by three points; they couldn't afford not to win, and aside from his team-mate Furino, no Italian footballer had ever won seven *Scudetti* before. What's more Toro were at home, and those are always the best derbies to win.

With 20 minutes remaining Juve were 2–0 up. They seemed to be coasting but then 'Beppe' Dossena, the one truly creative spark in a prosaic Toro side, reduced the deficit with a stooping header. Two minutes later he released left-back Beruatto, and when he crossed, Alessandro Bonesso stole half a yard on Scirea. He glanced a header beyond Zoff, and the place erupted. Juve kicked off, but within 90 seconds they'd capitulate entirely. Toro's right-sided Dutchman Michel Van de Korput clipped a ball back to the edge of the box, an acrobatic volley from Fortunato Torrisi flew beyond Zoff at his near post, and Juve's title challenge was extinguished. The derby of 27 March 1983 looms large in Turin sporting legend, but there was no happy ending for Roberto Bettega.

The derby was lost and the title was lost, but in dumping out holders Aston Villa in the European Cup quarter-final, Juve finally broke the English stranglehold. What's more Widzew Łódź, Boniek's former employers, seemed eminently beatable semi-final opponents. Prior to Boniek's arrival there in 1975, Widzew had been a provincial club operating in the second tier of Polish football. Boniek had changed all that. His signing for Juve derived in large measure from a stunning World Cup hat-trick against Belgium, but also from a UEFA Cup tie between the two clubs in 1980. He'd taken Juve apart in Łódź, and his excellence had propelled Widzew to successive domestic titles.

In Soviet bloc countries, sportsmen were regarded as 'diplomats in tracksuits'. Having represented socialism with such distinction at previous World Cups, Boniek's countrymen Gadocha, Deyna and Lato had been rewarded with transfers to ... capitalist clubs in the West. In return the Polish Ministry of Sport had acquired American dollars or, in the case of Deyna's move to Manchester City, X-ray machines and photocopiers. Juve had paid 2.3 billion lire for Boniek, but he hadn't been a prolific scorer and he'd struggled initially to work with Marocchino, Platini and Rossi. He was neither a striker nor a winger, he was a model of inconsistency and tactically a difficult fit. However, he was direct and riotously talented, and when his head was right he was immense. This was one such occasion; the real Boniek stood up, and Juve cantered to a 2–0 win.

Gianni once referred to Boniek as *bello di notte* ('beauty by night'). Legend has it that he was referencing the disparity between his Sunday-afternoon Serie A performances and those under lights in Europe. Supposedly Boniek wasn't interested in the muck and nettles of the league, and saved his spectacular best for nights like these. While it's undeniable that he was a big-game player, Boniek has always maintained that this has no basis in fact. Rather the nickname has its roots in a glitzy reception, and a meeting with Gianni's old pal Henry Kissinger.

Gianni liked football, and he liked young, sinewy, rough-hewn footballers. Mostly he liked to patronise them, and he viewed them in much the same way he viewed his art collection. They were expensively acquired ornaments to be shown off to his wealthy pals, and on this occasion he had them lined up to meet America's most famous statesman. When they reached Frenchman Platini, he's believed to have said, 'I call this one *bello di giorno*.' With his long black hair and saccharine good looks, Platini wouldn't have seemed out of place in a French new-wave movie. He was young, glamorous and wildly talented, and Gianni was making an oblique reference to Luis Buñuel's *Belle de Jour*, an art-house cinema masterpiece starring Catherine Deneuve. Standing alongside Platini was the red-haired, moustachioed Boniek. He was pallid and a wee bit brooding, and he looked not unlike a Mirafiori *operaio* stuffed into a fancy suit. One way or another he appeared rather less ethereal than Platini, and so Gianni, seldom lost for words, quipped, 'And this is *bello di notte ...*'

They reckon 50,000 *Juventini* descended on Athens for the European Cup final. It's quite a trip from Turin, but this being Juve they came from far and wide. Theirs had been a long, hard march to the summit of European football, and for them the match represented a coronation. It was the final hurrah for the giants Bettega and Zoff, and the Italian press imbued the whole thing with Homeric qualities. Of course they'd need to overcome Hamburg, but the reporting suggested that was but a formality. Having lost to the *blocco Juve* in the World Cup final the previous summer, the Germans would be no match for six of the same team reinforced by Bettega, Platini and Boniek. Would they?

The problem was that only one Hamburg player, right-back Manni Kaltz, had started that night in Madrid. Horst Hrubesch and Felix Magath had each been sat on the German bench, but World Cup football in Spain counted for nothing in the context of a club match in Greece. Amid the backslapping, Italy quite forgot that the German champions would likely be quite good at football, and that at one point they'd gone 30-odd matches unbeaten.

Heavyset, stooped and swarthy, Magath had about him the look of an alehouse footballer. He had an exquisite left foot, mind, and he used it to arc an absolute peach beyond a flat-footed Zoff after eight minutes. That wasn't in the script, and neither (by way of Teutonic cliché) was the monochromatic efficiency of Hamburg's offside trap. Rossi couldn't unlock it; Wolfgang Rolff neutered Platini almost entirely, and keeper Stein made a couple of half-decent saves when called upon. Italian football legend has it that the final was a travesty, the umpteenth manifestation of Juve's European curse. In reality that does a disservice to Hamburg. They won because, for all that Juve probably had more-talented individual players, they were the more coherent team. Hamburg had another perfectly good goal disallowed for offside, and Magath of all people blazed over with only Zoff to beat. If anything, 1–0 flattered Juve.

Over six games in twelve clammy late-June days, Juve won two secondary trophies. With Zoff having bowed out against Hamburg, one of the club's least conspicuous but best-loved figures kept goal. Luciano Bodini had signed four years earlier, when he'd been 25 and Zoff 38. He'd expected to replace him as first choice *portiere* in short order, but Zoff had kept on keeping on. Bodini now started home and away in the Coppa Italia final against Verona. Juve lost the away leg 2–0, but then Platini had his say. Following Rossi's opener he equalised with nine minutes left, and then ghosted in at the far post in the last minute of extra time. Bodini had himself a gold medal, and the following week he got another one. He played all four games in a half-arsed round robin featuring the best club sides from Italy, Brazil and Argentina. It wasn't up to much, but a trophy is a trophy. Sort of. More or less.

After having worn the number 12 shirt for four years, Bodini appeared to have earned a regular starting berth. Later that summer, however, the club went and signed Stefano Tacconi. He was younger and better, and so, occasional brief interlude aside, Bodini reverted to bench-warming. He only played 26 games in ten seasons, but in the pantheon of non-goalkeeping goalkeepers, the professional number 12s, he was the absolute master. He had plenty of offers elsewhere but stuck around, he always said, because he felt so proud that Boniperti considered him worthy.

Juventus hit the ground running in September. The opening league game against Ascoli was won 7–0, and three days later Gdansk were walloped by the same scoreline in the Cup Winners' Cup. With Platini simultaneously operating as midfield anchor, playmaker and false 9, Serie A was a foregone conclusion by Christmas. There may have been better, more entertaining teams in Europe, but none sprang readily to mind.

Many thought Platini the continent's best number 10, though the good people of Udine would probably have begged to differ. The ice-cream king Teofilo Sanson had sold their club to Lamberto Mazza, the owner of Zanussi. He didn't know much about football, but he loved showing off. He'd brought the final stage of the Giro d'Italia to Udine the previous year and announced that he was going to 'make Udinese great'. He had Zanussi's shareholders and Italy's financial institutions shell out 4 billion lire, while a nebulous PR company said to represent Adidas and Coca-Cola contributed 2 billion. That lot converted to about $4 million, more or less twice Manchester United's British record outlay for Brian Robson. For it he got reputedly the best footballer on the planet as the Brazilian virtuoso Arthur Antunes Coimbra, otherwise known as Zico, fetched up in the footballing hotbed which was … Friuli. The unions at Zanussi loved that one, but that's another story.

Zico looked set to go toe to toe with Platini for the *capocannoniere* award, but as homesickness and the winter set in, his form tailed off. The Frenchman won it for the second season in succession, and Udinese finished a distant ninth. Shit-or-bust Mazza wasn't deterred though. He'd promised the people of Friuli the earth and so, regardless of the massive losses at Zanussi, he'd go to the bank again that summer and spend almost $3 million on another exotic-sounding name, the mythical Cosmo.

That, in case you were wondering, was Europe's largest LCD screen, and in all probability its least reliable. It was ten metres wide and eight high, and it would be installed in time for Zico's second and last season in Italy. Like him, though, it would perform only fitfully. For the most part it was blank, though from time to time it would gurgle something vaguely intelligible. For his part, Zico would generally be indisposed. When he wasn't injured he was suspended for haranguing Italy's refs on the pitch and publicly impugning their partiality off it. He scored three times all season and then, his bank account replete, re-signed for Flamengo.

Electrolux (Swedish, prudent, reliable) would rescue Zanussi, but Mazza's life in football would come to an abrupt end in 1986. He was barred from the game for his part in a match-rigging scandal which centred around … Italo Allodi! He was in the employ of Napoli now, but he'd enough friends in enough high places to dodge yet another corruption bullet. History repeats in Italian football, and *Totonero-bis* saw poor, powerless, provincial Udinese demoted to Serie B. The club would spend the next decade yo-yoing between the divisions, a fairly hefty price for 39 games from Zico. Still, at least his erstwhile fans had Cosmo to remind them of his all-too-fleeting brilliance. And of the absolute futility of supporting a provincial football club in Italy.

With the *Scudetto* done and almost dusted, Juve drew Manchester United in the 1984 Cup Winners' Cup semifinal. They drew 1–1 at Old Trafford, before the best game of the season at the Comunale saw Rossi break Mancunian hearts in the last minute. The final, across the Alps in Basel, was a belter. Vignola and Boniek scored, and Juve outlasted a cracking Porto side to conclude a unique Cup Winners' Cup-Serie A double. Then, three days later, another good-news story arrived from Switzerland.

On 19 May 1984, FIFA delegates met in Zurich. Sixteen of them were invited to participate in a ballot to elect the host country for the 1990 World Cup. The candidates were Italy and the Soviet Union, and they chose the *bel paese*. Some 56 years on from Combi, Allemandi and the others, *calcio* was coming home.

The very best of times, then, and Italy's footballing sweetheart had never had it so good. Two major European trophies down, one to go …

TORINO – The dichotomy is net, crude: There are those who have tickets for Liverpool–Juventus, and those who don't. According to this distinction, everything rises and falls – happiness, the joy of life, pride, the sense of power. Those in possession exit Juventus' headquarters resembling the tribe's shaman. The touts, the tables turned upon them, approach and enquire whether they'll sell their tickets. They're offering very high prices; sell four standing tickets for 29 May and you'll have enough for a week in the sun in the Canaries, flight included. Only nobody in Turin has four tickets …

It's a crazy Italo-Belgian story, this. The Heysel stadium in Brussels, where Liverpool won the draw for the home dressing room, is 55 years old. It's handsome, but it only holds 58,000 and they're almost all standing. Juventus, like Liverpool, have 25 per cent of them, 14,500 tickets. The club received 66,000 applications, and it would have been 100,000 were they not so expensive. Sergio Secco, the club treasurer, spends his days explaining that it's not possible for them to multiply. Liverpool won't give theirs up, notwithstanding the fact that, in light of the previous acts of hooliganism committed by their fauna, their ability to leave their island and follow their team is conditional upon a sort of police profiling. The Belgian Federation, which manages 50 per cent of the tickets, is also playing hardball. Almost all their 29,000 tickets vanished within 90 minutes on 2 May, at the stadium's three ticket booths. It was thought they'd been bought *en masse* by the Italians (and *Juventini*) in Belgium, but it seems they've discovered touting there as well. In theory there were a maximum of five tickets per person, assuming they were in possession of a residency permit. In reality it seems that the black market was already in operation there at the ticket booths. You simply needed to ask and pay (even if it was more than face value) and the tickets were yours.

'A Kingdom for a Ticket', *La Stampa*, 9 May 1985

In Brussels, with Sandro (20) and Marco (21)

MARCO: Tickets weren't easy, but our mate said, 'I can get us tickets for Sector Z. We knew that meant being near the hooligans, and we'd already had experience of them. We'd been to watch England against Belgium in Turin at Euro '80, and we'd never seen anything like it. These people were insane, but the Italians had policed them really well. They'd basically just beaten them to submission, because they'd had the numbers and the armoury. The thing with the hooligans was that they were crazy, but they weren't terrorists ...

SANDRO: There were three of us, and we went everywhere together. This was the third European final we'd been to. We set off in the car on Tuesday afternoon, after I finished work.

MARCO: If memory serves we'd already exchanged our tickets when we got there, so we were in our section with the Juve fans at the opposite end of the ground. Our mate swapped his when we got there, and I've an idea he swapped it with an English fan. Outside the ground there were lots of bare-chested, drunk people. I'd never seen people carrying crates of beer to a football match before, but we just sort of laughed it off. I suppose you were a bit careful about where you went, but probably no more than usual. We'd been to loads of games, and it wasn't as if there weren't idiots in Italy as well.

SANDRO: There was nothing that suggested there was going to be a tragedy, but then why would there be? It was only a football match …

I'd say the way they did it was absurd. Everyone knew about hooliganism, so why on earth would you place a neutral sector, mainly populated by Italian fans and locals, right next to the Liverpool fans? Why, when you knew what these people were like, would you separate them with chicken wire and such a flimsy police corridor? I remember thinking, *Jesus, if they're wanting to provoke trouble, they couldn't have planned this any better*.

MARCO: So you're watching this thing, and you see the English crossing their section of the terrace in waves. They surge, they seem to be repelled, and on it goes. By now you're hoping that reinforcements arrive, because this isn't normal. You don't know exactly what's happening, but you can tell it's becoming sinister.

SANDRO: You can tell they're attacking, and you know that the people in Sector Z aren't exactly ultras. They're occasional fans, locals, older people, and they're getting scared. They're moving as far away from the danger as they can, because it's human instinct …

MARCO: I remember the *thud* the wall made when it collapsed – that's still with me. Obviously we'd no idea, but I remember turning to Sandro and saying, 'Somebody could be seriously hurt here!'

SANDRO: Then you started seeing ambulances, helicopters, first-aid people and what have you, and you knew something bad had happened. You didn't know *what* had happened, but people were saying there'd been fatalities. You assumed three, four, maybe five …

MARCO: By the time the game started you just wanted to be out of there as quickly as possible.

SANDRO: It was already spoiled by the time they kicked off. I don't really know how I'd describe the feeling. Disgust, probably …

MARCO: It was only really coming home that we understood the gravity of it. We stopped to call home, and that's when we heard the full extent of what had happened.

SANDRO: I couldn't go to the football any more after that. It took a couple of years for me to be able to go back, because I couldn't understand it. I tried to, but there was no logic to any of it. For me, football had always been something to be enjoyed. It was sport, and I'd always associated sports with fun. I couldn't understand this, and if I'm honest I still can't.

MARCO: My feelings about them having played the game? Obviously it's not worth anything, that trophy, but what if they hadn't? I guess it's something for the people who died. I don't know, but I'd probably lay about 20 per cent of the blame at the hooligans' door. They were idiots, but you like to think they didn't set out to kill people.

SANDRO: I still think a part of me died there. I don't know; maybe it's like that for everyone who went ...

†Rocco Acerra
†Bruno Balli
†Alfons Bos
†Giancarlo Bruschera
†Andrea Casula
†Giovanni Casula
†Nino Cerullo
†Willy Chielens
†Giuseppina Conti
†Dirk Daenecky
†Dionisio Fabbro
†Jacques François
†Eugenio Gagliano
†Francesco Galli
†Giancarlo Gonnelli
†Alberto Guarini
†Giovacchino Landini
†Roberto Lorentini
†Barbara Lusci
†Franco Martelli
†Loris Messore
†Gianni Mastrolaco

†Sergio Bastino Mazzino
†Luciano Rocco Papaluca
†Luigi Pidone
†Bento Pistolato
†Patrick Radcliffe
†Domenico Ragazzi
†Antonio Ragnanese
†Claude Robert
†Mario Ronchi
†Domenico Russo
†Tarcisio Salvi
†Gianfranco Sarto
†Giuseppe Spalaore
†Mario Spanu
†Tarcisio Venturin
†Jean Michel Walla
†Claudio Zavaroni

At the top table, with Silvio Berlusconi

Heysel was calamitous, and still today the debate rages about the decision to play the match. However life, like death, goes on, and the fact remained that Juve had reached the summit of the European game. They'd won eight domestic titles in fourteen years and, uniquely, all three major European cup competitions. Not even Liverpool could claim to have been so successful for so long, and Boni and Trap were rightly proud of the fact.

Brussels had been tumultuous and tragic, and Boni had known instinctively that only wholesale renewal would enable the club to get beyond it. Italy's *calciomercato* resembled a high-stakes sporting bazaar, and there was nothing Boniperti loved more than wheeling and dealing. It was what had attracted Gianni to him in the first place, but he also prided himself on his financial husbandry of the club. Boni had watched a succession of hotshot presidents come and go, gambling money they didn't have on dreams they'd never realise. He'd seen them all off because he'd had the Agnellis' backing, but also because he'd been sagacious in the marketplace. Trap had played his part by providing continuity, a high-energy 4–4–2 and a winning mentality, but Boni and Gianni had made the buying decisions.

While Gianni had a weakness for decorative footballers, Boniperti took pains to ensure that they bought only effective ones and that they were moved on at the right time. As Italian football's alpha males, they'd dominated the transfer market, and the prestige of playing for Juve had helped to keep the wage bill under control. The exception to that was Platini's salary, but he was a great player and the club had paid peanuts to get him. Saint-Etienne had probably misinterpreted the UEFA guidelines regarding fees for out-of-contract players moving abroad, but that had been their lookout and not Juve's. Gianni famously said they'd 'signed him for the price of a breadcrust, and he'd spread foie gras on it'. For three seasons Platini had been top scorer in Serie A and was a two-time Ballon d'Or winner. His worth to the club was inestimable, and alongside the likes of Cabrini and Scirea he'd become the heartbeat of a wonderful team.

Italian football was richer and more glamourous than ever before. At Gianni's behest, Serie A had become the go-to league for the world's best footballers, and the more they came the more the money flooded in. The two-foreigner rule had made Serie A more egalitarian though, and as a consequence new threats were emerging. Over at Verona, a consortium of local businessman had inherited a very workmanlike side. It had included the ex-*Juventini* Fanna and Galderisi, and to it they'd added buccaneering German left-back Hans-Peter Briegel and Danish striker Preben 'crazy horse' Elkjær. They'd confounded expectations by topping the league at Christmas, and won the 1984–85 championship by four points.

Inter's new owner, catering impresario Ernesto Pellegrini, had announced himself by acquiring Bayern Munich uber-striker Karl-Heinz Rummennige, while Fiorentina had landed the opulent Brazilian midfielder Sòcrates. His pal Júnior, ostensibly Toro's right-back, had finished the season as their top scorer. Júnior was a doozy of a footballer, but Napoli had broken the world transfer record to entice the greatest of them all. Diego Armando Maradona had flown in from Barcelona, and now the footballing omnipotence of the north would be stress-tested for the first time.

Rumour had it that, in signing for Roma, Boniek had doubled his salary at a stroke. Trap hadn't wanted to lose him, and nor had the fans. He wasn't as good as Platini – nobody was – but he had a big, generous heart, and one always had the sense that he cared about results more than personal glory. In his stead came dashing Michael Laudrup, eight years his junior at 21. The Dane had been bought two years before from Brøndby, and it had been Boniperti at his stealthy, connected best. He'd taken a

call from an old Juve team-mate who'd become a distinguished coach in Denmark. Mario Astorri had told him
that Laudrup was fantastic and he'd be a mug not to snap
him up. Boni had paid $1 million but forgotten to inform
Laudrup that he wouldn't actually be *playing* for Juventus.
With the two-foreigner rule in place he couldn't, because
Platini and Boniek were Platini and Boniek.

Boni had loaned the boy out to Lazio for two seasons,
but now Boniek was out and he was in. Elsewhere Rossi,
injury-prone and close to washed up, was shipped out
to Milan. Their latest chairman was the mighty Giussy
Farina, the man who'd almost bankrupted Vicenza to get
Rossi back in '78. Now he was on the verge of capsiz-
ing Milan as well, so he needed someone to placate the
ugly-looking mob which gathered each morning at the
training ground.

Juve spent the Rossi cash on 24-year-old Aldo Serena
from Inter, with veteran Tardelli going the other way
in part-exchange. Serena, who'd been scoring copiously on loan at Toro, was informed that he was being
sold while attending a Bruce Springsteen concert at the
San Siro. Lazio's stalwart holding midfielder Lionello
Manfredonia, one of those indicted for *Totonero*, completed this new black and white composite.

Uniquely, none of the big three began the 1984–85 season as favourites or as reigning champions. Verona were
both, but by December, when Juve travelled to Tokyo
for the Intercontinental Cup Final, the title was theirs
to lose. This brilliant match, won on penalties against a
really good Argentinos Juniors team, would redefine the
way football was consumed by Italians, and in the full-
ness of time the way they lived, thought and acted. RAI,

Italy's state broadcaster, had always had exclusive rights to broadcast major sporting events, but on this occasion the Italian rights were bought by FININVEST, a Milan-based private TV company owned by a former cruise-ship singer turned construction magnate.

Silvio Berlusconi had attempted to buy Inter in 1977, and three years later had dipped a toe into the pond of televised football. The Fascist junta in Uruguay had arranged the *Mundialito*, an invitation-only tournament for previous World Cup winners. It had taken place during the winter break, its aim to help reconstruct the country's shattered reputation abroad. RAI had turned down the chance to show the games, but Berlusconi, allegedly financed by the nefarious P2 masonic lodge, had not. The Italian team had treated the trip, quite understandably, as a jolly. They'd drawn one game and lost one, but Berlusconi made a killing anyway. Football fans would watch any old dross ...

Now he'd expanded his empire to a point where the advertising revenues of his three channels outstripped those of RAI. He hadn't yet breached the barrier that the state had constructed around live sports broadcasting, but with each set of accounts he was inching closer. The more wealth he accumulated the more influence he accrued, and everyone knew that the dam had to break eventually. Now he was almost there, but he needed one really big unmissable event. Notwithstanding the 4 a.m. kick-off and the fact that his broadcasting licence was limited to Lombardy, he outbid RAI and put the game on.

No European team had won the Intercontinental Cup since Bayern in 1976. In accomplishing it in Tokyo, Juve completed a clean sweep of the major club competitions. On a sporting level, that captured the imagination of the Italian public, and so did the promise, implicit in FININVEST having transmitted it, that stodgy old RAI was on borrowed time.

Berlusconi hit the headlines again three weeks later. In relieving Farina of AC Milan, he put him out of his self-imposed misery and completed another giant step in his inexorable rise to the top of Italy's sporting, political and (more's the pity) cultural pyramid. Farina always claimed that he had been solvent and that Berlusconi never paid a lira for the club. His assertion was that he owed only four months' income tax, while other club owners hadn't paid for years. The inference was that the potential social and political fallout from the foreclosure of Italy's football clubs had always indemnified them, and that he had been singled out by the tax authorities. He said he could have paid the debt at a stroke by selling the *libero* Franco Baresi, or indeed any one of a handful of players. Berlusconi's coup, he insisted, had been orchestrated by his friend Bettino Craxi, the socialist prime minister. The whole thing was a stitch-up, yet another example of the commodification – and criminalisation – of Italian football.

Little wonder that Gianni, who was seldom off the phone, took to calling Berlusconi most mornings. While the two of them professed to be friends, and the discussions were never less than cordial, *l'Avvocato* wasn't deluding himself. Silvio Berlusconi was a bit of a Luddite, but he was no fool. Sadly there's no record of what was said during those early-morning conversations, but one imagines a carousel of polite subterfuge and misinformation, a veritable Enigma Code of Italianate smoke and mirrors. In their world, calling a delicately honed, precision-engineered excavating apparatus a spade would have been to gravely insult its intelligence. Regardless, Silvio Berlusconi was the coming man in Italy, and Gianni knew it.

At the university of life, with Ian Rush

On 5 March 1986, a lacklustre Juve lost the first leg of their European Cup quarter-final in Barcelona. Their eight-point lead over Roma had been reduced to four, and the Italian press was speculating that Trapattoni was off to Inter. For a decade he'd been a bundle of nervous energy, but now the urgency which had characterised him and his teams was absent. Trap had won everything with Juventus, but unfriendly voices within Italian football still maintained that Boniperti – and not he – had been the catalyst. The suggestion was that Trap was a decent enough *functionary*, but that anyone could do what he'd done with the resources available to him. Meanwhile Inter, Juve's old rivals, had accomplished next to nothing. It was an open secret that Pellegrini had offered him a blank cheque, and Milan was Trapattoni's home.

Two days later he came clean. The rumours were true and, after 596 games, going on six championships and every meaningful cup competition there was to be won, it was almost over. There was this *Scudetto* to play for, but at the season's end he'd be on his way.

Try as they might, his team couldn't buy a win that spring. They came up short against Barça, and when Sven-Göran Eriksson's Roma drew level with them with two games remaining, it was all up for grabs. Juve were disjointed, injury-plagued and seemingly knackered. They would host Berlusconi's Milan in the penultimate game while Roma, unbeaten at home, entertained whipping boys Lecce. Promoted for the first time to Serie A, they'd been reunited with the Juve legend Causio. He'd grown up in the city, but he was 37 now and the team around him wasn't up to it. They were seven points adrift at the bottom, and – quite an achievement this – they'd failed to register even so much as a draw away from home. Come one, come all, it made no difference to the mighty Lecce. Football people are forever hacking on about consistency, and they had it in spades.

Before the match, Viola, the Roma president, did a lap of honour with the capital's mayor. Two years earlier they'd watched on helpless as their side lost a European Cup final penalty shoot-out to Liverpool on this very pitch. Today the memory of that would be swept away, and when Graziani headed in after seven minutes the party began in earnest. The avalanche, however, didn't materialise, and as Roma thrummed along in third gear, chances came and went. Of course that didn't really matter, because for half an hour Lecce were true to themselves and their apparent vocation. They barely crossed the halfway line but instead focused, as was customary, on arguing among themselves.

Then, inconceivably, they found themselves up the pitch, and their left-back wafted the ball in the general direction of the Roma goal. Nobody thought to track Lecce's Rome-born striker Alberto Di Chiara, presumably because he'd been the scorer of precisely one goal all season. He'd begun his career at the Olimpico, but they'd let him go before his 21st birthday. So far he'd done nothing to convince them they'd been mistaken, but now, unmarked, he stooped to head in the unlikeliest of equalisers.

The crowd, 60,000 of them, became fretful now, and as their tension turned their idols' feet to clay, Lecce took flight. They converted a penalty, and seven minutes into the second half scored *again*. In 20 cataclysmic minutes, Roma had contrived to concede three goals against the worst travelling side in the history of Serie A. In all probability there's a very good book to be written about the match, and the Italian football community has been attempting to untangle it all for over 30 years. It's proved to be one for the ages, but through the fug of it all the consensus is that Lecce were 'incentivised' (that old Italian footballing euphemism) to at least give it a go in Rome.

Whether or not that's true, give it a go is precisely what they did, and all subsequent attempts to subvert the result fell on deaf Pugliese ears. Some have speculated that there were *discussions* during the half-time interval, though Roma's talisman Roberto Pruzzo maintains that he and his colleagues just cracked. Following Graziani's opener something probably went haywire in their Freudian selves, and they just ran out of nervous energy. (That's my interpretation, by the way, not Pruzzo's. He was very good at heading it, but not so hot on rationalisation theory.)

Whatever. Lecce won the match fair and square. Meanwhile, on the hour, Laudrup rolled in a far-post cross at the Comunale, and in that instant Roma's pursuit was over. The following Sunday they conceded in the first minute at Como, and the next 89 were a wake. *La Stampa* wrote that Roma's championship dreams had been 'drowned in Lake Como', but in reality it had made no difference. Juve had edged a five-goal thriller (or a *thrilling*, as the Italians say) down at Lecce (them again), and the Trapattoni era ended on a high.

Juve appointed Rino Marchesi, the softly spoken Toro fan who'd masterminded Como's win over Roma that afternoon, to replace him. Though he inherited a title-winning squad, there was no *blocco Juve* at Mexico '86. Only veterans Cabrini and Scirea were selected, and that was a measure of the job Marchesi had taken on. The *Azzurri* just about made it through their group, but were knocked out by France in the last 16. Platini scored one and made the other that day, but the tournament was dominated by the sorcerer Maradona. They say that footballers can't win World Cups on their own, but at times Argentina seemed to be nought but he and ten anciliary staff.

By now preparations for *Italia '90*, the World Cup, were full steam ahead. Turin would host one of the semi-finals, but the Comunale was tired. It needed to be rebuilt or replaced, so Boniperti dispatched a team of architects to the citadels of European football. He told them to take the best bits from all of them and then design the club a wonderous all-seater stadium. They settled on a capacity of 60,000 and a site on the western fringes of the city in Corso Francia. Boniperti costed the stadium at 60 billion lire and set about finding ways to finance it. A PR agency declared itself ready to pay 25 billion to lease the advertising hoardings, while 2000 ten-year bonds would bring in a further 30 billion. The city was disposed to chuck in another 10 billion, and that would cover it. But then Romiti and company CFO Paolo Mattioli convinced Gianni not to go ahead.

Boniperti got on well with Romiti, but here he was dismayed by his obstinacy. As he saw it, the stadium was a no-brainer, and he failed to understand the logic in abandoning it. In reality it was pretty straightforward. FIAT was laying off employees in droves, and ordinary families were hurting. Spending that sort of money on a football ground would have been perceived as excessive, and Gianni was extremely sensitive to that sort of thing.

It was incumbent on the city, therefore, to build a new stadium. They engaged local architect Sergio Hutter and, notwithstanding the fact that he'd never designed a sporting arena before, he set to. At Lucento, on the north-western edge of the city, there was a scrubby area of wasteland formerly known as Continassa. There had been farmhouses there back in the day, and then a prison and a slaughterhouse. That had closed down in the mid-70s, and when the *comune* unadopted it a community of Roma had moved in.

Primo Nebiolo, *torinese* president of both CONI and the IAAF, had been a long-jumper in his youth. He agreed to contribute only on the basis that the facility be track and field compliant, and in December 1986 contracts were awarded. The 69,000-seater Stadio Delle Alpi, costed initially at 59 billion lire, would come in at 191 billion. It would host precisely one international athletics meeting – laughably, they forgot to provide a warm-up track – and would almost bankrupt the city of Turin.

Meanwhile the shifting sands within Italian football – and indeed Italian society – were epitomised by a transfer saga two hours' drive east. Roberto Donadoni was a refined young midfielder from Bergamo. He had two excellent feet, a great engine, and he played with his head up. Operating principally on the right, he'd broken into the Atalanta first team as a teenager. The big three had formed an orderly queue to sign him, and now, as he approached his 23rd birthday, the *bergamaschi* were ready to cash in.

Like most Serie A presidents, Atalanta's Achille Bortolotto had always been an Agnelli man. It was one of football's unwritten rules that Juve had first dibs in the transfer market, and besides Gianni had a certain affinity with the city of Bergamo and its football club. So, when Boniperti had come calling, Bortolotto had done what all serfs do – he'd doffed his cap and complied. Now, however, Bortolotto's son Cesare had assumed the presidency. At 35 he was the youngest in Serie A, and he wasn't particularly interested in the status quo. Invited by Berlusconi to dinner at his villa on the outskirts of Milan, he was soft-soaped into feeling really, really important. Berlusconi convinced Bortolotto Junior that he was his friend and in so doing overturned Italian footballing convention. Roberto Donadoni's transfer to Milan wasn't the highest profile that summer, but it was easily the most significant.

Berlusconi had resolved to out-Agnelli the Agnellis. He had a cheek on him, this Milanese lout, and Boniperti was furious. He was more furious still when, in November, Marchesi's side was swamped by Maradona and Co. at the Comunale. From there on in it was a procession, as the city of Naples abandoned itself to the infinitude of Maradona's genius. Gianni would later claim that Juve's failure to sign him was one of his biggest regrets.

In the circumstances second in 1986–87 was a decent finish for Juve, but at the season's end Platini announced that he was retiring aged 31. He'd had five golden years at 'the best club in the world', but his body could no longer cover the lung-busting distances or absorb the buffeting. Juve's best player – some say their best *ever* player – was leaving, and eight days later Boni wrote to Agnelli. For 40 years he'd been a *Juventino*, and a *Juventino* he'd remain. However with Platini and Trap gone and with Berlusconi having torn up the rule book, wasn't it time for a new broom in the boardroom as well? Gianni wrote back and told him, in no uncertain terms, not to be so ridiculous.

While Milan acquired the Dutch superstars Marco Van Basten and Ruud Gullit, *la vechia signora* replaced Platini with one of Europe's most prolific centre forwards. They'd actually bought Ian Rush from Liverpool the previous year, but left him there on loan for a season. In the meantime they'd sorted him out with an Italian tutor, but Rushy was fingers and thumbs with English grammar, never mind Italian. Interviewed after having completed the paperwork, he famously declared that Gianni spoke better English than he did.

He was right, but no matter. Aided and abetted by the great Kenny Dalglish, he had kept his hand in by netting 30 league goals that final season on Merseyside. That had the *Juventini* salivating over the prospect of him teaming up with Laudrup, but it seems the dog ate his homework. Rush, not the most articulate man at the best of times, touched down with barely a word of Italian. Fans, pundits and journalists had spent a year invoking the second coming of John Charles, but what they got was a tongue-tied, cloth-eared Joe Baker.

It would be a stretch to state that Rush spoke Italian badly because, quite simply, he spoke it hardly at all. He seemed perennially lost off the pitch but also, without Dalglish, lost on it. A month into the season, as Gianni left the ground following a particularly insipid performance against Pescara, the usual phalanx of journos pestered him for a few words. They enquired as to what was wrong with Rush, what he thought he was lacking. Gianni replied, 'A couple of Dalglishes.' Pithy, but painfully accurate.

Milan and Napoli, Italian football's *nouveau riche*, slugged it out for the 1988 title. Meanwhile Juve and Toro, its ugly sisters, bickered over sixth place. Rushy had been a duck out of water for eight months, but in his defence he had a very good final fortnight. He scored a stunning 88th-minute winner in the derby, and followed it with an even better interview. It went, verbatim, like this:

JOURNALIST: Rush, maybe your most important goal for Juve?

RUSH: Yes no most important for Juve because two points.

JOURNALIST: But not for you?

RUSH: Yes but also me because more important Juve because UEFA zone.

JOURNALIST: Did you use your lucky boots?
RUSH: Yes no English shoes here Italy.
JOURNALIST: Can we see them?

Rushy had the boots in his hand, but he didn't understand the question so he just stood there grinning politely at the guy.

Juve finished level with Toro. Thus, conversely in light of its having been abject, the season delivered a gripping epilogue. They played off for the final UEFA Cup place at a heaving Comunale, and a nervous, error-strewn 0–0 was followed by a nervous, error-strewn penalty shoot-out. Rushy was Juve's last man, and so it fell upon him, the not-the-new John Charles, to not cock up the deciding spot kick. It's not easy for a professional footballer to shank a dead ball, but Lorieri went the wrong way and it hobbled in off the post. After the match, north Wales' finest said he'd be happy to stay at Juve. At least that's what they *thought* he said, but it was never going to happen. *Arrivederci*, Rushy …

Arrivederci, Marchesi as well, as Juve sought to turn the page. He was replaced by Zoff as coach, and by the retiring Scirea as assistant. The *tifosi* loved that, but there would be no quick fixes for a team which had lost its champions and forgotten how to win. There would be no *blocco Juve* at the European Championships in Germany either; left-back Gigi de Agostini aside, no Juve at all. There was, however, a *blocco milanese*, as Inter and Milan supplied seven of the eleven starters for the semi-final against the Soviet Union. The *Azzurri* lost that one 2–0, before a wonderful Holland side starring Van Basten and Gullit outplayed the Soviets in the final.

By then Berlusconi had gifted Arrigo Sacchi, his new coach, another Dutchman. With Italian club sides now permitted three *stranieri* in their starting line-ups, the imposing central midfielder Frank Rijkaard arrived from Real Zaragoza. Over at Inter they had the German stars Lothar Matthäus and Andreas Brehme, and would later add their compatriot Jürgen Klinsmann. The presidents of foreign clubs loved Italian money, but they neither understood nor were interested in Italian politics. They'd no vested interests in Italian football, and that, along with Berlusconi's intervention and the burgeoning globalisation of the game, had swept away Boniperti's primacy in the marketplace.

Berlusconi, Pellegrini and Napoli's Ferlaino had initiated the sport's equivalent of an arms race, and by the early 90s Berlusconi in particular would be stockpiling designer footballers. The likes of Jean-Pierre Papin, Dejan Savićević and Zvonimir Bobin were inordinately talented. They'd have walked into any other club side in the world, but on matchdays at the San Siro were invariably sitting in the stand. There were six foreigners for three starting berths at Milan, and that was entirely the point. Competition for places was ferocious, and with money no object the club's interests were much better served by a redundant Papin than a *bianconero* Papin. A benched Savićević was an expensive ornament, but a *Juventino* or *Interista* Savićević didn't bear thinking about.

Meanwhile, over at Juve, Gianni indulged his predilection for all things mercurial. With the Soviet Union on the brink of collapse, he did a deal with Communism PLC (in liquidation) for Oleksandr Zavarov. The Ministry of Sport in Moscow got $2 million, and so too did Dynamo

Kiev. The State Department got another million, and Zavarov got Rushy's old flat. In all likelihood he also got the worst deal in the history of football. They reckon he was over the moon when they told him he'd be getting $1200 a month, but he was yet to become acquainted with the cost of vodka in Italian supermarkets.

As the first Russian to play in the West, Zavarov was nicknamed (you guessed it) 'the tsar'. He was reputed to be an intellectual on account of playing chess and speaking bits and pieces of English, but both his English and his Italian were about on par with Rushy's. So, for two roller-coaster seasons, was his football. He refused Platini's number 10, saying he wasn't worthy, and he wasn't wrong. His team-mates liked him, and there's no question he was talented. He sparkled intermittently, but he struggled with the tactical rigidity of the Italian game and missed home terribly.

In some way his travails during that first season symbolised Juve's malaise. By March 1989 they were way off the pace in Serie A, and out of the Coppa Italia. Zavarov scored an own goal as they lost at home to Ascoli amid conjecture that this was the most dysfunctional of all post-war Juve sides. That left the UEFA Cup as their last-chance saloon, and the tsar was outstanding as they beat Napoli 2–0 in the quarter-final first leg. A corner seemed to have been turned, but then they stumbled into a Milanese cul-de-sac. Sacchi's team smashed them 4–0 at the San Siro, but still worse was to follow.

Having travelled with the team to the return match in Naples, Zavarov wasn't selected by Zoff. Nobody quite knows why, but most seem to concur that it was 'disciplinary'. It was no secret that he liked a drink, and legend has it that Zoff had caught him enjoying a tipple on the team coach. Zavarov has always strenuously denied this, and it does seem scarcely credible. Either way, the team conceded a decisive third goal in the final minute of extra time, as this dreadful season reached its nadir. Ultimately they'd finish 15 points and several light years behind the champions, Inter, and the team – such as it was – would undergo root-and surgery. Laudrup would depart for Barcelona, and Cabrini, 13 years at the coal face, would be pensioned off to Bologna.

Another Soviet, Belorussian midfielder Sergei Aleinikov, would spend a season studiously avoiding the ball. The fans would nickname him 'Alentikov'. A play on *lento*, the Italian word for 'slow', it was painfully apt. Alentikov was forever finding himself where the ball had recently been, but never quite where it actually was. In addition, the Sicilian striker Salvatore 'Totò' Schillaci arrived from Messina, his cocksure partner Pierluigi Casiraghi from Monza. The former would become the star of Italia '90, but in the meantime there'd be a season of outrageous slings and arrows …

In the Dolomites, with Niall Quinn

In recent years FIFA has standardised and globalised the rules of association football. More accurately it's standardised the implementation of the rules, but for the best part of a century Italian players perceived the game entirely differently to, say, their English counterparts. In 1992, I watched a pre-season friendly in the Dolomites.

The protagonists were Manchester City and an Italian side, and ostensibly it mattered not a jot to anybody. However, it was one of the most interesting games of football I've ever seen, because it perfectly encapsulated the two countries' view of the game and how to play it.

Back in the day City were prosaic even by the lamentable standards of the English game. They pretty much bypassed midfield and larruped the thing forward as quickly as they could, because in Niall Quinn and David White they had a useful front two. For their part the Italian side had two very 'robust' stoppers, and so, to cut a long and extremely fractious story short, they played in precisely the same way Italian defenders had always played. They operated at the very end stops of legality, and where practicable beyond them.

White and Quinn, a likeable Mancunian and a mild-mannered Irish giant, had assumed they were going to be taking part in a pre-season kickabout with nothing riding on it. By half-time they were battered and bruised, outraged and incredulous. They didn't begin to understand why the Italians kept fouling them on and off the ball, nor why, in a meaningless 'friendly', they seemed so intent on provoking confrontation.

The game ended 0–0, and at the end they refused to shake hands with their markers and stomped off in a huff. That deeply upset the Italians. I got to talking to one of them later, and he said he couldn't fathom it. Niall Quinn – he told me in his best pidgin English – was 'the best animal' and 'a great champion'. He'd been in awe of him, and so he'd treated him with the respect he deserved. He'd tried to stop him by fair means or foul, and that had included winding him up so tight he wouldn't be able to think straight. That had been the marker's *compito* – his task – and he didn't understand why Quinn was offended by it. In no way was it personal. He'd very much wanted Quinn's shirt as a souvenir, and he was hurt that it hadn't been proffered. It had been a *friendly*, he stressed, and Quinn had 'behaved badly'.

So that's the difference, right there.

When it comes to football the English are as thick as mince, but like everyone else they have their World Cup idols. They revere the blond, blue-eyed, quintessentially cockney Bobby Moore, and Nobby Stiles was 'They don't like it up 'em' personified. The Germans had the great Franz Beckenbauer, symbol of honesty and détente. Across the border in Holland, Wim Van Henegem was a major star in the 70s. Crujff and Neeskens were more gifted, but he was considered a great patriot. He'd lost his father and siblings during the war, and he wore his contempt for the Germans like a bruise. In Portugal, Eusébio is renowned for his brilliance on the pitch, but also for the profound impact he, a black player from the colonies, had socially and culturally.

Gaetano Scirea had been a great player for Juventus but also, 78 times, for his country. There's a school of thought that he was the greatest *libero* of all, better even than Milan's Franco Baresi. Whether he was better defensively is open to question, but he was infinitely more expansive. In 377 games for Juve he scored 24 goals – many of them very important – and had a hand in countless others. There was very little that Scirea couldn't do on a football pitch, and nothing at all that he couldn't foresee.

The likes of Gentile, Tardelli and Sergio Brio were nice guys off the pitch and, in common with the guy who'd tied Quinn in knots, absolute thugs on it. Gaetano Scirea wasn't like that at all, and even the most jaundiced *anti-Juventino* would concede that he was scrupulously fair-minded both as a footballer and a man. He was modest, compassionate and highly intelligent, and he enjoyed listening much more than talking. In a country predisposed to hypocrisy and a profession given to chicanery, he refused to subscribe to Italian football's win-at-whatever-cost doctrine. If, therefore, Tardelli's iconic goal was the abiding image of the 1982 World Cup, Scirea was the individual with whom most Italians wished to identify. His team-mates were generally cut from the same coarse working-class cloth, but he had about him a certain nobility. In his integrity he embodied everything Italy aspired to be (but mainly wasn't), and everything good about sport. That was why he'd been club captain, why they'd appointed him to assist Zoff, and why the assumption was that he'd one day become manager, or chairman, or as likely as not both.

Juve were drawn against Górnik Zabrze in the first round of the UEFA Cup, and it was decided that Scirea would travel to Silesia to watch them play. Before leaving he spoke briefly to Boniperti, who told him to be careful. The roads over there, he said, were full of curves and hidden dips, and the Poles were crazy drivers. Scirea told him not to worry, and he was waved off by wife Mariella and by Riccardo, their 12-year-old son.

On the evening of 3 September 1989, Sandro Ciotti – he of *Clamoroso al Cibali* – was presenting RAI's *Domenica Sportiva*. At a certain point, Italy's voice of football, clearly shaken, announced that he was interrupting proceedings because news had reached him of a terrible tragedy in Poland. Because of petrol shortages there, the car in which Scirea had been travelling had been carrying four jerrycans full of it. After colliding with a truck the car caught fire, and Scirea had been pronounced dead on arrival at hospital. Among the studio guests was his old team-mate, room-mate and friend Marco Tardelli. While the others eulogised about Scirea the man and the footballer, he was simply too distraught to continue.

Nobody will ever forget Tardelli's flight from the studio, and no Italian – football fan or otherwise – will ever forget the death of Gaetano Scirea.

At Florence, with Roberto Baggio

Boniperti had toyed with the idea of leaving when Trap left, and again over the fiasco with the new ground. He'd also sent Gianni a resignation letter in the wake of Platini's retirement, but it hadn't been accepted. Scirea's death left him distraught, the more so because in his heart he'd known the trip to Poland hadn't been necessary. He carried on, but his heart was broken and so was the spell football had cast over him 60 years ago. The game seemed increasingly dominated by spivs, and there were smart-arsed 'executives' everywhere. They talked and talked and talked, but for the life of him he couldn't figure out what they were on about.

Umberto's son Giovanni Alberto – 'Giovannino' – had been earmarked as a future president of both club and company. He was smart; people liked him, and he'd inherited the Agnelli free-enterprise gene. Schooled in Rhode Island, he'd begun his FIAT career on the factory floor. They'd given him a false identity for security reasons (he'd been 'Giovanni Rossi') before assigning him the Piaggio scooter brand by way of preparation for the big job.

His cousin Edoardo couldn't have been more different. Gianni's boy was ten years Giovannino's senior, so the age difference more or less mirrored that between their respective fathers. Like Gianni, Edoardo loved Juve and even had a seat on the board for a time in the mid-80s. That, however, was about the only thing he had in common with his old man. He'd been sent off to Lehman Brothers in New York to begin his career, but he'd hated it. Edoardo was more taken by spiritualism, Shi'ite theology and philosophy, all anathema to his father. In rejecting materialism, he was rubbishing not only his family's calling, but also Gianni's very being.

He converted to Islam and spent considerable time in Iran, and was arrested in Kenya for possession of heroin. Ultimately he was cleared of the charges, but his apparent disinclination to kick the drug had his father tearing his hair out. The two of them struggled to establish common – or even neutral – ground, and the more clueless Gianni appeared, the more alienated Edoardo seemed to become.

Edoardo wasn't a *bad* person, but where his father was concerned, he was an angry, conflicted one. Gianni hadn't been present often enough, and when he had been he'd had more interesting things to do than frumpy old parenting. There's a story that Margherita, Edoardo's sister, once shaved her hair off in the hope that her father would notice she existed. Gianni knew he was a hopeless dad, but he was far too self-absorbed and hedonistic to do anything about it. Parenthood is about patience, altruism and unconditional love, and he was ill-equipped on all three fronts.

Giovannino was the chosen one, then, but in the interim Luca di Montezemolo would replace Boniperti. He'd distinguished himself as manager of the Ferrari Formula 1 team and Italy's America's Cup campaign, and was perfectly attuned to the notion of sport as a commercial activity. At present, Montezemolo was head of the organising committee for Italia '90, but would take over at Juventus when, in June 1991, Boni's mandate expired.

Boniperti understood all of this, but he wasn't comfortable in a holding role and he now barely recognised football. Clubs were spending money which wasn't theirs on players they couldn't afford and paying them movie-star salaries. To his generation, debt – in this case borrowing against future TV revenues – was simply wrong. He knew that the new breed of chairmen thought and operated differently, but he couldn't reconcile their behaviour with his upbringing, his values and his mindset.

In November he travelled with the team to Udinese. As he left the ground at half-time, he was reminded by a journalist that this was his 555th game as president. He'd played in another 445, and so this was quite a landmark. He waffled mindlessly to the reporter about carrying on, but he had a distracted, careworn look about him. In late January, with Juve seven points adrift of Napoli, the club announced that it had accepted his resignation.

Vittorio Chiusano, a 60-year-old lawyer, was installed as a stopgap in advance of Montezemolo's arrival. It was understood that Zoff, another old-school type, would be leaving as well, but in the meantime his team focused on an improbable cup double. In the third round of the UEFA Cup they drew Karl-Marx-Stadt, the socialist utopia formerly known as Chemnitz. Two weeks before the fall of the Berlin Wall it was a city in turmoil, but Juve came through with their ideology (among other things) intact, and drew their old nemesis Hamburg on the far side of East Germany's 'anti-Fascist rampart'. They exacted revenge of sorts with a 3–2 aggregate win, and then survived 90 helter-skelter minutes in Cologne. The following week they sealed the Coppa Italia with an unlikely 1–0 win at Milan and readied themselves for the first all-Italian European final. Their opponents would be Fiorentina, and one way or another there was a hell of a lot riding on it.

Juventus had been losing out in the transfer market and, as a consequence, in Serie A. They were without a *Scudetto* in four years, and fourth in Serie A was a fair reflection of where they were in the great scheme of things. They weren't quite as good as Inter, while Napoli and Milan were streets ahead of both of them. Boniperti's thrift had served them well prior to Berlusconi's incursion, but football had moved on. The old 'Winning isn't important – it's the only thing that matters' schtick was all well and good, but to implement it they needed to keep up with the big-spending Joneses. They urgently needed top players to arrest the slide. Deals were lined up to bring in wingers Thomas Hässler and Paolo Di Canio, and for the teenage midfielder Eugenio Corini. All three were talented, but the real prize lay elsewhere.

The Fiorentina president, Flavio Pontello, had been sucked into the spending vortex. It hadn't worked – Fiorentina hadn't won a trophy in fifteen years – and now he needed to get his money back. Word on the Ponte Vecchio was that his building empire was in dire straits, but in 23-year-old Roberto Baggio he had Italian football's most valuable asset. Baggio was a magical *fantasista* (playmaker), a number 10 destined for the World Cup and for greatness. By all accounts he didn't want to leave Florence, but Pontello had no option but to sell. Juve, the sworn enemy of *Viola* fans, needed to buy him at virtually any cost, and ahead of the first leg at the Comunale the papers were full of it.

Fiorentina's march to the final had been a genuine odyssey. With their stadium undergoing refurbishment for the World Cup, they'd become an itinerant team. Most home games had been played in Perugia, and it was there that they'd come through a penalty shoot-out against Atlético Madrid. They'd survived temperatures of –15° in Kiev, while in Sochaux they'd hung on for 86 minutes with ten men. In the semi-final they'd drawn Werder Bremen, and Pontello had sacked his manager four days before the first leg. They'd scored a crucial away goal, but then it had all gone off during the 'home' game in Perugia.

Fiorentina had parked the bus in the best Italian tradition, and after 45 stop-start minutes the game remained goalless. Upon taking the field for the second half, the Werder keeper Oliver Reck had started removing toilet rolls, flares and other detritus from his six-yard box. As he'd done so, however, two Fiorentina ultras had run on and assaulted him. Reck had been fine to continue, and the game had finished goalless. His club had been magnanimous enough not to appeal, so Fiorentina had scraped through. However the football world had been watching, and UEFA needed to act.

Its disciplinary committee would sit, and in light of Werder's sportsmanship the club might just get away with it. That being the case, the home leg of the final would probably be played in Florence, because the ground was all but ready and they might just have a safety certificate in time. Failing that they'd be back to Perugia, but if they insisted on a sanction then a neutral ground (as likely as not Rome or Genoa) would have to do. Worst-case scenario would have them playing it behind closed doors, but that was highly unlikely. This was one of UEFA's showcase events, and one of its cash cows. An all-Italian final was bad enough, but an all-Italian final in an empty stadium didn't tick too many televisual boxes.

The committee would meet on 7 May, five days after the first leg in Turin. This was Zoff's last home match in charge and, fittingly enough, Juve's final competitive match at the Comunale. It was also billed as a de facto memorial match for Scirea, so one way or another it was a really big occasion. As sporting contests go, though, it would be everything he'd abhorred.

Baggio was a sensitive soul, and his misgivings about the move derived to a degree from an interview Gianni had given the previous November. Agnelli had been invited to compare him to Platini, and had noted, quite correctly, that he still had a way to go. But here he excelled as Fiorentina dominated the first half. They went in at 1–1, but after the break the game came over all Italian. Juve's second goal was scored by Casiraghi following a blatantly obvious push on *Viola* defender Celeste Pin. Quite how the referee missed it is anybody's guess, because Casiraghi literally shoved the bloke to the floor before the ball arrived. A goalkeeping error rubbed salt in the Florentine wound, and they boarded their coach 3–1 down.

Four of the Fiorentina players were referred to the UEFA disciplinary committee for 'violent comments' aimed at the (Spanish) referee. To be fair he had been diabolical, but on Monday 7 May 1990 the committee pronounced judgement on both issues. The miscreants got off with a warning for verbally assaulting the ref, but the second leg would indeed take place in a neutral venue. And that venue would be …

The *comune* of Avellino, population 50,000, is the unofficial capital of Irpinia, a beautiful, lush mountain district in Italy's deepish south. Nothing much happens there, and in 1990 it had a Serie B team and, in the Stadio Partenio, a decidedly Serie B ground. Juve keeper Stefano Tacconi had begun his career in it, and the people down there were proud of his having become a *Juventino* and an *Azzurro*. Everyone had family or friends in Turin or, post-*boom economico*, family or friends who'd returned from Turin. Regions like Irpinia are almost as *Juventino* as Turin itself. Figuratively, therefore, Avellino was closer to Juve's Comunale than Fiorentina's Artemio Franchi. Fiorentina were seething about this, because it guaranteed a stadium full of black and white. However the logical choices, Rome and Genoa, were inadmissible. A neutral venue had to be a minimum of 300 kilometres from where the match would have been played (Florence), and so, eight years to the day since the

'*Meglio secondi che ladri*' game, Avellino it was but neutral it wasn't.

It finished 0–0, and it was awful: petulant, violent and bleak. The old lady had another UEFA Cup, and the very next day she had Roberto Baggio. Florence, which had neither, literally burned. There were fires. Lots of them. And riots.

Chapter 8

Good Men and True

It's not true that I don't like to win. I like to win respecting the rules.

Zdeněk Zeman

At the Delle Alpi, with a pair of binoculars

It was stunning on the outside, the Delle Alpi, and rubbish on the inside. The pitch would flood because the drainage was useless; the seats were uncomfortable, and the 'atmosphere' was funereal. I remember watching a game in the third tier, and the old boy sitting next to me pulled out a pair of binoculars. I looked at him and shrugged, and he shrugged back. '*Fa schifo,*' he said – 'It's crap.' He was right. The stadium was crap, the all-new corporate branding was crap, and by Juve standards the team was utterly crap.

Juve's new manager was Gigi Maifredi. In his previous job at Bologna he'd eschewed Italy's trademark sweeper system in favour of a zonal defence. It had made him flavour of the month, and what with the Catholicism and his natty suits, everyone had seemed convinced. Only it transpired that Maifredi wasn't the messiah after all, but rather an overpromoted prance. Maifredi was a former champagne salesman, but the football he 'coached' resembled the cheap spumante they made up the road in Asti. He'd inherited a deluxe group of players, but he denuded them of the ability to play.

They lost the opening game of the 1990–91 season, the Supercoppa, 5–1 to champions Napoli. Maifredi suggested it was just a spot of teething trouble, but that was wishful thinking. Júlio César, the Brazilian World Cup star tasked with coordinating the new back four on the field, couldn't make head nor tail of it. Schillaci, *capocannoniere* the previous year and star of the *Mondiale*, proved to be a bit of a one-season wonder. His bark was much worse than his bite, while poor, displaced Baggio just looked plain miserable.

Things came to a head over four calamitous games in the spring. Down in Florence, the ultras had been preparing for Juve's visit for almost a year. The mayor appealed for calm, but Baggio's presence was always going to be divisive. He was an inoffensive young man and a great footballer, but great footballers tend to induce idiocy in otherwise balanced human beings. His wearing the wrong coloured T-shirt here was a case in point, and it split Florence down the middle. Almost everyone had known he'd have to be sacrificed, but for some going *there* was unconscionable. For others he was the victim of Pontello's treachery, but in reality he was just a piece of meat like the rest of them. One way or another, Baggio couldn't do right for doing wrong.

Five minutes into the second half, with Juve trailing 1–0, Baggio had his shirt pulled inside the box. He was Maifredi's penalty taker, but he couldn't bring himself to take this one. Gigi De Agostini stepped up instead, and it was duly saved. Maifredi hauled Baggio off soon after, and as he walked around the perimeter some hurled insults and bottles while others sent love and kisses. When someone threw a *Viola* scarf, Baggio bent down and picked it up. That seemed to do it for the home crowd, and to a man they melted. He trundled off to tumultuous applause, and his former team won thanks to his having demurred on the penalty.

The following week, newly promoted Toro were the 'visitors' to the Delle Alpi. Champagne Gigi had some very talented individuals, but Juve had no discernible method. They lost 2–1 and then played out an anodyne 0–0 draw at Cagliari. When Milan took them apart at the Delle Alpi the following Sunday, Maifredi's fate was sealed.

Juventus failed to qualify for Europe for the first time in 28 years, and now ever-ready Boniperti took a call from Gianni Agnelli. He told him to forget all that nonsense about travelling and to cancel the English lessons he'd been meaning to get round to. He wasn't cut out for any of that, and he *certainly* wasn't cut out to be a full-time grandad. Rather, Gianni said, he had a new role as managing director of Juventus Football Club. Montezemolo was to be redeployed elsewhere, and the rest of the board would be invited politely but firmly to vacate their positions. Maifredi was out (back to relegated Bologna), so Boni's first task would be to speak to Pellegrini over at Inter. He'd been forewarned that Trapattoni was wanted back in Turin, so they'd just need to sort out the compensation for the final year of his contract.

When Boniperti asked if that would be all, Gianni said that yes, that would be all. Boniperti put the phone down, and then picked it up again. He rang Pellegrini and they agreed that Dino Baggio, a brilliant young midfielder Juve had signed from Toro, would be loaned to Inter for a year, and in exchange Trapattoni would be released from his contract.

The ground, the choice of Montezemolo as president, Maifredi as first-team coach – all big mistakes, but none of them altered the fact that football had moved on. The respective squads of Juve and Milan, the new power in the land, told their own story. Trap, who employed *Juventino*' favourite Sergio Brio as his assistant, began the season with a first-team squad of 17 just as he'd always done. That had always seemed to make sense to Boniperti. You needed 11 starters, a backup keeper, striker and centre half and a few utility scufflers. Your backups wouldn't be as good as the starters, but assuming you didn't get too many injuries you ought to be able to get by.

Among this season's new arrivals at Juventus were goalie Angelo Peruzzi and Antonio Conte, a trojan right-sided midfielder from down in Puglia. Conte was straight out of HH2's *Juve operaia* playbook, and he'd compete with Corini, Roberto Galia, Giancarlo Marocchi and Angelo Alessio for a place in the side. Over at Milan, Gullit and Rijkaard would rub shoulders with Donadoni, Demetrio Albertini and Carlo Ancelotti. Throw in the artist Diego Fuser and crafty Alberigo Evani, and Milan's midfielders would amass 347 international caps. Juve's would cobble together 34.

The point is that these *milanesi* saw things differently. They had 21 extremely good players, rising to 28 by the time the Champions League started in 1993. Their second string was *Scudetto*-winning good, because what sense was there in risking unproven players when you could just as easily go to the bank and buy ready-made champions? Boniperti's ability to spot a bargain had been laudable, but nobody wanted that any more. Money was cheap and easy to borrow, and so borrow it they did. Suddenly the likes of Foggia and Parma, unremarkable clubs in small provincial cities, were 'investing' in world-class players.

Toro, relegated two years earlier, had been acquired for a song by one of Bettino Craxi's minions. Gian Mauro Borsano had brought them straight back up, appointed Moggi as sports director and secured funding for brilliant midfielders Rafael Martín Vásquez and Enzo Scifo. As a result Toro – yes *Toro* – had finished above Maifredi's Juve. Under Borsano the club would win the Coppa Italia and reach the UEFA Cup final. For a few years a galaxy of stars would wear *granata* but then – who'd have guessed it? – there was a massive fire sale. By 1996 the club was back in Serie B, and Borsano was arrested for (among other things) false accounting and tax evasion. The upshot of his spending spree was 15 years yo-yoing between the divisions, bankruptcy in 2005, and no derby win in two decades.

Parma's president was Calisto Tanzi, founder and CEO of the Parmalat food conglomerate. Having embezzled €800 million, he'd go to prison following the biggest bankruptcy in European history. His collection of Modiglianis, Cézannes and Matisses would be auctioned off, and so would his Thurams, his Crespos and his Zolas. Sergio Cragnotti, the president of Paul Gascoigne's Lazio, would similarly find himself behind bars, but Berlusconi would just keep right on. Milan would win three successive *Scudetti* (losing only five games), become easily the best club side on the planet and contest five European Cup/Champions League finals in seven years.

Football had become a game of high profiles, high stakes and high finance. It was *the* global sport, and almost without exception its best exponents were found in Italy. Young men like Baggio were world famous, and their employers were increasingly adept at monetising their popularity. What the owners of minnows Udinese and Perugia had started with local ice cream and pasta, Berlusconi et al. had appropriated, developed and inflated out of all proportion. Through sponsorship, merchandising and above all TV, the money rolled in as never before. Serie A was the most glamorous league in the world, and by a distance the most corpulent.

This, broadly, was the context for Trap's second tenure at Juventus. He and Boniperti were almost anachronisms, and the mess they inherited meant they were always going to be playing catch-up.

Though far too introverted to be a dressing-room leader, Baggio was a wonderful player. Juve had broken the world transfer record in signing him, but if ever a footballer was worth 25 billion lire, it was 'Roby'. He'd win the Ballon d'Or in 1993, and by then Juve had assembled a half-decent supporting cast. Gianluca Vialli was one of the world's best centre forwards, Conte a trojan, the German Andreas Möller a scorer of outstanding goals. Over time his countryman Jürgen Kohler developed a solid partnership with Júlio César. They were living in a material world, but from time to time even a sport as mercenary as *calcio* threw up a heart-warming story.

Moreno Torricelli had grown up in Brianza, a sprawling Milanese satellite town. Like everyone he'd dreamed of Serie A, but like most he hadn't made it. He'd therefore found himself a packing job at the Spinelli furniture factory, and plugged away at park football of a weekend.

Torricelli was an aggressive, energetic full-back. He was also reasonably talented, and Caratese, one of 200-odd teams operating in Italy's regionalised fifth division, spent 20 million lire (£7000) on his signature. That was a break for Moreno, and so was the fact that they paid him £400 a month expenses. Soon enough Serie C2 sides, those in the fourth tier, started sniffing around. One of them was Pro Vercelli. He turned them down convinced he had enough to get into a club higher up, though an unsuccessful trial at Serie B Verona suggested otherwise.

One of the local clubs, Serie C2 Lecco, had taken on Juve legend Claudio Gentile as *direttore sportivo*. In conversation with Trapattoni, he mentioned that the kid was as ballsy as they came, had bags of initiative and wasn't without ability. Something in that appealed to the romantic in Trap, probably because he himself had worked in a print shop before Milan had offered him a contract. His great friend 'Billy' Salvadore had started his adult life as a joiner, and they'd each gone on to represent their country. Thus, in June 1992 Trap told Boniperti he wanted to give Torricelli a trial over three of the traditional end-of-season friendlies, because what possible harm could it do?

Boni was sceptical. Torricelli was 22, and logic suggested that if he was any good he wouldn't be playing for Caratese. That said, Gentile was no fool, and besides if the guy was hopeless they'd send him back whence he came. If he was OK, then one of the Serie B or C1 sides would likely give him a leg up, and if he was *really* good they'd move him on at a tidy profit. Either way the cost to Juve would be zero, and they'd be seen as benevolent in giving the kid a chance.

Torricelli had his trial, and he felt like he did pretty well. The club told him they'd let him know *pronto*, and his old man told him he'd been fantastic. Then, day by heartbreaking day, the dream died. There was no phone call, no telegram or letter, and so no hope. There was nothing whatsoever, and in the end Moreno Torricelli resigned himself to the idea that it just wasn't meant to be. The trial had come to nought, but at least his mum, a lifelong *Juventina*, had fleetingly lived the dream. She'd seen her boy play for the *bianconeri*, and how many mothers could say that?

Then, on 17 July 1992, a telegram appeared at *casa* Torricelli. It was from Juventus, and it informed him that he needed to get in touch asap. He did as he was told, and it transpired they hadn't forgotten him after all. They'd just forgotten to ask him for his home address, so the previous telegram had been sent to a different Torricelli. They'd taken an educated guess that the address they'd found would be his, or at least that of a family member. It wasn't, and the recipient hadn't thought to do anything about it. Whatever. He needed to get himself to Turin, because he'd a contract to sign with Juventus Football Club. He signed it – Boniperti said he'd fill in the numbers afterwards – in the hope that it would help towards a new car. The one he'd spent four years savings on had just been stolen.

Then he packed his bags and flew to Bavaria for pre-season *ritiro*. Ten months later he found himself on a podium in the centre circle of the Delle Alpi, receiving a gold medal from some sort of dignitary with 62,000 people waving at him and cheering. He was standing next to Baggio and Vialli, and they were passing round a giant silver trophy. Borussia Dortmund had been over-whelmed, and Moreno Torricelli, the packing guy from the Spinelli furniture factory, had won the 1993 UEFA Cup.

The win over Dortmund was great, but the football club – *the* football club – had been seven years without a championship. If Berlusconi's Milan was a mirror on its upwardly mobile city then so, conversely, was Agnelli's Juve. The Milanese economy had always been more diverse than that of FIATville, and in consequence was better placed to adapt as the traditional engineering/manufacturing sector contracted. As cheap Chinese steel and consumer goods flooded the Italian market, the smart *milanesi* pivoted towards banking, service industries, media and tourism. But as Milan reinvested, reinvented and reconfigured itself for the post-industrial age, Italy's Motown atrophied. FIAT remained the largest employer for now, but day by day and week by week the shutters were coming down. The long goodbye had begun with the closure of Lingotto back in 1982, and now Mirafiori was shrinking. In 1967 the factory had produced 5000 cars a day there and employed 52,000 people, but 30 years on only half that number clocked in.

Moreover, the company wanted to lay off 5000 of them, and a further 3000 were to go at Rivalta.

With the state committed to paying half the costs, the company agreed to build its new plant in the deep south. The new Punto would be produced not in mighty Turin, but in a small market town in Basilicata. Melfi was (is) on the road to nowhere in particular and, as Carlo Levi eloquently reminded us, Christ stopped at Eboli. That explained the chronic unemployment and the fact that it tended to be missed out of guidebooks. Regardless of all that, Piedmont's loss was most definitely Basilicata's gain, and the plant has produced over five million Puntos. That's five million more than Turin, but the defection denuded the city of much more than employment. Once more it lost prestige, identity and direction, and what remained, as living standards declined and unemployment increased, was a feeling of impotence. People felt betrayed, and many of them *still* feel betrayed. Melfi was a clear line in the sand and for some a clear sign that what FIAT giveth, FIAT taketh away. It was the end of Turin as a manufacturing powerhouse, and the beginning of its ongoing fight for post-industrial employment, investment and relevance.

Gianni had been clear from the outset that Boniperti's mandate would expire in the summer of 1994. That had suited both of them, and besides *l'Avvocato*'s time was up as well. He'd always promised himself he'd take a back seat when he turned 75, and he was 72 now. It was time to start thinking about a successor, and in a roundabout way he informed Boniperti that Umberto was doing just that. He'd be taking the reins, and he had very different ideas about the way the football club should be run.

Umberto's had been a life spent in Gianni's lee. That hadn't necessarily been his fault, but as he approached his 60th birthday he felt the need to assert his identity, his ideas and his abilities. He'd struggled to prove himself in the public domain, but if he could return Juventus to the top of Serie A it would be tangible, highly visible proof that he was a great manager in his own right. Meanwhile his associate Antonio Giraudo had successfully relaunched the ski resort at Sestriere, and he'd been a very capable manager of the family's insurance company. The two were agreed that Roberto Bettega would be an excellent vice president, and everyone knew that Moggi had to be brought in as sports director. (That's the fancy Italian term for head of player recruitment, and nobody recruited footballers quite like Moggi.)

In effect Gianni was telling Boniperti that their race was run, and so was that of Trapattoni. The times were a-changin', and on 26 January 1994 Roberto Bettega began his second *Juventino* life. The idea was that he'd work alongside Boniperti for six months, but that was wishful thinking. Boni barely recognised him any more, and the language he and Giraudo talked might as well have been Norwegian. There was a certain smugness in the way Giraudo in particular conducted himself, and Boni had the distinct impression they couldn't wait to see the back of him. By late April he could stand it no longer. He explained to Gianni – rather than his little brother – that it was best for everyone if he went before it turned sour.

On 29 April he did precisely that, and Juventus Football Club turned another page.

At the San Siro, with the hunchbacks

Boniperti was out, then, and the Giraudo–Bettega–Moggi troika installed Marcello Lippi in Trap's stead. A 46-year-old former *libero* who'd spent most of his playing career at Sampdoria, he'd started his coaching life with their youth team. He'd moved on to Serie C2 side Pontedera, and from there he'd chipped his way up through the divisions. Latterly he'd distinguished himself at post-Maradona, post-money Napoli. The club had sold just about anyone who was any good, but somehow Lippi had guided them to a UEFA Cup place. He was charming and Paul Newman-handsome, and Moggi and Bettega were convinced that he was the man to end the drought.

Boniperti's last meaningful act had been to secure 18-year-old Alessandro Del Piero from Padova under the noses of Milan. He'd become one of the great Juve playmakers, in all probability *the* greatest. Baggio was similarly gifted but not as robust, while Platini played only 147 times for the club. Del Piero would play over 500, more even than the great Boniperti. He'd score in excess of 200 goals, and conduct himself with humility, grace and class. He was the professional footballing exemplar, and his value to the brand was immeasurable. Gianni famously referred to him as 'Pinturicchio' – Little

Artist – after the Renaissance painter of the same name. Say what you will about Boniperti, but there's an absolute rightness in him having bequeathed Del Piero, his true heir, to the Agnelli family. What *Juventini* they each were.

Del Piero aside, Umberto didn't invest too heavily at the beginning. The Portuguese floater Paolo Sousa adorned the midfield, and against the odds the stopper Ciro Ferrara was persuaded to leave his beloved Napoli. French destroyer Didier Deschamps was signed initially as backup, Atalanta prodigy Alessandro Tacchinardi as one for the future. All were fine players, and all would contribute as the old lady reasserted herself as Italy's pre-eminent team. However the *real* story of the Lippi era lay elsewhere.

The Delle Alpi was hopeless. Costs were exorbitant, and those sitting in the lower tier simply couldn't see the pitch. To those in the second it resembled a wind tunnel, and for those in the third the players were dots on the horizon. The public voted with their feet, and the club fell out with the company contracted by the city to manage the place. The situation reached its nadir one tragicomic evening in September 1994, when CSKA Sofia visited for the opening round of the UEFA Cup.

Two years earlier, Toro had defeated Real Madrid in the home leg of the UEFA Cup semi-final. They'd filled the place for that, but the old enemy still hadn't accomplished it. U2 (twice) and Vasco Rossi (multiple times) would sell it out, and three weeks before the CSKA game 80,000 had been shoehorned in to see Pink Floyd. Here silver-haired striker Fabrizio Ravanelli scored five times, but only 2475 paid to watch. It was pitiable.

Giraudo was exploring the possibilities of a new home, but that would be a project 15 years in the making. In the here and now the row over the management fees escalated, and in April the club took a decision which was as provocative as it was totemic. Juventus Football Club, domiciled in Turin but harbouring pretensions to represent the entire peninsula, would play the UEFA Cup semi-final first leg in ... Milan.

The San Siro is one of the great temples of the sport, and the *tifosi* travelled from far and wide. Italy's sweetheart sold out a stadium some 135 kilometres from home, and the troika congratulated themselves on having made good on their threats to the management company. The game itself was a struggle though, as goals from Borussia Dortmund's former *Juventini* Möller and Stefan Reuter overhauled Baggio's opener. With two minutes remaining, the Milanese experiment was starting to look extremely ill-advised, but then another footballing expat intervened. Having stayed forward from a corner, Kohler lashed a loose ball home to salvage a 2–2 draw.

In the away leg, Juve dispatched the Germans in much the same way they'd been dispatching Italians for the preceding seven months. Under Lippi they were a team transformed, and the credit went to the new staff. Riccardo Agricola, promoted from the youth sector, had become first-team doctor, and Giampiero Ventrone had assumed responsibility for their fitness. As Serie A adopted three points for a win, they'd outrun, -jumped and -muscled the rest, and now only Parma stood between them and a unique treble.

The two sides were slated to meet five times in as many weeks over May and June, first in the UEFA Cup final. Juve old boy Dino Baggio scored the only goal in Parma, and the two teams reconvened at a heaving San Siro for the second leg. There Vialli opened the scoring for the 'hosts', but Baggio equalised as Juve's strategy backfired. They'd chosen once more to play the home leg at what amounted to a neutral venue. It had more or less worked against Dortmund, but then Dortmund hadn't had Dino Baggio, Gianfranco Zola and Tino Asprilla in their side.

In explaining the defection to Milan, Juve had trotted out the old *anti-campanilismo* line. That had been a tidy little construct, but a construct all the same. The Delle Alpi, for all its manifest shortcomings, was home. Turin was home as well, but the club had sacrificed its players' competitive advantage on the altar of hard currency. The age-old *Juventino* arrogance had revealed itself once again, and this time they'd paid a heavy price.

Whether they liked it or not, *campanilismo* was the heart and soul of the game, and four days later Lippi's men proved it by hammering Parma 4-0 at the Delle Alpi to seal the championship. Two weeks later they overpowered them there once more. This time it was in the first leg of the Coppa Italia final, and the *coup de grâce* was applied with a comfortable 2-0 win in Parma.

Del Piero was to have learned his craft from Baggio, but the 'divine ponytail' wasn't much of a mentor and his relationship with Lippi was catastrophic. They didn't know how to be around each other, and by the season's end it was clear that it was never going to work. Baggio joined Milan and embarked upon a peripatetic footballing existence which would see him fetch up in provincial cities like Bologna and Brescia.

By the time they reached the 1996 Champions League final, Juventus were bigger, stronger and fitter than almost any side they encountered. There were more technically gifted teams across Europe, but none so powerful. Nobody had full-backs who covered the ground like Torricelli and Gianluca Pessotto, nor a trio of midfielders as rapacious as Conte, Sousa and Deschamps. Ravanelli and Vialli were fast and immensely strong, and Del Piero's physical transformation was sensational. He'd arrived coltish and half-formed, but now he allied muscularity to creativity. No parvenu, but a worthy successor to Baggio and, aged just 21, one of the most expansive players on the continent. It took extra time and a penalty shoot-out to finally subdue a wonderful young Ajax team in Rome, but when Peruzzi saved from Sonny Silooy it was done. Eleven years from Heysel, the club finally had a European championship with no apparent strings attached.

That summer, Vialli and Ravanelli joined the Premier League gravy train, as freedom-of-movement restrictions were lifted for EU players. All told seven of the first team squad departed, and a completely new group emerged. Zinedine Zidane and Del Piero constituted its brain, Ferrara and Uruguayan hard man Paolo Montero its defensive brawn. The engine room was peopled by bothersome, tireless snappers like Deschamps and Angelo Di Livio. Their role was to get it and courier it to the soloists quickly and unfussily, and they were extremely good at it.

In November 1996, 32-year-old Giovannino married American architect Frances Avery Howe. By way of a wedding present, Juve travelled to Tokyo for the

Intercontinental Cup final. Their opponents were River Plate; Del Piero scored the only goal, and the Argentines scarcely had a kick. Their manager, Ramón Diaz, remarked on the 'enormous physical difference between the two squads'. Athletically it was men against boys, but River Plate weren't alone in being overpowered. Walter Smith, the Glasgow Rangers manager, reckoned Ravanelli's thigh muscles were the biggest he'd ever seen on a striker.

Back in the day Umberto had done it with Charles, Sívori and Boniperti, and now he'd repeated it with Bettega, Giraudo and Moggi. The troika had clobbered the philistine Berlusconi, and *la vecchia signora* embarked upon her 100th birthday celebrations as officially the world's best football team. Paris Saint-Germain were beaten 9–2 on aggregate in the European Super Cup, before Lippi's team bludgeoned its way to another *Scudetto*. The Champions League final was lost to Dortmund, but Juve were firmly established at the very top of the European game.

Heading into the 1997–98 season, Giovannino Agnelli was gravely ill. He'd gone public with the fact that he had intestinal cancer, and each time he appeared in the *tribune d'onore* he looked more jaundiced. Notwithstanding the efforts of the world's best oncologists, he watched his last match on the evening of 10 December. The players bade him farewell by beating Manchester United, and he passed away peacefully three days later. This was the Agnelli story – triumph at work and tragedy in their private lives – perfectly distilled. So was the media coverage; Umberto had lost his son, but the press reported the death of 'Gianni's nephew'.

By now Juve had signed former Ajax midfielder Edgar 'pitbull' Davids. He'd spent a season at Milan, but Alessandro 'Billy' Costacurta, their veteran stopper, had famously labelled him a 'bad apple'. There's a body of opinion that Moggi was instrumental in that. The story goes that Davids had set out to make his position at Milan untenable, but by now that was part and parcel of the game. It's fair to say – as they do in Italy – that Davids didn't need to work hard to appear *antipatico*. Gianni said he wouldn't have fancied running into him down a dark alleyway, and off the pitch he could be prickly. On it, though, he ran, tackled and scrapped like two men. He could play as well, and with him in the cockpit the domestic season developed into a two-horse race with the old enemy Inter. On 26 April 1998 they met for the *derby d'Italia* in Turin ...

That season, Juventus had been the beneficiaries of two dreadful refereeing decisions. In November, Udinese had been visitors to the Delle Alpi. With the score at 1–1, German striker Oliver Bierhoff had beaten Peruzzi's understudy, Michelangelo Rampulla, to a punt down the middle. He'd toed it towards the goal, and the ball had been the best part of a metre over the line when Ciro Ferrara hacked it away. The linesman hadn't noticed though, and Juve had gone on to win the match 4–1.

At Empoli a week before the Inter game, Stefano Bianconi's header was a good foot inside the goal when Peruzzi clawed it away. Referee Pasquale Rodomonti was just about the only person in the ground who failed to notice, despite standing a few metres away with a clear view. A Tuscan magistrate initiated an investigation and would find that while Rodomonti hadn't *set out* to cheat, in common with many Italian refs he'd developed a 'psychological allegiance' to Juventus. Either way, Juve won 1–0, and they led by a point heading into the Inter game.

Early in the piece, Inter's Ronaldo, the best striker in world football, received the ball 30 yards out. His first touch took him beyond his marker, but Torricelli then intervened with a late, high, clumsy challenge. It was patently bookable, but referee Piero Ceccarini let him off scot-free and Del Piero gave Juve the lead shortly after. On 28 minutes, the Inter *fantasista* Youri Djorkaeff intercepted an underhit pass from Zidane. Torricelli lunged in once more, and kicked Djorkaeff in the midriff. It was another stone-cold booking, and Ceccarini was standing no more than fifteen yards away. However, he neglected to caution Torricelli, and failed to book Davids when he cleaned out Benoit Cauet from behind.

After the break, Mark Iuliano pulled Ronaldo's shirt, whereupon Ceccarini awarded a free kick but didn't issue a yellow. Then Deschamps hacked down Cauet under the linesman's nose. Still nothing. Three minutes later Ceccarini *did* produce a card, booking Inter's Iván Zamorano for a foul on Davids in the centre circle. Next, Davids retaliated violently following a Diego Simeone foul. The incident is similar to David Beckham's red card offence against the same player during France 1998, but Ceccarini elected not to send Davids off. Instead he booked Simeone for the initial infraction, leaving the *nerazzurri* apoplectic.

With 20 minutes remaining, Ronaldo raced onto a loose ball in the Juve box. He toed it round Iuliano, but the Juve stopper was committed. His momentum caused him to body-check Ronaldo, who finished on the floor in a heap. It was the clearest foul you're ever likely to see, and yet Ceccarini somehow saw fit to wave it away. As Inter's incredulous players protested, the ball was transferred quickly downfield. Del Piero went down under challenge from Taribo West, and Juve were awarded a *rigore*. Inter manager Simoni lost it completely at this point, and was sent off for encroaching onto the pitch.

Del Piero's penalty was saved, but that wasn't the issue. Inter had been denied a stonewall penalty, and neither Davids nor Iuliano had any right to be on the field of play. By the time Inter midfielder Zé Elias was dismissed for a stray elbow, the whole thing had become a grotesque caricature. Rhetorically, the front page of Monday morning's *Gazzetta dello Sport* screamed, CECCARINI WHAT HAVE YOU DONE?

What he'd done was insult the intelligence of the Italian sporting public – again. On the Ronaldo body check he subsequently blathered that he might have awarded an indirect free kick for obstruction had he seen it, and in so doing offered an alternative interpretation of the laws of football. Obstruction is when there is no bodily contact, but Ronaldo had been poleaxed.

There was a debate in parliament about it, as even the *Juventino* vice president Walter Veltroni admitted there was a 'problem'. One minister, Roma fan Domenico Gramazio, was moved to ask, 'How many FIATs are the refs getting?' before getting into a bust-up with a former Juve player. Massimo Mauro had won the *Scudetto* both in Turin and in Naples, and upon retirement had become a centre-left politician. It took four people to separate them, but after it all calmed down the parliamentarians concluded that, while there was no evidence that Ceccarini was crooked, the refs were in some way 'conditioned'. There was a case for using foreign ones because it was impacting share values on the stock market and compromising the emotional wellbeing of Italian society(!)

Unlike Iuliano, Gramazio was suspended for 15 days. Then everything carried on as normal, which is to say Juve won the league and Inter were climbing the walls.

In deepest, darkest Wallonia, with (of all people) the Gewiss cycling team

Have you heard the story of Gewiss, the famous Italian cycling team from the mid-1990s? Of the legendary 1994 edition of the Flèche Wallonne, a single-day classic synonymous with that era of bike racing?

You haven't? I'll try to be brief ...

Back then most of the really big races took place in one of three countries, France, Belgium and Italy, and most of the winners came from there. In 1993, a number of the Italians started working with a brilliant new *preparatore*, a sort of sports doctor/trainer. His name was Michele Ferrari, and he attached himself to the riders of the Gewiss team. It had always been a middling sort of outfit, but under Ferrari its riders morphed into champions. Their results were astounding, but the official team doctor employed to ensure the riders' well-being wanted nothing to do with it. He quit, but Ferrari didn't care and nor, apparently, did his acolytes. He was turning carthorses into racehorses, and they were rewarded with bigger, fatter, better contracts.

By the spring of 1994, the Gewiss boys were turning bigger gears than everyone else, and turning them faster and for longer. By April one of them was winning pretty much every time they pinned on a number, and they seemed to be taking it in turns. Hitherto-second-rate-Italians, guys who'd been anonymous for years, were humiliating the best of the rest.

Sections of the Belgian and French cycling press suggested something was afoot, but the Italians carried on regardless. Training methods, nutrition and tactics were moving on apace, and the others would do well to refrain from insinuating and get their own houses in order. The president of the UCI, the sport's governing body, even waded in. He took out a full page in one of the big cycling magazines and stated that unless 'certain journalists' desisted, they'd be barred from attending all future events under its auspices. Cycling, he blustered, was a clean sport, and to suggest otherwise was ridiculous. His statement was published on April Fool's Day.

The Flèche Wallonne was on 20 April, and what happened was that three guys from Gewiss just rode away from the other 184. Nothing like it had ever been seen before, and nor had the speeds they rode up the hills. Ultimately Italian-based riders occupied nine of the top ten places, as world-class riders, authentic champions who didn't subscribe to the Ferrari 'method', were annihilated.

One of the three Gewiss riders was a former Soviet citizen named Evgeni Berzin. In previous years he'd been a *gregario*, his job to help better, stronger, more accomplished riders win. He'd finished 90th in the 1993 Giro d'Italia, over two hours behind the great Spanish champion Miguel Indurain. Now, though, he rocked up at the Giro having won a bunch of big, important races. Suddenly he was being touted as one of the favourites, and when the race began he smashed it out of the park. Indurain hadn't lost a three-week stage race for years, and nor had he been beaten in a time trial. Here he lost both, as a supercharged Berzin beat him by almost three minutes over 44 insanely fast kilometres in Tuscany.

At the time, Berzin's strength beggared belief. As we've discovered, however, professional athletes in Italy have been transgressing for decades. Physically demanding, highly remunerated sports are predisposed to it, and the overwhelming consensus within the cycling community is that Ferrari and the Gewiss riders were simply ahead of the curve. For all the spiel about evolved training methods and power thresholds, most seem to believe that Ferrari was extremely skilled in the deployment of synthetic EPO (erythropoietin). It dramatically increased the riders' red-blood-cell count, and consequently their strength, recovery and stamina. Ferrari repeatedly denied any wrongdoing, but following a wide-ranging investigation into his relationship with Lance Armstrong, he was banned from involvement in professional sports. At this point you're probably asking yourself what any of this has to do with a book about Juventus FC, and the short answer is nothing.

The *short* answer is nothing whatsoever …

In court, with Raffaele Guariniello

On 3 July 1998, a French side containing Zidane and Deschamps knocked Italy out of the World Cup in Paris. That was nice for the natives, but five days later France's other great sporting festival was prostrated by the mother of all doping scandals. At the end of the Tour the Italian Marco Pantani wore the yellow jersey in Paris, but his blood was like treacle.

Planet football paid no heed. Everyone knew that cycling was filthy, and besides it was nobody's business but their own. Only then Roma's bellicose manager Zdeněk Zeman broke Italian football's *omertà*, its conspiracy of silence. Famously and explosively he stated, 'In football there hasn't yet been an explosive scandal, but the more important the sport the more people are inclined to turn a blind eye to the negative elements. I know of many doctors who've moved from cycling to football, and of many Serie A clubs using pharmacological products. Football can't be allowed to become like the Tour …'

Good grief.

Zeman insisted that the game was 'in the hands of the pharmacists', and made specific references to Vialli and Del Piero. Juventus rubbished the interview, and Vialli insisted it was 'bullshit from a terrorist'. Then, however, the coach of Bologna piped up.

Very few in *calcio* were more credible than Carletto Mazzone. Few were more worthy of respect, and no coach had ever been so popular with his players. Mazzone was as about as straight as they came, and he asserted that everyone within football was aware that there was an issue. Blood doping was injurious to the players' health, and it was abundantly clear that the game's custodians were burying their heads in the sand. Football needed an inquest in the first instance, and to introduce blood testing in the second.

As a young prosecutor back in 1970, Raffaele Guariniello had discovered the secret files FIAT had held on its staff. Later he'd launched an investigation into Cesare Romiti's activities at the firm and had generally distinguished himself by holding powerful industrialists to account. In Italy there was no greater power than the Agnellis, but Guariniello – seemingly alone – had the courage to take them on. He was a lifelong Juventus fan, and that, he said, was entirely the point. If what Zeman said was true, then the Lippi miracle was a hoax. If, on the other hand, it was without foundation, then he and millions like him could rest easy in their beds at night.

In the absence of a test for synthetic EPO, Guariniello launched an inquiry into 'sporting fraud through the abuse of medication'. He centred it around Giraudo and Agricola, Juve's team doctor. Guariniello obtained a search warrant for his offices, and 281 different drugs were turned up. When, in 2002, the case finally made it to court, the judge was informed that this was in no way consistent with the requirements of a football club. There were, as Guariniello put it, 'hospital quantities'.

The club was accused of administering antidepressants like Narcan and Samyr, often used to increase respiratory capacity after drug overdoses. There were industrial doses of creatine, but most of all there was synthetic EPO. Proscribed if not yet detectable, it had made cycling a pariah sport, ridiculed and abhorred in equal measure by the wider sporting community. If it was true that Juve were using it, then by definition its administration was performance-enhancing as distinct to medicinal.

The players were called in to testify, and for the most part their responses followed a similar pattern; they 'couldn't remember' or Agricola had assured them the stuff they were ingesting was 'vitamins'. In that respect at least the whole thing recalled the state-orchestrated anabolic steroid programmes of the former Soviet bloc. Slowly, though, the fog began to lift, and a picture began to emerge. Zinedine Zidane's testimony was indicative, if not entirely conclusive.

'I only ever took creatine at Juventus. I never used it in France beforehand, and never at Real Madrid subsequently. I'd take two or three grams during the week if the workload demanded it, and also at half-time. Sometimes Dr Agricola gave us it, and sometimes Dr Tencone. The intravenous drips? Yes, on the eve of the match in the hotel room – vitamins, or so the doctors told us. Samyr I took often, before and after games. They told me it was a vitamin. Esafosfina? Yes, I took that.'

On and on it went, hour after hour of circumstantial evidence and red-blood-cell count levels pointing to Agricola having operated a systematic doping programme. In 2004 he was sentenced to 22 months for sporting fraud, including the administration of EPO. The judge found that Giraudo's knowledge couldn't be proved beyond reasonable doubt, and he got off.

Predictably enough, Agricola (in other words, Juventus) won at appeal, and the club made great play of having been 'cleared'. In reality it was simply a technicality; the Italian statute made no provision for doping as a criminal offence at the point at which the fraud had occurred. The substance of the case remained unaltered though, and the facts remained unaltered. Dick Pound, president of WADA, was unequivocal. He stated that it 'hadn't happened by chance – the doping was deliberate and programmed. The players were naive and unaware? Ridiculous! I don't believe for one minute it was all the fault of one crazy doctor. Juventus committed fraud, and profited from that fraud. In fame, wealth and publicity.'

Italy's statute of limitations saw the case archived in 2007, and none of the players was ever sanctioned. Agricola went on to run J Medical, the giant health facility outside Juve's stadium. A lot of water has passed under the bridge, but the wording of the Supreme Court judgement hasn't gone away. Between 1994 and 1998, Juventus had operated 'a criminal scheme designed to alter the outcome of matches through the illicit administration of medication'.

The case for the defence often descends into whataboutism – the notion that everyone was at it and that Juve were singled out. That's entirely without factual basis, but also entirely besides the point. The record books inform us that in just four seasons Juventus won three *Scudetti*, the Champions League and the de facto world club championship. They've never been stripped of any of these titles, but then again nor has Pantani. He wasn't the only doper at the 1998 Tour de France, but that doesn't mean he wasn't doping. So while Juve *did* beat Ajax that night in Rome, Evgeni Berzin *did* beat Miguel Indurain to win the 1994 Giro. Gewiss *did* obliterate the opposition that afternoon at Fléche Wallonne, but with the benefit of hindsight it merely proves that they were the best at cheating.

The crux of all this is probably to be found in the hearts and minds of ordinary Juve fans. For generations of them, the European Cup had been the impossible dream. Their failure to land it was always portrayed – not least by the *tifosi* themselves – as a curse upon the club and the family. It was one of the ties that bound them, as much part of the Juve identity as FIAT and the Agnellis, as Allemandi, Boniperti and Platini. For obvious reasons, Heysel made the longing still more acute, and if they're honest with themselves Rome didn't make it go away. There are two European trophies in the Juventus Museum. The first of them means everything and nothing, but it's questionable whether the second one is worth the plinth it stands on. It besmirches the memory of those who lost their lives at Heysel, and that tells us everything we need to know about the Lippi years.

Juve began the 1998–99 season well enough, but an injury to Del Piero at Udinese in November prompted a slump. The team went 511 minutes without a goal, and Lippi departed on 7 February amid rumours that he'd lost the dressing room. Rome had been the peak, and so by definition it was all downhill from there.

His replacement was deeply unpopular. Carlo Ancelotti was a nice man, and he'd been a terrific midfielder. Unfortunately, he'd been terrific for Roma and Milan, two sworn enemies of Juventus. Your average fan tends not to distinguish between football as a career and football as a religion, so Ancelotti's starting position wasn't ideal. He had more than enough phlegm to cope with that, but the squad he'd inherited was breaking apart. They staggered through a mediocre Champions League group stage with one scuzzy win and five draws, and then scraped past Olympiacos. In the home leg of the semi they folded against Manchester United, and their league form was woeful. They finished seventh and earned – if that's the right word – a place in the mythical Intertoto Cup.

That summer they sold World Cup winner Deschamps to Chelsea, and replaced him with Middlesbrough's 20-year-old Irishman Ronnie O'Brien. He'd never started a game for the club, and his manager, Bryan Robson, had decided not to renew his contract. Robson had also made remarks to the effect that he wasn't perhaps the very best, so it must be assumed that O'Brien's agent, Steve Kutner, was a seer.

As his new club congratulated itself on offloading the ineffectual Thierry Henry to Arsenal, O'Brien began his Italian job by coming off the bench in an Intertoto game against Rostov. He never played again on account of being the proverbial ashtray on a motorbike, but he'll be able to tell the grandkids he played for Juve. For his 15 minutes of fame (or more precisely his 13 minutes) he has an Intertoto Cup winners' medal kicking about somewhere at home.

Having debased themselves to qualify via the Intertoto, Juve's UEFA Cup ship ran aground in the Galician port city of Vigo. Celta put four past them, but domestically their form was extremely good. On 19 March 2000 they hosted a Toro side in relegation trouble in a derby characterised by extreme violence off the field and *nervosismo* on it. Juve led through an own goal, before Toro levelled with the first penalty conceded by Juve in 40 Serie A matches. A second Toro own goal and a disputed penalty saw Ancelotti's team stretch out to a 3–1 lead before Pierluigi 'the Mekon' Collina, the ref of refs, awarded Toro a consolation penalty in the last minute. Quite how he did so is anybody's guess, because there were at least six players between him and Zidane's 'foul' on Fabio Tricarico. Some speculated that maybe he was the Mekon after all, that he had extra-sensory powers. Given that Zidane hadn't touched Tricarico, it didn't *appear* to be a penalty, but Collina was Collina so who knows?

Juve led Serie A by nine points, but successive defeats by Milan and Lazio saw the latter close to three. Juve lost again at Verona, but held on to beat Parma in the penultimate game. Del Piero, the best-paid player in the world, scored for the first time in Serie A open play for eighteen months, and Fabio Cannavaro's equalising free header was inexplicably ruled out for a 'foul'. Thus, heading into the final fixture, Juve led Lazio by two points. Each would conclude with an away fixture against a provincial side, Lazio at Reggina and Juve at their old nemesis Perugia.

In one of those madcap Serie A days, Lazio scored two penalties in four first-half minutes, before a deluge in Perugia saw Collina suspend the match at half-time. The pitch was close to waterlogged, but Collina restarted the game just over an hour later. On 49 minutes he awarded the home side a free kick just inside the Juve half, close to the touchline. Perugia defender (and Juve fan) Alessandro Calori trundled forward, and when it broke for him 15 yards out, he clumped it into the bottom corner of Edwin van der Sar's goal. He'd later claim that Luciano Gaucci, the club president, so detested Juve that he'd threatened the team with a month of *ritiro* if they failed to win.

Juve huffed and puffed, but this time to no avail. The only thing they'd blown was a nine-point lead, and this amid a widespread consensus – even among sensible people – that the refereeing had been more lopsided than ever. Interviewed after the match, monosyllabic Moggi whined that he was a 'decent person', and that those trying to sully his name should hold their tongues 'until they had proof'. It would arrive soon enough.

Regardless, the Agnelli family began the new millennium in good heart. Gianni, Turin's patriarch, had been instrumental in the city being awarded the 2006 Winter Olympics. *L'Avvocato* was 78 now, but his sense of *spettacolo* was undiminished. He'd also a keen eye for his place in Turin history, and he felt like he wanted to bestow one last great gift. Gianni being Gianni he wanted something in return, and he knew that a new stadium would be needed for the opening ceremony ...

The troika was engaged in soft-soaping Valentino Castellani, Turin's mayor. The Delle Alpi was costing Juve 2 billion lire a year (about €1 million), and it made nothing from pitchside advertising, parking, merchandising and the rest. Season tickets sales were 34,000, the average gate 42,000. It always looked half-empty on TV, and the fans hated it. For a club like Juve the stadium was an embarrassment, hence the cup games played elsewhere and the endless (empty) threats to abandon the city altogether. For ten years there had been a stand-off, but with the Olympics around the corner an opportunity presented itself. Juve needed a ground of their own, and the city needed to rid itself of a white elephant.

Over at Toro, the wheels were off yet again. Following the glory years of the early 1990s, a slew of sharp-suited, slow-witted chancers had bled it dry. With each passing season the playing staff and the financial situation had worsened, and now they found themselves back in Serie B. They were also insolvent, and that was the background for a discussion between Paolo Cantarella and Franco Cimminelli – between the Toro-supporting CEO of FIAT and one of the company's most important suppliers.

Cimminelli's ERGOM made dashboards for FIAT, and FIAT alone. He was a migrant from Calabria, and it followed that his allegiances lay with Juventus. On the face of it, therefore, buying rubbishy old Toro made no sense. However, Cantarella seemed to be saying that it would be good for business, and that to decline probably wouldn't. That's the way it worked in FIATville, and that, more or less, is how Franco Cimminelli became the 'proprietor' of Torino.

They say business improved no end – that was the way it worked in FIATville as well. He promised to increase production by building two strike-free new plants, and FIAT promised to assist with the financing. It was all very cosy, though in his gut Cimminelli must have known he wasn't the *real* owner of Toro. FIAT was, because in practical terms it controlled everything and everyone in the supply chain. That didn't matter though, because he was a vain man and football clubs are status symbols.

Having referred to them as 'arseholes who still go and cry at Superga', Cimminelli was *deeply* unpopular with Toro fans. That made becoming president of the club he nominally owned a little tricky, so Tilo Romero was installed. As a young man he'd broken *granata* hearts (including his own) by running over Gigi Meroni on Corso Re Umberto. He'd gone on to enjoy a successful career though, latterly as Gianni Agnelli's spokesman. Now he was mandated to cure Toro's ills, because ... well because that was the way it worked in FIATville.

All this suited just about everyone, and it suited Juventus most of all. It meant they had full control over Toro's liquidity or, more precisely, ensured that Toro didn't *have* any liquidity. That being so, a deal was done for Torino to buy the Comunale for a knockdown €2.5 million. The catch was that Cimminelli would need to spend €30 million rebuilding it in time for the Olympic opening ceremony. If he did that the ground would be his, but if he didn't then ownership would revert to the city.

The point of all this, in case you haven't noticed, is tit-for-Turin-tat. Gianni had got Turin the Winter Olympics, and so, having given Toro a stadium for peanuts, the *comune* was obliged to do the same for Juve. They bought 260,000 square metres of land (the Delle Alpi included) for only €25 million, and would immediately sell a slug of it to the CONAD supermarket chain for €20 million. Toro would continue to share the Delle Alpi while the Comunale was being refurbished, paying Juve an annual rent of €1.5 million. Then, when the Comunale was done (and renamed the Stadio Olimpico), Juve would reciprocate by lodging there. That would enable work to begin on their new home at Continassa, which would be a veritable theatre of dreams. Plans were drawn up for a spectacular, wholly owned 41,000-all-seater stadium unlike anything else in Italy. It would set Juve apart from the twenty-first-century also-rans of Serie A and lead to a period of unparalleled dominance on and off the pitch.

Any teenage maths student could see that the costs were going to be difficult for Toro. Cimminelli was going to have to make serious money out of football to cover them, and with Italian attendances and revenues contracting that was unrealistic. Toro would win promotion back to Serie A in 2005, but by then he was in hock to the tune of €60 million. The Italian taxman was demanding €20 million of that *pronto*, and the rules stipulated that the club couldn't play in the top flight until the debt was cleared. With the banks unprepared to underwrite it, Cimminelli would present a fraudulent guarantee he'd acquired from the former president of Venezia. When it became apparent it was fake, he'd be left with no choice but to offer ERGOM as surety. That was highly problematic for FIAT, because if ERGOM went into administration they wouldn't be able to build cars.

With the revenue refusing to sanction a staged payment plan, FIAT prevailed upon a lawyer named Angelo Benessia to divest them of the risk. He would assist Cimminelli, the useful idiot, in uncoupling the club's debts from ERGOM's. In essence it was OK for Cimminelli to fail personally, and if need be for Toro to go under. Italian law made provision for bankrupt clubs to be renamed and readmitted to a lower division, by way of protecting fans from people like Cimminelli.

Toro would indeed fold that summer, whereupon Turin's mayor, Toro fan Sergio Chiamparino, called a former personal assistant of Silvio Berlusconi. Urbano Cairo had been tried for false accounting as part of the *mani pulite* corruption scandal, but had plea-bargained a suspended sentence. Now, as the head of a low-brow magazine-publishing empire, he assumed ownership of what amounted to a shirt, a big chunk of Italian history and an ageing fan base. He walked into Bar Norman, where the lunatic Alfred Dick had formed the club 99 years earlier, and changed its name from Torino Calcio to Torino Football Club. It would start again from scratch in Serie B, and it was as simple as that.

In 2007 FIAT would buy ERGOM, its eleven factories and its massive accumulated debts, for a symbolic €1. Some say they deliberately bankrupted Cimminelli, and that's entirely conceivable. Some say they deliberately bankrupted Toro, but that's not. Toro were no threat to Juve, and contrary to popular misconceptions, installing Cimminelli hadn't been some evil plot. It was *absolutely* in Juve's interest, but neither Cantarella nor the Agnelli brothers set out to destroy Toro. There was no value for them in it folding, and Gianni Agnelli was anything but a bully. Toro was simply collateral damage, and Gianni would have been mortified if it had disappeared altogether. Not only would it have been counterproductive, but for all Juve's global aspirations he loved his city far too much to have countenanced it.

Anyway all of this was in the future, and *l'Avvocato* always was one for the here and now. It was the first November of the twenty-first century, and he had a very important appointment with CNN …

Into the void, With Edoardo Agnelli

Gianni Agnelli stayed up half the night as the United States elected a useful idiot of its own. George W. Bush was sworn in, and Gianni claimed he belonged to a 'nice family with nerves of steel'. In the normal course of events he'd have been there, because America was his second home. He liked to be around when history was made, and he'd seen Kennedy, Carter and Reagan elected. His son Edoardo had been born in New York during the McCarthy trials of 1954, but this time he just had 'great fun' calling his American friends. On the Saturday he watched Juve draw 1–1 with Lazio (that wasn't so great), and on Tuesday the company's quarterly report came in. It was better than expected, and so *l'Avvocato* was in high spirits.

As was his wont, he was up and at it at six on the Wednesday. He'd have eaten a light breakfast and read the papers (Italian and International) as usual, but then mid-morning there was a knock on the door of his office. It was police superintendent Nicola Cavalieri, and Gianni would have known that something was wrong. Terribly, terribly wrong.

Edoardo, the son he'd never known how to father, had been up earlier than was usual for him. Shortly after 7 o'clock he'd slipped away from his minders and climbed into his FIAT Croma. Where he'd been heading at that hour still wasn't clear, but Cavalieri explained that his car had joined the Turin–Savona motorway at 8.59. FIAT had constructed it in 1960 to connect the city to the Ligurian coast, and near Fossano there was an infamous viaduct. The drop from there was 73 metres, and not for nothing was it known as Suicide Bridge.

Where the deaths of his uncle and grandmother had never been fully elucidated, here the prosecutor was clear that Edoardo had taken his own life. It transpired he'd driven the same route each of the three previous mornings. He'd taken the same exit and then, some minutes later, re-entered the motorway and returned to Turin. Like all suicides it was unspeakably sad, and many believe that it marked the beginning of the end for his 78-year-old father. It wounded him profoundly because, though it wasn't his fault as such, he'd been responsible for the life which preceded it and informed it. That Edoardo was predisposed to addiction and depression couldn't be helped, but Gianni's negligent parenting was perhaps his most grievous failure.

Sunday afternoons at the match had always been his haven, and never more so than now. The love affair with Juve was unconditional and entirely reciprocal, and it was there that he went to forget. He routinely called the management for updates and football-related gossip, and often dropped in to the dressing room. That sort of thing was increasingly rare in the modern game, but the club belonged to him and he to it. Everyone knew that, and everyone knew it had been one of the few things he and Edoardo had been able to share.

In the summer of 2000, Juventus acquired David Trezeguet from Monaco. Over ten years and 138 goals he'd become 'Le Roi', but in his debut season a front four of he, Del Piero, Zidane and Inzaghi mainly just got in one another's way. Aided and abetted by Edwin van der Sar's goalkeeping meltdown, Juve somehow contrived to not win the title, and Ancelotti paid for it with his job. Lippi returned, à la Trapattoni, to the club which had made him, and by November his predecessor had fetched up in Milan.

The catastrophist van der Sar went as well, to Fulham. In his stead, at a jaw-dropping €50 million, came Parma's Gianluigi Buffon – and the rest is history – while Pavel Nedvěd replaced Madrid-bound Zidane. Gianni described the world's most expensive footballer as 'more enjoyable than useful', and the club spent the change on Lilian Thuram. He had designs on being the best central defender in the world, but for now had to settle on becoming the best reluctant right-back.

In December, Juventus became the third Italian club to float on the Italian stock exchange. The difference was that shares in the other two, Lazio and Roma, were worthless. They'd been issued in financial extremis to shore up two overspending, loss-making institutions, while Juve had a healthy balance sheet, a credible vision for the future of the business and that old Agnelli magic. Investing in Juventus offered both prestige and potential for a return, and so institutions – and of course rose-tinted punters – lined up to do precisely that.

This time, the final-day debacle was all Inter's. Thirteen years without a *Scudetto*, they led by six points at the end of March. Then, however, they lost at home against Atalanta and conceded an injury-time equaliser at Chievo. Nedvěd's 88th-minute winner at Piacenza saw Juve close to a single point, with Roma a further one adrift. Now the apparent formality of Inter's championship became contingent on them winning at Lazio, whose fans declared themselves favourable to the idea in no uncertain terms. Roma were odds on to win at Toro, which of course would have suited *granata* partisans down to the ground, while Juve were at Udinese.

Confused? It's all quite simple.

Lazio fans wanted their team to lose against Inter in order to deny Roma (and of course Juve) the title. Thousands of them therefore turned up with blue and black scarves and flags. Roma fans held their noses in the hope that Lazio would beat Inter (and that Juve would lose in Udine). Toro fans wanted nothing more than for their side to go under against Roma, and of course, for Juve to lose in Udine. The common denominator, as ever, was that everyone wanted to see Juve beaten.

All clear? Then we'll proceed …

Juve didn't lose, but rather galloped into a 2–0 lead at Udinese. By half-time Toro had failed to concede against Roma and Inter were 2–1 up at Lazio. In effect the top two were as was, and Roma were done for. Then Lazio's shaggy-haired Czech winger Karol Poborsky threw a spanner in the works. He'd already been fool enough to equalise once, which suggested he'd failed to grasp just how much Lazio's fans had riding on this. Everyone knew it was his last game for the club, but no one quite knew just how much he hated it. The Lazio fans started booing him, because for them the notion that he might hand Roma (or Juve) the title didn't bear thinking about. Problem was the booing was counterproductive, because now he latched onto a headed back pass and poked it home. You could hear a pin drop as he wheeled away to celebrate. On his own. Like a bloody idiot.

Worse still, Poborsky's enthusiasm was contagious, and Lazio scored twice more after the break. Inter so wanted to win that they forgot about the playing football part. They were paralyzed by fear, and with Udinese failing to make inroads into Juve's lead, a 26th championship fell right into a euphoric *gobbo* lap. The lesser of two evils for the *laziali* and another unmitigated disaster for the *interisti*.

Into the great beyond, with the Agnelli brothers

On 21 January 2003, 47-year-old Margherita Agnelli left her home in Geneva. Dolefully she made her way to the airport and boarded a flight to Turin's Caselle airport. From there she was taken to Villa Frescot, her parents' home.

Margherita had known for several months what all of Italy had suspected. The previous May, her father had missed the FIAT AGM for the first time in 60 years. Its share value had subsequently nosedived amid rumours he had passed away, and he'd been compelled to deny it in *La Stampa*, his newspaper. He'd admitted there was a 'small problem' with his prostate, and he'd be spending a few weeks in the States to undergo treatment. Gianni Agnelli's prostate was 81 years old. There was no such thing as a 'small problem'.

Margherita had been present when he'd decided that the endless journeys back and forth to New York were simply too debilitating, that his race – the one he'd undertaken for, with and on behalf of a nation – was run.

Cancer had done for Italy's twentieth-century boy. For the quintessential, irrefutable, indefatigable boy of Italy's twentieth century.

They say 600,000 attended his funeral, about half of metropolitan Turin. They like to draw comparisons with the service for the *Grande Torino* and with the funerals of Elvis Presley, Princess Diana and JFK. That's probably inevitable given that it was transmitted live by the state broadcaster, but also rather simplistic. Though doubtless twentieth-century icons, the lives of Elvis, Diana and John Kennedy were truncated in dramatic circumstances. More importantly, their contributions were ephemeral in relative terms. Kennedy governed for less than three years; Diana was essentially a media construct, and Elvis a popular-culture phenomenon. They were synonymous with and indivisible from a moment in time, but their legacies were more cultural than societal.

Gianni Agnelli's FIAT accounted for 5 per cent of Italian GDP, but even that doesn't begin to tell the whole story. Much of the other 95 per cent was contingent upon it and conditioned by it, and his company dominated his country's financial, political and, yes, social trajectory for fifty post-war years. For all his shortcomings as a father, a husband and a manager, *l'Avvocato's* elan, his charisma and his genius for international statecraft were without parallel. Nobody – not anybody – was ever so stylish, so funny or so eternally youthful. Like all great men he was loved and loathed in equal measure, but nobody in Italy was ambivalent.

Today, as post-industrial Italy continues to wrestle with the political and social *campanilismo* he so abhorred, his achievements, personality and legacy are woven deeply into its fabric. Whether Italians like it or not, FIAT was their century and their journey perfectly distilled. If the 1946 referendum taught us nothing else, it was that Italians still had need of a royal family. The Agnellis were that family, and Gianni Agnelli was their king.

Whether they like it or not, they just did, and he just was.

Moreover, the football club he, his father and his brother built was Italy's most potent sporting metaphor. It was unique not because it was so successful on the pitch, but because for almost a century its pre-eminence had been underpinned by family, that most Italian of all values. From the day in 1925 that four-year-old Gianni set foot on the training ground with his dad, the club had remained his passion, his refuge and his greatest, most enduring joy. He hadn't necessarily appreciated its twenty-first-century iteration, and he lamented what he saw as football's transformation from sport to cheerless corporate behemoth. That hadn't, however, undermined his love for Juve, nor had it spoiled the infinite romance he associated with Sunday afternoons at the stadium. There he'd been able to feel like just one among 40,000. Of course he wasn't – he was the chosen one – but he'd never failed to feel inspired by that unity of Italian purpose.

It's a fact that he was a man of many parts and many sports, but long after Father Time deprived him of the sailing, the skiing and even the Formula 1, Juventus remained one of the bulwarks of his extraordinary life. He'd always said that a team with 14 million supporters was much bigger than him, and in Italy he'd been much, much bigger than everyone else.

Juve announced that the new stadium, when it came, would bear Gianni's name, although they'd can that idea for thirty pieces of silver or, more accurately, for €3 million a year from the German financial services provider Allianz. Gianni wouldn't have liked that, but not because he was particularly vain. He'd have disapproved on the basis that Juve – his Juve – ought to be above that sort of thing. Modern football, though, is show business. Actually no. Strike that. Modern football is 20 per cent show and 80 per cent business.

His death saw Umberto assume the FIAT presidency, with the splendidly named Franzo Grande Stevens replacing him at Juve. With Nedvěd irrepressible, the team raced to both the *Scudetto* and an Old Trafford Champions League final against Carlo Ancelotti's Milan. There, however, the curse was more powerful even than Gianni's legacy.

Nedvěd was the most complete midfielder in Europe. With his Stakhanovite attitude, his altruism and generosity of spirit, he'd become one of those players who could and routinely would do anything to dig his team out. However, he had picked up two yellow cards and was suspended for the final. That handed the psychological initiative to Milan, who began at breakneck speed. With Davids and defender Igor Tudor limping off, Juve struggled increasingly to impose themselves. They survived 120 goalless minutes with the dream still intact, but it died when three of their takers failed in the penalty shoot-out.

Some more of Juventus died the following spring. With the team embarrassed by Deportivo in the Champions League and off Milan's pace in Serie A TIM

– the league was now sponsored by Telecom Italia – Lippi was replaced by old *Juventino* Fabio Capello. It would be the last significant act, for now at least, of the Agnelli dynasty. Umberto Agnelli had delivered the *trio magico* and the troika, but now he had terminal lung cancer. He passed away at his country home north of the city on 27 May 2004, and for the first time in over 60 years there was no Agnelli at the summit of Juventus.

Chapter 9

Back to the Future, with Andrea Agnelli

There are people wanting football to die from scandals, fraud, excessive money and debt. I preach financial fair play.

Michel Platini

Across the Swiss border, buying SIM cards with Luciano Moggi

You've probably heard this one already, in which case forgive me ...

Juve are playing; it's 0–0, and it's the last minute. There's a 50–50 on the edge of the opposition box, and the referee blows for a free kick. On hearing the whistle, one of the Juve players turns to him and shouts, 'Who to?' Quick as a flash, the ref shouts back, 'To us!'

One miserable, sodden Sunday in December 2004, perennial escape artists Bologna travelled to Fiorentina. The *bolognesi* tended to be abject until April and miraculous in May, and this 'derby of the Apennines' was precisely the sort of game they were expected to lose. Lose it they duly did, and the 28,000 fool enough to attend couldn't wait for it to draw to its turgid conclusion. The travelling fans hadn't really expected to get anything in Florence. They were in the drop zone again, and once more their home form would be crucial. They had two big games coming up at the Dall'Ara before the Christmas break. Reggina were beatable, but first they had to entertain runaway leaders Juve. That was one hell of an ask, not least because Bologna would be without two of their better defenders. Referee Massimo De Santis had booked Romanian Valentin Năstase and veteran Fabio Petruzzi, and both would be suspended.

Shortly after the match, Juve's Luciano Moggi was in telephone conversation with Tony Damascelli, a football journalist from the Milanese paper *Il Giornale*. The transcript of the call is as follows:

> DAMASCELLI: So De Santis committed the prefect crime, eh?
>
> MOGGI: What did he do?
>
> DAMASCELLI: Eh, We have three play— three Bologna defenders out. Suspended, all three of them.
>
> MOGGI: Who was cautioned?
>
> DAMASCELLI: All three. What do you call them? Petruzzi, Năstase and Gamberini.
>
> MOGGI: Mm.
>
> DAMASCELLI: Not bad, eh?
>
> MOGGI: That's good, just as well. What more is there to say?

The panel awarded the Bologna–Juve game to *genovese* referee Tiziano Pieri. Earlier in the season, he'd officiated as Bologna hosted Roma. They'd raced into a 3–0 lead, and then striker Giacomo Cipriani had been upended in the Roma box. It was a foul, but Pieri booked Cipriani for simulation. Given that he was already on a yellow, Bologna began the second half with ten men. Five minutes after the restart they'd become nine, as Theo Zagorakīs received a second yellow for a nothing foul on Francesco Totti. They'd hung on to win the game 3–1, but it's safe to say Tiziano Pieri wasn't on their Christmas-card list. Now they appealed against the awarding of the Juve game to him, but to no avail.

Bologna played really well against Juve, but you know what it's like when you're at the foot of the table. Things just don't go for you, and they didn't go for Bologna when Jonathan Zebina brought down Cipriani in the box. Pieri told him to get up and get on with it, but then Thuram went and brought him down in the box as well. He'd no choice but to get up and get on with it, but the *bolognesi* couldn't quite believe what they were witnessing. They informed Pieri that he was a 'son of a whore', but that seemed only to make his decision-making worse.

With four minutes left and the score 0–0, a ball was punted towards Zlatan Ibrahimović, Juve's talented Swedish striker. He and Ciro Capuano went for it and, notwithstanding the fact that Ibra's arm was against his throat, Capuano headed it clear. It was nothing, but Pieri awarded Juve a free kick on the edge of the box anyway. Incensed, virtually the entire *rossoblu* team rounded on him, and when Nedvěd smashed home the free kick the home fans did something highly unusual. They stood up and gave a standing ovation.

To Pieri, that is, not Nedvěd.

Juve won a 28th *Scudetto* and the following season they carried on where they'd left off. Then, just as they were wrapping up the 29th, the wiretaps of Moggi's phone conversations were released. And so, as briefly as I know how, to perhaps the grimmest, most wretched episode in the history of football's grimmest, most wretched and most compelling league. Apologies if this all feels a bit like déjà vu, but this is a book about Juventus. As such, whether we like it or not, here's the story of *Calciopoli*.

Moggi and Giraudo were the central figures in an elaborate scheme designed to ensure that Juventus-friendly refs were appointed to the games – their own and those of their closest rivals – that most mattered to them. Using Swiss-registered SIM cards to avoid detection, they not only subverted sporting justice, but also journalistic impartiality. Through his friendships with Damascelli and his like, Moggi set out to ensure that any suggestion of corruption was strangled at source.

Gerrymandering aside, Moggi admitted to having locked one referee, Gianluca Paparesta, in the dressing room following Juve's defeat at Reggina. In the recording he's heard boasting of having torn a strip off Paparesta and his assistants. After the match he called Aldo Biscardi, the famous host of a popular football programme. He claimed to have given Biscardi a watch worth €20,000 (Biscardi disputed the value, though not the gift) and during the conversation insisted that he call for Paparesta to have his refereeing licence suspended. When Biscardi came on air he did as he had been told, railing against Paparesta's 'scandalous' performance before a rabid studio audience. Biscardi was later relieved of his own licence, the one you need in Italy to practise journalism.

The scandal took down the presidents of the Italian football association and the Lega Calcio, the body which managed Series A and B. Pierluigi Pairetto, one of the two officials responsible for allocating Serie A match officials, was sentenced to two years in jail, while the presidents of Fiorentina and Lazio each received 15 months. Moggi got five years and four months, Giraudo 20 months. Because this is Italy, the statute of limitations came into play, and neither went to prison. That's perfectly normal because, as a lawyer friend of mine told me, it's 'practically impossible' to serve time for this sort of thing. He also confirmed that in the upper echelons of Italian business a CV without some sort of conviction (overturned or otherwise) is considered highly dubious. Regardless, *Calciopoli* cost Juventus the *Scudetti* of 2005 and 2006 and saw them demoted for the first time to Serie B. Inter inherited the 2006 championship, though it later became apparent that they'd been up to no good as well.

The minutiae of it all is infinitely complex. In simple terms though, of the nineteen 2004–2005 games originally investigated, seven directly involved Juventus. Most of the others involved Fiorentina, Milan, Lazio and Reggina, and each would be docked points. As the net spread, a number of officials were convicted. Among the referees, Pieri was acquitted, but not so De Santis. He was sentenced to 23 months, reduced on appeal to 12. When the story broke, he was set to be Italy's representative at the 2006 World Cup. Quite what that says about Italian football doesn't bear thinking about.

For Gianluca Pessotto, it was too much. For 11 years he'd been a popular and highly accomplished full-back. He'd been one of the Champions League winners in Rome and a mainstay of six *Scudetto*-winning sides.

Pessotto was a sensitive and intelligent man, and the club had just rewarded him with a management role. On 27 June he fell, clutching a rosary, from the fourth floor of the Juventus headquarters. Mercifully he survived.

Juve's share value was decimated. When the club was listed in 2001, each was valued at €3.70. When the tapes were released, there were some 201 million shares in circulation, and they were valued at €2.50 each. Five years later, as the various retrials, appeals and recriminations rumbled on, they were 90 cents apiece. In real terms that's a depreciation of €328 million, about 64 per cent. By then the global financial crisis had hit share values in every sector, so not all of the decline can be attributed to *Calciopoli*. Some estimate the immediate cost to Juventus of Serie B football at only €130 million, but it's also clear that sponsors ran a mile. The medium-term damage to the Juventus brand and to Italian football as an industry was incalculable literally, but also figuratively.

Prior to his death, Umberto had chosen the brilliant Sergio Marchionne as future CEO of the FIAT group. Now Marchionne and the family prevailed upon 78-year-old Boniperti to return to the club, as much as a sop to the shareholders as anything else. It goes without saying that a side containing Del Piero, Nedvěd, Buffon and Trezeguet was only ever going to come straight back up, and many *Juventini* view the year they spent in Serie B as having been something of a catharsis.

They point to days out in dreamy La Spezia and canal-side Treviso, lunchtime picnics in comely central Italian market towns like Arezzo and Frosinone. The revamped squad included two talented local boys, Claudio Marchisio and Matteo Paro, who played most of the games. Some *gobbi* would have us believe that through them they were reacquainted with age-old Juve values which had been temporarily misplaced under the troika, while others like to portray themselves as standing shoulder to shoulder with their poor, provincial, long-suffering Serie B brethren. The suggestion is that glorious, technicolour Juventus would burst into their humdrum lives, anoint them with gold dust and leave their smitten, starry-eyed kids with the memory of a lifetime. It's a very endearing depiction, but it infers a virtue which was entirely absent. It wasn't the players' fault, nor the fans', but the club had been kicked out of Serie A for one reason and one reason only. It had cheated. Again.

All of which begs some big, ugly, urgent questions. Was Juventus intrinsically and institutionally corrupt? Is it conceivable that Umberto hadn't known what he'd be getting when he employed Moggi and Giraudo? Given that winning is 'the only thing that matters' is the Juve credo, was *Calciopoli* its inevitable consequence?

That, dear reader, is for you to deduce.

Back where it all started, with Boniperti and Del Piero …

On 8 September 2011, Juventus hosted Notts County in their wonderful new stadium. Evoking the time and place that the club is thought to have been formed, the footballing gods spirited a park bench into the centre circle. On it sat giants Boniperti and Del Piero, and they articulated what it had meant, for 114 years, to be *Juventino*.

Needless to say it was impossible not to be moved by the *spettacolo*, nor by the beauty and humility of Del Piero's words. Boniperti concluded, as he would, with the old 'Winning isn't important – it's the only thing that matters' refrain. It's the direct inverse of de Coubertain's life-affirming Olympian ideal, and it had got Juve into a whole heap of trouble down the years. The apostles seemed not to mind though. Not a dry eye in the house.

Five years on from *Calciopoli*, there was a new Agnelli at the helm. Umberto's 35-year-old son Andrea had installed newer, younger staff and, following eight fallow seasons, a new manager. The old midfield tyro Angelo Conte inherited Italy's best keeper in Gigi Buffon, its meanest back three in Chiellini, Barzagli and Bonucci. Chilean Vidal and *torinese* Marchisio never stopped, and illusionist Andrea Pirlo induced neurosis in Italy's defences. After eight undefeated months a 28th title was theirs, and the latest *rinascimento* was complete.

Had Juve not been stripped of the two *Calciopoli* titles, Conte's team would have been entitled to a third gold star, so Andrea made great play of eschewing the bauble his own father had lobbied for back in the day. Instead the new shirts bore the legend 30 ON THE PITCH. This was classic Juve, a rebuke to the plebs who'd had the temerity to revoke the two *Scudetti*.

Andrea has been a wonderful chairman, objectively the best of the dynasty. He hasn't stopped spending and, domestically at least, Juve haven't stopped winning. There have been eight Serie A titles in succession, and as I write only Coronavirus stands between them and a ninth. In sporting terms Juve no longer compete with Milan, Inter, Lazio and poor old Toro. The club has more supporters than that lot combined, and these days there are any number of ways to monetise their devotion. Turnover has increased from €170 million to over €500 million, one hell of an achievement given that the Italian economy has been stagnant for over a decade.

Overcoming Italian teams is but a means to the end that is the Champions League. In recent times, Andrea has called into question Atalanta's right to participate in the competition, on account of them being 'without international history'. Roma, he informed us, have contributed to Italy's UEFA ranking, and were being punished for one bad season. That's kind of been the bedrock of professional football for a century, kind of how sport works. Evidently Andrea doesn't much like it though, because you need to 'protect investments and costs'. Thankfully though, he and his team were hard at it 'analysing the dynamics to understand what consumers want', so good-o.

The club reached the final in 2017. Once more, however, the curse had its way. The *comune* installed a giant screen in Piazza San Carlo, but a gang of guttersnipe thieves fired pepper spray into the crowd to create panic. A stampede ensued, and 38-year-old Erika Pioletti was crushed to death. Another woman, Marisa Amato, was paralyzed. She wasn't a football fan, just happened to be in town with her husband. She'd die two years later from her injuries.

The inquiries rumble on, but while Juve has become the global icon that Uncle Gianni always dreamed of, the rest of Serie A are still mired in their age-old *campanilismo*. They're stuck in a football paradigm which is 25 years behind the times and hamstrung by the massive debts which are its direct consequence. They can't generate sufficient revenue to compete, and nor will they until they own the stadiums they play in, understand that fans are consumers and recast their players as brand ambassadors.

Or find a chairman like Andrea Agnelli.

FIAT is FIAT-Chrysler now. Margherita's son John is president, and the family holding company still owns two thirds of Juventus. The rest is in the hands of banks, investment funds and private investors, and in November 2019 Andrea told them that the club needed a €300 million cash injection. He'd stump up the family's share, but they needed to find the rest. Nine months earlier it had issued a bond of €175 million against debts of €310 million. These numbers, for a club which only barely sells out its 41,000-capacity stadium in the era of UEFA Financial Fair Play regulations, are bewildering. Best to probably just suspend disbelief.

There's a financial chasm between Juventus and the rest of Italian football. It widens every year, although the absence of any sustained, meaningful competition at home is probably detrimental to Juve's bottom line. The hope is that Inter can start to challenge once more, because Juve's monopoly and all the cheating has rather devalued Italian football as a brand. Sport's not terribly interesting when you know the outcome before the start, so its image at home and abroad has taken a bit of a battering. Besides, young people in Italy watch TV progressively less. The final of League of Legends, an 'online multiplayer battle arena video game' (it says here) attracted a global audience of 58 million. Juve, much the biggest draw for the domestic TV audience, get under 2 million on average. The good news for Juventus is that domestic TV revenues account for less than 20 per cent of its turnover; for those outside the Champions League it's 40 to 60 per cent.

Juve's rivals are to be found in Manchester and Madrid, in Italian high streets and in low-cost airline destinations across the continent. The club is in the leisure business, and it's extremely good at it. Among its business partners are a Chinese cruise company, a Japanese deodorant manufacturer, a multinational food corporation and an online bookmaker. The club offers myriad ways to spend your disposable income, just as it affords its owners myriad ways to spend theirs. While FIAT has become an Italo-American fusion, the Juventus brand remains a byword for Italian excellence. It's a means by which Italian identity is disseminated to the world, and that's why people like my friend Albi support the team. When Juve win at home they make him feel like a winner, and when they win abroad they make him proud to be Italian.

The pride of Italy rebranded in January 2017. The Turin bull disappeared altogether, replaced by two asymmetric letters J and a catchy 'Juve and more' strapline. The second J, the 'more', refers to all the ancillary stuff they do to generate revenues. The new logo is a radical departure from traditional football club crests. It's not at all unattractive, but it's more Giorgio Armani than Giorgio Chiellini.

Talking of which, in 2019 Juve's Notts County stripes disappeared. Amid general bemusement they were replaced, at a stroke, by black and white halves. Some say it's because black and white stripes are associated with referees in the emerging North American market, others that it was a ploy to keep one step ahead of the counterfeiters. That would seem to make sense, because goodness knows there are enough of them. The club's 'chief revenue officer' cut right to the chase though, when he stated that one way or another the old one just didn't earn its keep. It was light years behind the best-performing kits, and precedent told him this sort of change could work wonders if done well. Many of the fans weren't best pleased – they said it looks like something you'd see at a *palio* – but needs must and they'd get used to it. The 'chief revenue officer' reiterated that a shirt is just a shirt and, salivating now, informed us that Barcelona and Bayern Munich had increased their revenues dramatically by changing theirs.

Actually the bit about it only being a shirt isn't 100-percent accurate. What he meant was the *old* shirt had been just a shirt, but the new one was actually an act of faith. The €130 you would need to find for one amounted to a renewal of your bond or, as the (English) voiceover guy on the promo video called it, your 'oath'. The problem there was that he pronounced it 'oaf', and the shirt itself is just that. It's clumsy and quite ugly, and a lot of the fans feel like the club has taken them for a bit of a ride. If they feel like that, then it's probably true, but it can't be helped. There will be further rebrandings along soon, because Juve are still way behind in terms of shirts sold. For every one they sell, Barcelona shift two and Liverpool three.

Juve's problem is that their *earned* revenues are half those of United, Real Madrid and Bayern. They're in line with those of Dortmund and Spurs, but the immediate objective is to leapfrog fourth-placed Bayern in the

UEFA rankings. For that to happen they need a successor to the show pony, alleged sex offender and world's greatest player Cristiano Ronaldo. Someone calculated that he added 34 million followers to Juve's social media channels, someone else that his average monthly wage (€2.5 million) was equal to the unemployment benefit of 3,125 *operai* laid off when FIAT closed the plant at Termini.

Production at Mirafiori and Grugliasco is almost at a standstill now. They're only producing a Maserati-branded SUV, though in a nod to its heritage the company has chosen Turin for the electric version of the FIAT 500. There are progressively less workers and more robots though, and FIATville sometimes feels like a city in retreat. Somehow Juventus feels too big for it, and that's probably because it is. It's much more than the football club of a medium-sized European city, which probably explains why at times it feels so separate from it.

I write this having just watched the final night of the Sanremo Music Festival. For millions it's the televisual highlight of the year, and has been for 70 years. At peak viewing time on the decisive evening, before an audience of almost 11 million, they effectively interrupted it because Juventus had lost a football match. Now try to imagine that happening in England, in Holland or in Germany. You can't. It wouldn't happen. Manchester United, Ajax and Bayern are merely football clubs.

Juve – and the Agnelli saga – are much more. They are among the central narrative planks of everyday Italian life, and that largely explains why the devotion of its fans is liturgical. For those who understand Italy's history it's tempting to view them not as supporters, but as subjects.

They prostrate themselves because, as they gleefully inform us, *la vecchia signora* transcends mere football. They're right of course. It's Il Duce, the economic boom and the years of lead. It's post-Catholicism, post-industrialisation and the cultural and intellectual train wreck that is post-*Berlusconismo*.

For Juve's disciples it's also their unshakeable faith that poor, wretched Italy will somehow prevail. Somehow it will survive itself, and the core *Juventino* attributes of simplicity, seriousness and sobriety will see it through. To believe in Juve is to reject Italian *campanilismo*, and to line up behind the sanctity and destiny of the *bel paese*. It's to cast aside Italy's age-old inferiority complex, to place one's faith in the Agnelli protectorate and, fundamentally, to believe.

And yet …

Millions of rational, balanced Italians are convinced that the thing is irredeemably corrupt. They say with 'Winning isn't important – it's the only thing that matters' it can't be otherwise, and it's not as if there's no evidence. With reason they point to *Calciopoli* and the doping scandal, and to Moggi as the living, breathing, festering embodiment of what amounts to a giant sporting con trick. Tellingly, Andrea Agnelli maintains that the club was the victim of *Calciopoli*, not its promoter. He's a Juve fan, so he blames *La Gazzetta dello Sport* for having published the transcripts. Andrea says it's 'ridiculous', and blames anyone and everyone that is not Juventus. He insists that Moggi was one of the many, and apparently continues to fraternise with him. He seems unable or unwilling to acknowledge the fact that what the club did was wrong and that his own father employed Moggi knowing *precisely* what kind of individual he was. He couldn't not know, because everyone in Italian football knew. Everyone knew, just as everyone knows that for Juve winning is the only thing that matters.

The Juventus story, like that of FIAT, encapsulates what and how it is to be Italian. It's two European championships and 35 (37 if you're a Juve fan) Serie A titles, the greatness of Boniperti and Zoff, of Platini and Del Piero. By the same token it's the sleaze of *Calciopoli*, the calamity of Heysel, the death of Scirea and the apparent suicide of Edoardo Agnelli II.

Albi and Luca are two years older now. They don't agree on much, but they both think Juve are the best. When I ask Luca why he switched he says it's just easier. He says there's no point trying to explain, but if I were in his shoes I'd understand. When I ask, 'But what about Toro?' he says, 'What about them? It's a joke club for *sfigati*; the team is garbage and nothing ever happens.'

I still don't have an answer to that, and nor, if I'm honest, does anyone else.

It seems Albi was right all along.

Aveva ragione, Albi . . .

Index